413527

D0267905

Minding the Close Relationship

In this informative volume, social psychologists John H. Harvey and Julia Omarzu describe a new concept called "minding," which demonstrates principles by which couples can achieve and maintain long-term closeness and satisfaction. *Minding the Close Relationship* brings together the latest scholarship on relationships, with practical advice, and it compares the theory of minding with several other theories about maintaining closeness. The activity of minding yields a cooperative, consensual approach that cannot be achieved by either partner's individual acts and, once achieved, makes partners feel validated and special in their relationships.

Minding the Close Relationship will serve as a supplementary textbook for undergraduate and graduate courses in social psychology, communication, family studies, and clinical and counseling psychology.

John H. Harvey is Professor of Psychology at the University of Iowa.

Julia Omarzu is currently a doctoral candidate in Personality and Social Psychology at the University of Iowa.

Minding the Close Relationship

A THEORY OF RELATIONSHIP ENHANCEMENT

John H. Harvey
University of Iowa

Julia Omarzu
University of Iowa

CAMBRIDGE
UNIVERSITY PRESS

PUBLISHED BY THE PRESS SYNDICATE OF THE UNIVERSITY OF CAMBRIDGE
The Pitt Building, Trumpington Street, Cambridge, United Kingdom

CAMBRIDGE UNIVERSITY PRESS
The Edinburgh Building, Cambridge CB2 2RU, UK   www.cup.cam.ac.uk
40 West 20th Street, New York, NY 10011-4211, USA   www.cup.org
10 Stamford Road, Oakleigh, Melbourne 3166, Australia
Ruiz de Alarcón 13, 28014 Madrid, Spain

First published 1999

Printed in the United States of America

Typeface Palatino 10.25/14 pt.   System DeskTopPro$_{/UX}$® [BV]

*A catalog record for this book is available from
the British Library.*

Table 1 and portions of the text are reproduced from J. H. Harvey and J. Omarzu,
"Minding the Close Relationship," *Personality and Social Psychology Review*, 1: 223–239.
Reprinted with permission of the publisher.

Library of Congress Cataloging-in-Publication Data
Harvey, John H., 1943–
    Minding the close relationship : a theory of relationship
enhancement / John H. Harvey, Julia Omarzu.
        p. cm.
    Includes bibliographical references and index.
    ISBN 0-521-63318-4 (hardbound)
    1. Interpersonal relations.   2. Man–woman relationships.
3. Couples.   4. Cognition.   I. Omarzu, Julia.   II. Title.
HM132.H347   1999
302—dc21   98-51562
                    CIP

ISBN 0 521 63318 4 hardback

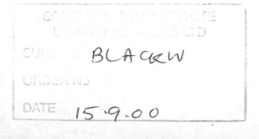

This book is dedicated to Pamela and Michael,
who have been indispensable
to our understanding of closeness and minding

Contents

Preface and Acknowledgments   *page* ix

1 *Introduction to the Minding Concept*   1

2 *Minding: Definition and Components*   11

3 *Knowing and Being Known by One's Partner*   31

4 *Attributions in Close Relationships*   61

5 *Acceptance, Respect, Reciprocity, and Continuity*   84

6 *Beginnings and Endings*   97

7 *Minding in the Close Relationship Literature*   120

8 *Minding and Other Major Concepts of Closeness*   137

9 *Evidence about Minding in Close Relationships*   157

10 *An International Perspective on Minding*   168

11 *Minding in Couples Therapy and Counseling*   182

12 *Limitations and Future Directions*   201

   References   215

   Index   223

Preface and Acknowledgments

We wrote this book to describe a new approach to close relationship maintenance. As described in Chapter 1, minding refers to a process that we believe is essential if a committed couple is to feel the special joy and satisfaction that may be associated with long-term closeness.

The history of this book is traced in Chapter 1. As we note there, the book began to be developed about four years ago from early musings by the first author on how little is known about the maintenance of close relationships. We know a lot about how people start and end relationships, but much less about how they make their relationships work over time. As described in Chapter 1, we were fortunate to begin our association in 1995 and began to consider the minding idea as a new approach to factors that may contribute significantly to relationship enhancement.

Part of this book overlaps with our earlier 1997 article that first articulated our theory of minding. We are indebted to Norbert Kerr, Associate Editor of the *Personality and Social Psychology Review,* who handled the review of our article, and to the anonymous reviewers who challenged us to make the argument more coherent and better fitted to many more works in the extensive close relationships literature than we had initially conceived to be relevant to minding. While these reviewers did not agree with our conception, they along with a long list of commentators who are accomplished relationship scholars literally helped us build the theory and its many implications that are presented here. These scholars include: Carolyn Ellis, Susan Hendrick, Constance Jones, Susan Lutgendorf, Terri Orbuch,

Susan Sprecher, and Mika Uematsu. Further, we are indebted to the following student colleagues at Iowa who provided invaluable help in developing a research program on the minding ideas: Charles Busch, Alexis Chavis, Joel Clutts, Michelle Papadopoulos, Johanna Reyes, Wendy Schulte, Elizabeth-Anne Trevino, and Joanne Whalen. We thank Julia Hough, Editor for Psychology and Cognitive Science at Cambridge University Press, for her support of this book's development. Finally, we are most grateful to our spouses, Pamela and Michael, who contributed ideas and support for our work on the book.

Iowa City, Iowa   John H. Harvey and Julia Omarzu
January 1999

CHAPTER 1

Introduction to the Minding Concept

> More has been written about how relationships
> don't work than about how they do. We have virtu-
> ally no language, other than banality, to describe the
> couple who has been happy together for a long time.
> We would like them to have a secret, we would like
> them to have something they could give us. Or that
> we could give them, other than our suspicion. There
> is nothing more terrorizing than the possibility that
> nothing is hidden. There is nothing more scandalous
> than a happy marriage.
>
> Adam Phillips, *Monogamy*

What's on your mind? In answer to this question, the January 6,
1997, issue of *USA Today* indicated that 64 percent of adults in the
United States said that "relationships with loved ones" were "always on their minds." This survey's outcome hints at the substance
of this book. Clearly, one of the things that matter most to most
people is the status of their close relationships. These relationships
give them psychological sustenance and provide a sense of meaning
in life. Thus, our loves, or our hopes for love, are "always" on our
mind. A main thesis of this book is that we can use our minds in a
much more powerful and enduring way to achieve closeness than is
often recognized in either popular or scholarly treatments of how to
achieve satisfaction in close relationships.

The opening statement by Adam Phillips also resonates with a
second theme of this book: We do not know very well how to talk
about couples who achieve and maintain closeness over a long pe-

1

riod. We do not understand well the processes by which their love is preserved and even enhanced over time. Furthermore, Phillips's implication that perhaps "nothing is hidden" regarding such long-term closeness overlaps with the concept of "minding" that is articulated in this book. Minding may seem at first glance terribly simple – too simple to be scientific or even valid in terms of common sense. Yet we believe that it represents a central process by which people maintain closeness.

Minding is hypothesized to be a process by which couples can maintain close, satisfying relationships over long periods of time. While perhaps simple on the surface, in its detail and execution minding is complex and requires the development of finely tuned interpersonal skills. Before discussing the details of minding, however, we introduce it by describing how the concept developed.

MUSING ABOUT THE WHYS AND HOWS OF THE MAINTENANCE OF CLOSENESS

The idea for this conception of minding goes back to the spring of 1995. The first author began to jot down notes about the fact that in the relationship literature, there have been more than thirty years of research on the ingredients of what attracts people to one another and what eventually leads to closeness. However, despite this work and a burgeoning interest in close relationships in the social and behavioral sciences, we still have too little understanding of the processes involved in *long-term,* successful relating.

How do people maintain their closeness and satisfaction over an extended period of time? Students in relationship classes frequently ask this question. Many have observed their parents' divorces and subsequent start-ups and dissolutions with different lovers, and their own relationship peaks, valleys, and dissolutions. They have seen many relationship endings in their twenty or so years, but few "lastings." They may have seen their grandparents make it to their golden anniversary, but they wonder whether relationships are now so different that their situations may not be comparable with those of their grandparents. This seems discouraging to those who hope for true "life partners" to share the ups and downs of their futures.

In answer to these kinds of questions about the dynamics of long-term closeness, we as instructors tend to stammer out answers about the importance of making wise selections of mates in the first place, as if what happens over the "extended period" is not similarly critical. Or we come up with platitudes, responses such as "It takes a lot of work" or "It takes regular communication." It was partly frustration with the insufficiency of these answers that led to the conception of minding. Thus, in the wee hours of the morning, the first author began to write a short paper on this enigma.

Then, in the early fall of 1995, the first author had the good fortune to begin to work with the second author in the Personality and Social Psychology graduate program at The University of Iowa. The maintenance question was a puzzle that intrigued both of us. We also shared an interest in exploring an emphasis upon the *mind's* role in relating. Very soon we began to trade our individual guesses about the correct formulae or interrelated components for minding. We eventually integrated our ideas in a 1997 article published in the *Personality and Social Psychology Review*.

When we speak of the mind, and the use of the mind in relating, we mean cognition, the "thinking" work we do each day. This could specifically include our thoughts, memories, knowledge acquisition, decisions, judgments, and attributions. Although we consider emotion to be an important aspect of relationships, our theory of "minding" addresses how our thinking processes may impact those emotions.

As we note in the Preface, we are indebted to Norbert Kerr and to the anonymous reviewers who challenged us to make the argument more coherent and better fitted to other works in the literature than we had initially conceived to be relevant. These reviewers, and others, helped us build the theory and delineate the implications that are presented here.

So, the "short" article on the mystery of maintaining close relationships became an essay about the importance of the *mind* in achieving long-term closeness. But the elaboration of this idea re-quired a lot of "minding" itself and study of the relevant literature. And it turned into a very long article. Strangely enough, *there was no previous analysis in the vast close relationship literature that empha-sized the mind and its functioning as vital to relationship closeness*. It is this emphasis and an accompanying delineation of the hows of relationship functioning that our subsequent writing, including this book, has attempted to provide.

A further compelling stimulus for this book has been the many discussions of "minding" we have had with students in interper-sonal relationship classes, with research colleagues, and with parti-cipants in our research on the topic. From the beginning, students have been drawn to the idea of minding. And why not? What do we do in higher education other than espouse and argue the role of the human mind in regulating and affecting the course of our lives? Students seem to appreciate the logic of the minding approach. It has a set of criteria that makes sense in terms of their attempts to be close to others in daily life.

But the larger community of scholars and interested readers has never questioned whether people use their minds in close relation-ships. Of course, they do. Rather, their questions are about how and when, especially regarding the search for long-term closeness. An-swering these questions is a daunting task. While trying to describe the ways in which the mind operates in relationships in general, we also need to take into account the major categories of social and personal differences among people. People have different personal-ity qualities, grow up and live in different cultures and social situa-tions, and are socialized in vastly different types of families with different experiences and backgrounds. Individuals are born with differing biological systems and sometimes develop different tem-peraments in conjunction with those systems and different social situations. Further, various circumstances also affect literacy, intelli-gence, and physical health, which in turn may influence social skills and memory. Thus people are most likely to have very different abilities in carrying out close relationships.

A theory of relationship closeness and satisfaction, which minding is, must be quite carefully constructed so that it applies to as many different people in as many different social milieus as possible. So far, as we will elaborate in this book, we have good reason to believe in the generality of our theory. It covers much territory in addressing what we know about long-term closeness. As will be discussed, other conceptions (e.g., a general theory of intimacy) exist that also cover much of the same territory. We will try to distinguish minding from these conceptions. Our hope is that minding can be used as a framework theory that will enable relationship scholars, students, and laypersons to better understand and discuss what keeps people together, and happy together.

SYNERGY: A CENTRAL QUALITY OF MINDING

In the dictionary, "synergy" refers to "combined or cooperative action or force." In this book, it refers to a central quality of minding that will be defined and discussed: Couples working together can create more of a general, consensual meaning of closeness than they do separately. "Together" is a vital aspect of minding (see the discussion of reciprocity). Minding first creates this working-together synergy. Then, once created, the synergy reinforces and produces further minding. We will argue that minding does not fully occur without the existence of this synergy.

Relationship synergy does not represent only "holy moments" or the rare occurrence of special times – what have been referred to as epiphanies – in couples' mutual experiences. Rather, in our view, synergy is more of a prosaic continuing feature of minding. It encompasses a sense of bonding and completeness that couples may carry with them throughout days, weeks, or even years.

We also argue that minding is not something a couple can do one day, neglect for a week, and then resume with effectiveness. It is a thought and activity pattern that must be built into the day-to-day realities of the couple. To continue in a state of relationship synergy, the minding process must not stop.

Synergy therefore reflects what we see as the ultimate goal of the minding process. All of the components we describe – the patterns of thinking and behaving, the striving for relationship stability – are centered on the goal of relationship synergy. A well-minded couple feels stronger, better, and healthier together than apart.

LOOKING FOR DATA

Some readers, especially scholars in the area of relationship research, may feel this book is premature. We do not have large amounts of data collected specifically to validate the concepts behind minding theory. We still feel, however, that this book can make an important contribution. Our reasons include the following:

(1) The theory involves several interrelated components, which require time-consuming research to test thoroughly and to evaluate carefully in the context of other conceptions of closeness and satisfaction. Although that technical enterprise can be and is being pursued currently, we believe that efforts to amass data can be done simultaneously with presenting the theory.

(2) We also believe that there is enough evidence of various sorts available to begin to support the theory. Part of what we have done in creating minding theory is to combine some of the principles established by other researchers, some working in the area of relationships, some in other areas of psychology. In many ways we have not "invented" the theory so much as put the pieces together in a new way. The evidence collected by others validates the ideas behind our theory, if not its exact form and application to relationships. This book, in part, explores some of the diversity of this evidence.

(3) Because we believe in the theory, we want to present it as widely as possible so that varying audiences can evaluate it and "use" it, if they find elements of its argument to be compelling. Such an outcome would be marvelous to us.

Other scholars have already contributed to the development of our ideas by being cynical, challenging, or supportive. Many have offered points of revision. Some have suggested that the ideas are "too obvious." Ironically, minding may seem both too involved to be studied easily, and at the same time too obvious and simple.

We recall that the ideas in Fritz Heider's book *The Psychology of Interpersonal Relations* (1958) were circulated in memo form for over fifteen years in the 1940s and 1950s, but were scoffed at and thought to be much too transparent to have any value for our understanding of social perception processes. Today, scholars in social psychology recognize Heider's ideas as profound and as having been seminal in their impact. Probably all thinkers and writers should be warmed by this story.

We have no illusions that minding will be as important to understanding closeness as have Heider's ideas for understanding social perception. Still, we have confidence that there *is* something new and potentially valuable here.

As apparent in various parts of this book, we are writing for multiple audiences. We are partially writing for scholars of close relationship phenomena, but we also want to produce this book now for laypersons, thoughtful general students of close relationships, and clinicians or family therapists. The reactions of our students have encouraged us to believe that the message of the book will have value to these broader audiences. We have written some chapters with them specifically in mind.

We hope also that teachers will find the book of use as a supplement in courses on close relationships. In addition to our argument about the merit of minding, we provide integrative discussions of many major concepts pertinent to relationship closeness. These should be of value to classes studying the maintenance of close relationships.

AN OVERVIEW OF THE BOOK

In this book, we present the concept of minding as an invaluable process involved in long-term closeness and satisfaction in human relationships. On initial scrutiny, the idea may seem quite simple. It centers on the use of one's mind to facilitate relating to a partner. We use the gerund "minding" to emphasize the role of the mind in this process.

We stress that the process is far from simple, especially in its execution in close relationships. Even though we emphasize the mind as critical to closeness, we also recognize the role of behavior as similarly essential. We believe that the mind should take precedence in our understanding of closeness because it can regulate behavior and social interaction.

People plan much that they do. People can calculate and anticipate outcomes. People can imagine what others think and feel, especially others to whom they are close. People can learn from their mistakes. These are minding acts when they occur within a framework of caring about a close other and taking actions consistent with that caring.

In this book we emphasize minding as it applies to relationships *after people have made a commitment* (whether in marriage or otherwise). By commitment, we mean a mutual expectation that a couple's relationship will continue for an indefinite, long-term period. This expectation can be manifested in explicit agreement or in the implicit private judgments of partners (Parks, 1997). However, parts of the minding process may be useful both in courtship prior to commitment and in movement away from a close relationship. Hence, we include a chapter on minding in courtship and relationship dissolution.

We most frequently use heterosexual, romantic relationships as our examples. Most of the research in the close relationships field has involved this type of relationship. We do believe, however, that our ideas apply equally well to homosexual romantic relationships, to close, nonromantic friendships, and to some familial relationships.

Throughout the book we examine some related concepts that have special relevance to the use of the mind in achieving closeness. These include Beck's (1988) explanations of why "love is never enough" in achieving closeness, Schwartz's (1994) descriptions of the "peer marriage," and the ingredients of "the good marriage" delineated by Wallerstein and Blakeslee's (1995) book of that title. We expand on and compare these and other conceptions of close relationships with the logic of minding. The concerns of these scholars are at the center of our inquiry into minding as well.

For the sake of convenience, we refer to close relationships as being "well minded" or "not well minded." We recognize that there is most probably a continuum of minding. Some couples may be very skilled at minding, while others are clearly not. It is probable, however, that a couple could fall between these two extremes as well.

A brief outline of the chapters is as follows. Chapter 2 presents a description of the minding theory; Chapter 3, an in-depth discussion of the knowing-other component and its relevance to other psychological and close relationship concepts. How do people both learn about their partners and allow themselves to be known by their partners? Is there a critical balance between knowing and being known in order for minding to be effective? We consider these matters in Chapter 3.

Chapter 4 discusses in detail the attribution component and its relevance to other psychological and close relationship concepts. Given that attribution is frequently going on in our minds, is it always relevant to minding? Or is it a certain kind of attribution about our partners and the relationship that matters most? These questions are considered in Chapter 4.

Chapter 5 presents an overview of evidence pertaining to the remaining components of minding: acceptance, reciprocity, and continuity. How are these elements integrated into the minding package? What do they bring to a relationship that facilitates its survival?

Minding in courtship, casual friendship, dissolution, and familial relationships is addressed in Chapter 6. We consider possible differences in how much people use their minds in developing approaches to relating in these kinds of situations. Is minding a part of close friendships? How can minding be of use when relationships are just beginning or ending?

Chapter 7 discusses minding in the context of current close relationship literature and other general concepts of closeness. The minding concept is applied to mainstream relationship literature questions and lines of work. We compare and contrast these, and try to make the case that minding is an original and useful idea for this literature.

In Chapter 8 minding is compared to treatments in major relationship books about closeness, especially the concepts of "love is never enough," "peer marriage," and "the good marriage." In this discussion, we have selected three major approaches to maintenance of relationships to which we believe minding is highly comparable.

Evidence from various sources about minding is presented in Chapter 9. At the time of the writing of this book, we have collected various types of evidence pertinent to minding from young couples, college students, and middle-aged persons in and out of relationships.

Further evidence about issues in relating and minding-type activities, from an international perspective, is presented in Chapter 10. The first author spent several months in Romania interviewing couples and singles about close relationships there. The perspectives provided by these respondents are valuable to the overall picture of how people try to make relationships work in very difficult socio-economic conditions. At the time of the interviews, Romanians averaged about $100 per month in income and faced about 150 percent annual inflation. Situations of loss, as evidenced by the large numbers of orphan children, orphan pets, and beggars, are pervasive there. How do relationships work in such a climate? How do these and other potent external conditions influence the maintenance of close relationships? These questions are considered in Chapter 10.

Chapter 11 examines how the minding ideas may be extrapolated to therapy and applications contexts. We believe that minding has considerable merit for counseling couples interested in the growth of their relationships. We articulate how the minding strategy might work, and we contrast it to other "self-help" approaches.

In the final chapter, we conclude with a discussion of the overall issues and questions arising from the conceptualization of minding. We consider possible alternatives for maintenance and speculate about future directions for minding theory and research.

CHAPTER 2

Minding: Definition and Components

We've got this gift of love, but love is like a precious plant. You can't just accept it and leave it in the cupboard or just think it's going to get on by itself. You've got to keep watering it. You've got to really look after it and nurture it.

John Lennon, December 30, 1969, MTV

"Minding" is a combination of thought and behavior patterns that interact to create stability and feelings of closeness in a relationship. We officially define minding as: *a reciprocal knowing process that occurs nonstop throughout the history of the relationship and that involves a complex package of interrelated thoughts, feelings, and behaviors.* There are five specific components of minding, which are described below. In the following chapters, they will be discussed in relation to other contemporary close relationship ideas.

KNOWING ONE'S PARTNER

The first component of minding refers to behaviors aimed at knowing one's partner. These include questioning your partner about his or her thoughts, feelings, and past experiences, as well as disclosing appropriately about yourself. This search to know a partner can lead to and includes intuition. Partners often "read between the lines" to know that something is wrong with the other; often the knowledge they have about each other makes it easier for them to pick up nonverbal cues. Knowledge about a partner can facilitate

11

this ability to see beneath surface behaviors to the emotions and motivations below.

In well-minded relationships, each partner will recognize that people change in many ways over time. These changes can involve their physical bodies and their psychological compositions; they can be ever so subtle. Minding partners will also recognize that continuous change makes the process of knowing each other a major challenge. It takes energy and time for both partners to find the right forum to discuss certain issues and to feel comfortable being open and expressive.

Most important, the focus in minding is on *wanting to know* about one's partner. There is great motivation to know about the other's background, hopes, fears, uncertainties, and what keeps him or her awake at night. Emphasis is often placed on "good communication" in a relationship, sometimes stressing the ability to express one's feelings often and fully. Minding theory acknowledges that accurate and frequent communication is important, but it changes the emphasis on one's own self-expression to an emphasis on the active seeking of the other's self-expression or information. It is this overt desire to really know another person that, we believe, creates an atmosphere that allows more open disclosure and "good communication."

This search to know and understand the other should also be reflected in acts explicitly designed to facilitate the relationship, and which are based on this knowledge. Everything from doing an errand to smiling at one's partner may be included. If the errand in question is one you know your partner dreads doing himself, or if the smile is given across the room as a response to a private joke, these are facilitative acts based on knowledge that partners have shared. Buying your partner flowers is an affectionate act, but it is much more meaningful when you choose a particular variety because you know they are your partner's favorite. It is a loving gesture regardless, but the latter has the extra impact of minding the relationship behind it. It will move the relationship that much closer.

RELATIONSHIP-ENHANCING ATTRIBUTIONS

The second component is the attributional activity that partners engage in regarding their partner's behavior. Attributions refer to the interpretations or explanations that people make for events in their lives. One of Heider's (1958, 1976) invaluable contributions was to describe human attributional patterns. He suggested that attribution was a broad, pervasive type of activity that occurred almost anytime a person interacted with or encountered an event in his or her environment. One of his examples was an occasion when he heard the back door of his home slam shut and immediately hypothesized that his wife Grace had returned from the grocery store. The slamming of the door created the need for an explanation: his wife's return. In Heider's view, we continually create these explanations (attributions) for each incident in our daily lives.

One of the most common types of attributional patterns Heider identified is the way in which we tend to explain the behavior of other people in terms either of the situation or of their personalities. Imagine that someone walking past you trips and stumbles. Is the sidewalk uneven (situational attribution), or is the person clumsy (personality or dispositional attribution)? A situational attribution explains the event in terms of external, environmental factors. A dispositional attribution explains the event in terms of internal, personality-based factors.

In relationships, the critical attributions pertain to the dispositional explanations (Jones & Davis, 1965) that people make when they observe their partner act in certain ways. For example, a wife comes home and begins screaming that she wants to be left alone, then goes into the bedroom and says that she does not want to talk about how she feels. The husband compares this act to her typical behavior after returning home from the office. If this type of behavior is rare, he may conclude that a unique external event must have occurred, perhaps at work, and caused her negative behavior. If, however, she often acts in this way, he likely will attribute the behavior more to her disposition to be grouchy and unhappy than to some particular incident.

As Heider asserted that attribution constantly occurs in everyday life, we reassert that attribution is literally always occurring at some level in close relationships. Attributional activity is a central way in which we develop a sense of meaning about our relationships. In a way, attributional activity reflects our trust and belief in our partners. When we attribute our partners' negative behaviors, such as rudeness or insensitivity, to outside causes we are essentially telling ourselves that they are *not* really insensitive; it's the situation. We believe better of them. However, if we attribute our partners' positive, caring acts to outside events or to self-interest, we are convincing ourselves not to believe in their love, not to trust their sincerity.

Relationship-enhancing attributions tend to be those that attribute positive behaviors to dispositional causes: He came home early to spend time with me. She called me at work because she cares about me. Negative behaviors, on the other hand, are attributed more often to external causes: She yelled at me because she's stressed at work. He is late for our date because his car broke down. Attribution theorists such as Heider recognized that people's attributions of causality and responsibility often are mixtures of internal and external attribution. For example, the husband in the foregoing example may emphasize his wife's stress at work, but also attribute part of her temper display to her susceptibility to such stresses. In well-minded relationships, these attributional activities will be carefully carried out, which includes working to develop fair mixtures of internal and external attributions. Partners will recognize how easy it is to be mistaken about a partner's behavior, feelings, intentions, and motivations, and how important it is to feel firm about attributions regarding behavior of their partner in different situations. Flexibility and willingness to reexamine attributions about one's partner and the relationship characterize well-minded relationships.

Partners who are minding well can use the knowledge they have gained about each other to help ensure that they do not blindly attribute all good, or all bad, to their partners. Parts of the minding process build on each other. The knowledge and attribution components work together to help couples build trust and positive beliefs that are based in real knowledge and that they can feel confident about relying on.

ACCEPTANCE AND RESPECT

Acceptance and respect for what is learned via the knowing, self-disclosure, and attributional activities are essential aspects of minding. Invariably, we discover qualities of our partners that may be flaws, unflattering to the partner, or that may conflict with our own ideals of background and behavior. In well-minded relationships, there will be respect and acceptance for what is discovered about a partner. Again, the minding components work together to make this acceptance possible. The active search for knowledge about a partner should help serious potential problems or conflicts surface early in a relationship. Ideally, this ensures that "critical flaws" most often will be discovered during the courtship or uncommitted stage of relating and not after a commitment has been made. Critical flaws would be any qualities that would make long-term commitment and long-term satisfaction unlikely.

Our definition of acceptance is not intended to be all-encompassing or completely unconditional. Students have mentioned to us that sometimes, after commitment, one partner may learn that the other has had a very troubling history (e.g., infidelity, sexual or physical abuse) that was not divulged during the early courtship stage. It is possible that in this situation, the relationship may be strained to the point of termination.

We believe that people need to find out a lot about people with whom they become involved. They need to look at family albums, listen carefully to relationship stories, and indeed "read between the lines" about what everything they learn tells them about this prospective mate (see Harvey, Weber, & Orbuch's 1990 analysis of accounts and their role in relationships). If they have done their homework, people will not be as surprised by what they may later discover. They will have done enough preliminary minding early on that they can generally accept and respect what they learn later when they are minding for maintenance of the relationship.

Lesser "noncritical" problems or differences between partners are probably unavoidable. Acceptance is always needed eventually to establish relationships that are stable and long-term with partners who are, after all, only human. In the television series *Seinfeld*, a running joke is the way in which the characters break off relationships with romantic partners because of superficial annoyances or quirks. One eats too slowly, another laughs too loudly, still another wears a favorite outfit too often. That's it – the relationship is over. While fictional, the romantic travails of these characters illustrate the importance of accepting a partner's minor faults and respecting a partner's differences, if the ultimate goal is long-term closeness.

RECIPROCITY

Minding involves reciprocity in thoughts, feelings, and behaviors between partners. In short, minding is not a one-way street. The idea of synergy suggests this cooperative interdependence. Interdependence refers to an intertwining of partners' behaviors, thoughts, and feelings. In an influential analysis of relationships, Kelley and colleagues (1983) developed a definition of closeness that also embraces this type of interdependence over a long period of time: "The close relationship is one of strong, frequent, and diverse interdependence that lasts over a considerable period of time" (p. 38).

It is critical that this mutuality of responses, or reciprocity, occurs. In relationships, both partners think, feel, and behave. To be close, we and our partners need to coordinate these thoughts, feelings, and behavior. Well-minded relationships epitomize this coordination or synchrony. If we are minding our relationships, we will be aware of our partner's patterns of behavior, and we will attempt to act out similar or complementary patterns that our partner, in turn, recognizes and appreciates. For example, well-minded relationships do not involve one partner exclusively playing "therapist" and getting the other partner to talk and express her or his feelings and concerns. Rather, each partner will recognize the value and necessity of listening and caring about what is heard and of being honest and expressive in return. They are confidants at a very basic level.

Does this mean we do tit-for-tat in each area? That there is a scoreboard for behaviors? No, not so formally, nor necessarily in a conscious way. Partners have different strengths and weaknesses. For instance, one partner may be especially good at verbally expressing affection, while the other may express caring in more nonverbal ways, such as giving gifts. Minding partners, for the most part, know about these differences and accept them. They are able to make the accurate attribution of caring and affection to a partner's actions, even when those actions are different from their own methods of showing their love. In time, couples who are minding their relationships well will achieve a rhythm or flow of interaction (Csikszentmihalyi, 1982) that reduces the need for conscious consideration of whether reciprocation is occurring.

It also may be possible that one member of a couple will be the leader and initial worker in taking constructive activity on behalf of the relationship. This person's leadership may then influence the partner to be likewise engaged in the constructive work. Over time, each partner may take turns as the leader and "front person" in dealing with issues and making things work in the relationship. While each partner then may not be working strongly for the relationship at the same time or in the same manner, each partner should have occasion to take such a role. Such is the imperative of the reciprocity component of minding.

CONTINUITY OVER TIME

A final component of minding is that the process of trying to know one's partner, understand the relationship, carefully engage in attributional activity, and maintain respect and acceptance for one's partner requires a substantial period of time to become firmly established. Once developed, the process needs to continue throughout the life of the relationship.

The "substantial period of time" requirement derives from the complexity of minding and the many details involved in the knowledge of another human being. Time is also necessary to stabilize and develop the "third party" that is created when a relationship is created. Two individuals, "you and me," also become a single unit, "us," a new, third entity.

Couples in well-minded relationships also recognize, possibly at an implicit level, that ceasing to care about knowing the other or the relationship, ceasing to be careful in making inferences, or becoming contemptuous and disrespectful are steps in the direction toward deterioration of the relationship. Every single act in a relationship certainly cannot reflect the highest form of minding. Our daily lives are far too complex, with far too many demands, to maintain that quality of concentration on the relationship through every minute. However, in a well-minded relationship, a majority of acts will reflect the minding process. As important, one's partner will be aware that such a motivation to care for the relationship exists and that there are the very best of intentions behind this composite reality. Remember, too, that this "meaning of closeness" must apply to both partners in a couple. One cannot be the caretaker and the other the cared for; each must nurture and each must be cared for in some general equivalence of thought, feeling, and action.

VARIABLES REVEALING HIGH AND LOW DEGREES OF MINDING

Table 1 shows a list of variables that we believe will differentiate couples who are engaged in high versus low degrees of minding. This list is only illustrative of the many specific acts, including behavior, thought, and feeling, that relate to the five minding criteria.

As can be seen in the table, there are many behavior – thought – feeling manifestations of well-minded and not well-minded relationships for each of the criteria. The final set of variables refers to "process" for well-minded relationships and to "discontinuity" for not well-minded relationships. It represents an outcome of the first four categories. Note that for each criterion, emphasis is on qualities such as effort to achieve accuracy, empathy, and fullness in how partners carry out their behavior toward one another.

Some criteria are very basic and crucial to the rest of the minding process. For example, they include listening and attention to accuracy, acts that facilitate knowledge acquisition, as well as appropriate attributional activity, acceptance, and respect. Without listening and attention, all of the other criteria of minding are negatively affected. It is easy to see how many minding acts and criteria are interrelated and interdependent.

MEASURING FEELINGS OF CLOSENESS AND SATISFACTION

How can we measure whether a couple has achieved closeness and/or satisfaction? By their responses to a questionnaire? Through a specially designed interview? By observing their behavior as they interact with each other? These are all methods researchers have utilized in their studies of close relationships and of relationship satisfaction. As discussed in Chapter 12, we believe that closeness and satisfaction may be best understood via multivariate techniques, a combination of these and other methods. We need to evaluate closeness and satisfaction with as many means as possible, as long as they make sense within the context of the theory we are trying to test.

At the heart of the social psychology of minding is the assumption that within limits, people can know and articulate what they are doing in general in their close relationships. If you ask them, as we have, what pleases and what troubles them, and how they address the troubles, they have answers. These answers may or may not correspond to what actually occurs in their daily lives. Hence, as has been contended by some investigators (e.g., Gottman, 1994, 1995), it may be informative to engage in other measuring techniques, including observing couples solve problems, talk over the dinner table, and respond to scenarios about other couples and their dilemmas.

Still, we believe that couples' own self-reports about their processing of major events in their relationships (e.g., whether to have a child at a certain time in their relationship history) are vital items of

Table 1. *Relationships involving high and low degrees of minding*

WELL-MINDED RELATIONSHIPS

Behavior-facilitating disclosure
• Questioning partner about feelings/behaviors
• Utilizing effective listener "responses"
• Accurate repetition of partner's disclosure
• Accurate, detailed knowledge of partner's preferences/opinions

Relationship-enhancing attributions
• Generally positive attributions for partner's behaviors
• External attributions for negative relationship events
• Partner attributions for positive relationship events
• Attributions for partner matches partner's self-attributions

Acceptance and respect
• Reconstruction of history/memory emphasizing positives
• Pride in the other's abilities
• Expressed feelings of trust and commitment
• Behaviors that acknowledge the other's preferences/concerns
• Behavior/verbal expressions that acknowledge self-disclosures

Reciprocity
• Estimates of relationship effort match partner's
• Can identify partner's contributions to relationship
• Recognition of the other's support and effort
• Perception of synergy (stronger together than separate)

Process
• Sense of "we-ness," togetherness permeates relationship
• Agreement in charting ups and downs of relationship over time
• Optimistic view of future of relationship
• Feeling of control over relationship
• Hope for the future in general

NOT WELL-MINDED RELATIONSHIPS

Behavior that avoids disclosure
- Poor listening behavior
- Lack of interest in the other's disclosures
- Distorted repetitions of partner's disclosures
- Ignorance of the other's preferences/opinions

Relationship-disruption attributions
- Overall negative attributions for partner's behaviors
- Partner attributions for negative relationship events
- External attributions for positive relationship events
- Nonmatching attributions (self and partner)

Criticism and contempt
- Negative reconstruction of memory/relationship history
- Little overt recognition of the other's preferences/concerns
- Inability to recall the other's disclosures
- Ability to extensively list the other's faults

Inequity
- Nonmatching estimates of relationship effort
- Expressed feelings of inequality
- Inability to recognize the other's contributions
- Nonsynergistic

Discontinuity
- Sense of separateness
- Inability to agree on relationship ups and downs
- Pessimistic view of future of relationship
- Lack of perceived control over relationship
- Inability to perceive future

information that often cannot be obtained by more indirect methods (see Harvey, Hendrick, & Tucker, 1988). We view the couples' own reports on their *sense* of these states as being of great value in determining the amount or level of closeness and satisfaction in their relationships. This sense of closeness should be one that they experience regularly and reciprocally, one that is manifest in their behavior, and one that each believes to exist in the other. This sense is their abiding, comforting, and transcending feeling about the relationship.

BEING MINDLESS VERSUS BEING MINDFUL

While we believe that our minding conception is unique to the close relationship literature, Ellen Langer (1989) has presented an argument that, in general, being mindful is more conducive to an adaptive and healthy life than is being mindless. Her argument did not treat close relationships per se, but her general points can help set the foundation for our treatment of minding in couples.

Langer's work in this area in part stems from evidence that a feeling of control and a belief in one's ability to make a difference in one's environment can improve overall health and well-being. In a well-known experimental study by Langer and Rodin (1976), one group of elderly residents of a nursing home were each given a choice of houseplants to care for and were asked to make a number of small decisions about their daily routines. Another similar group of residents did not receive this opportunity to make small changes in their nursing home environment. A year and a half later, not only were people who had been given the choices more cheerful, active, and alert than were the people in the comparison group, but many more of them were still alive. While Langer and Rodin's evidence cannot be used to show definitively that mortality is influenced by having a degree of felt choice and perceived control, the evidence is quite suggestive that health and vitality are associated with feelings of having choice and control.

Langer (1989) assimilated this evidence into her theory of mindlessness and its counterpart of mindfulness. Mindlessness refers to behavior that is carried out with little or no thought, reacting to the environment without thinking about it in any depth. It is like the "knee-jerk" responses that people sometimes make automatically, without thinking. It often is highly scripted, or routine, as is the act of pushing down on a car's accelerator when a light turns green. Mindfulness, on the other hand, involves conscious thought about behavior and the environment.

Langer identifies the following qualities of mindless behavior. First, mindlessness involves being trapped by categories – "good guys versus bad guys," with few shades in between. Stereotyping others is a fast and easy way to mentally categorize people; it reduces our cognitive effort and our need to be "mindful." We are often likely to stereotype others as being a particular way, without due consideration of behavioral evidence. We may lock in on our stereotypes without observing enough of a person's behavior across different situations and different times.

Second, mindlessness involves automatic behavior, such as an automatic angry curse in reaction to being cut off in traffic. This idea can be compared to one of Beck's important ideas in his work *Love Is Never Enough* (1988) about "automatic thoughts." Couples sometimes encounter difficulty in their relationships when they develop patterns of automatic thoughts that often are negative in valence. An example is a wife's thinking, "He's out drinking with his friends; he doesn't care about me." Beck says that people need to be careful in making such automatic assumptions. Over time, these assumptions may become self-fulfilling. After hearing his wife's automatic accusations, the husband may begin to feel that she is correct: He must *not* care as much about being with her as about being with his friends.

Mindlessness also involves acting from a single perspective. Langer says that we often act as if there is just one set of rules guiding behavior. These rules are our rules, the ones we are accustomed to, perhaps grew up learning and abiding by. When we are mindless, we are not flexible enough to entertain different systems

23

of rules and ways of doing business. We want everything to stay the same, the way we are used to and the way we feel most comfortable. This enables us to keep avoiding mindful work.

Why and how do we allow ourselves to stop using our minds to actively interact with our environments? How do we become "mindless" in our behavior? Langer identifies several causes of mindlessness: repetition, premature cognitive commitment, belief in limited resources, the notion of linear time, being educated to focus on outcome rather than process, and the powerful influence of context.

We are always repeating acts, and this repetition allows us to become automatic in our behaviors. Couples may say "I love you" to one another each morning until it becomes automatic. They stop thinking enough about the meaning of the words, and do not consciously recognize how deeply indebted they are to one another and how invaluable the other is in their lives.

Premature cognitive commitment is like the stereotyping described above. It involves developing and committing ourselves to our ideas too quickly. We make a quick, easy judgment and then move on to the next person, the next event, without stopping to consider enough evidence to make an accurate decision or appraisal. In our fast-paced, complicated world, this is all too easy to do.

Belief in limited resources is the view that there are only very limited amounts of any desired commodity, perhaps not enough to go around for everyone. Langer gives the wonderful example of a couple who fight for custody of a child after a divorce. They may talk about the importance of "who gets the child." She suggests a more reasonable view is that the child can continue to love and be with both parents. They have to plan how best to execute that quest. The belief that all valuable things must be limited fosters the tandem belief that we must always fight and compete for the things we want. This assumption saves us the mental work of planning other strategies, working out compromises with others, or acknowledging that some situations are qualitatively different from others. In our chapter on relationship endings, we indeed suggest that minding needs to continue at the point of termination, since it facilitates the well-being of ex-partners, as well as children and other third parties. Such minding would lead to a facilitation of a child's continued love for a parent and former partner.

In using linear time people sometimes become fixed on the idea that time is an asset that is running out and in which a certain amount must be accomplished. We often are stressed by our thoughts about time, such as, "There is not enough time to get done what must be done." As Harvey (1995) has suggested, people have great capacity to stretch and create time to act in accord with their values. They can work the "seams" of time, such as doing a moderate writing project on an airplane trip of a couple of hours. Or, if they wait a lot, they can learn to take work along, as the thousands of commuters using laptop computers or cell phones do nowadays. Again, though, by fixing our thoughts on the idea of completing a series of tasks in a particular segment of time, we free ourselves from the mindful work of really evaluating how our time is spent. Instead, like computers programmed to carry out a set of commands, we don't want to be interrupted or delayed. This would require a "reset" and mental effort aimed at rescheduling our lives.

Langer also sees mindlessness in our system of education, which primarily focuses on outcome. She notes that we are trained from very early on in our lives to value outcome more than process. "How do I get an A in this class?" versus "What values and information will this class teach me?" We want to be "winners," even if we trample over a few values to get there. This focus on outcome keeps our attention solely on the superficial symbols of our goals rather than on the experiences and learning they represent. What, after all, does an A mean, if it does not reflect the process of change and growth that should be inherent in education? This outcome focus thus induces mindlessness; in fact, it is mindless.

The final "cause" of mindlessness that Langer identifies is the power of social context over our behavior. The power of social context is readily demonstrated by the way in which we automatically begin whispering when we enter a church or a hospital. We are conditioned to behave in certain ways in certain contexts. When we enter these contexts, or see cues to these contexts, we mindlessly begin to act out this conditioning. Sometimes that behavior is highly maladaptive, especially when it involves other people. For instance, we may fail to see the "humanity" of officials such as police officers, the frailties of "experts" such as doctors, or the beauty of a poverty-stricken or homeless person. We see only the social contexts surrounding them: a marked police car, a hospital, a shelter. We automatically assume the rest. Langer's example of social context is George Bernard Shaw's play *Pygmalion*. It illustrates the power of context-based perceptions when Eliza Doolittle, a ragged, cockney-accented girl in London, is transformed into a charming and beautiful woman by Professor Higgins. He makes this reality happen largely by building a completely new social context and identity for Eliza.

BECOMING MINDFUL AND ITS RELATION TO MINDING

In a very general way, Langer's analysis of mindlessness versus mindfulness has considerable bearing on minding a close relationship. In the conclusion of her writings, Langer argues that becoming more mindful about our lives gives us both a stronger sense of control and more actual, literal control over our lives. We are healthier, happier, and more capable of contributing to others' welfare.

At the heart of being mindful is the flexible, creative use of the mind. This applies equally well to the minding of a close relationship. Langer says that we must use second-order mindfulness: making decisions about what we will make decisions about. This concept is important if a couple is minding their relationship well. Partners should examine their values and priorities and make choices that allot time and energy to those causes most important to them and to their relationship.

Minding in close relationships emphasizes many of the qualities of mindfulness that Langer pinpoints. Couples *must be creative and flexible in their thinking much of the time* to mind their relationships well. Couples that become caught up in stereotypic thinking about one another or about how a relationship should be carried out cannot mind well.

Couples should not get caught up in focusing too much on competitive outcome goals such as the acquisition of material goods, their children's comparative abilities, or the attainment of social status. These do not constitute the important accomplishments of a couple or family. Rather, the process of relating and growing together should be the center of their focus and behavior.

Couples must be "realistic optimists" about time and resources. They must rely on each other and seek new ways to achieve their life goals, without becoming trapped in the mindlessness of the daily treadmill. With creativity new methods will be found. Closeness and satisfaction will occur, not at some point when goals have been achieved, but at each point at which they perform in a manner consistent with a well-minded relationship.

MEANING AND MINDING

Meaning is a topic found throughout this book and deserves special comment in this chapter. As Heider (1976) suggested, people may make attributions about their partners, themselves, and their relationships quite frequently. Attribution, or "meaning making" in general, contributes to people's desire to be effective agents in their environments, to feel that they can control and make predictions about important events in the future. In making meanings, people are creating both specific and general structures of understandings of their close others, environment, and themselves.

We believe that in a well-minded relationship, the partners will have a shared vision about the nature and the big issues of the relationship. When their separate visions diverge, they will develop a process to resolve disagreements. Throughout the life of the relationship, however, they will concur in ascribing the meaning of a "strong relationship" to their nexus, their "togetherness," which will be based on the particular criteria of minding.

SUMMARY AND A FEW CAVEATS

In this chapter, we introduced the concept of minding, delineated its components, and provided foundation assumptions about how mindlessness/mindfulness relates to our minding analysis. We noted that there has been inadequate previous emphasis on the role of the mind and how it functions in the achievement and maintenance of long-term closeness. We define minding as a never-ending, reciprocal knowing process involving a complex package of interrelated thoughts, feelings, and behaviors. We suggested that there was a continuum of minding, such that some couples mind their relationships very well and others mind their relationships poorly. We discussed the more general ideas of mindlessness versus mindfulness and how minding in close relationships resembles general strategies of living that involve being mindful.

Some caveats should also be mentioned. It is important to note that we view minding as a necessary but not necessarily sufficient condition for the achievement of closeness and satisfaction in a close relationship over a long period. Why do we believe it to be necessary? Because the research literature suggests, in bits and pieces, that processes quite similar to those we have consolidated into the concept of minding are strongly associated with long-term relationship satisfaction and closeness. Additionally, we do not believe that any closeness and satisfaction literature exists that shows the operation of processes quite different from those which we propose.

Why is our conception of minding not necessarily sufficient in itself to produce this greatly desired state in life? Because relationships are complex constructions, they may vary dramatically based on the individual personalities and backgrounds of each set of partners. There are also likely to be situations in which minding, no matter how skillfully and carefully performed, may not be enough to surmount social or personal obstacles to relationship success. Thus there may be other elements to the formula for long-term closeness and satisfaction that may operate on occasion, or with certain people, that do not in any clear way relate to the elements we articulate for minding. We do not know what all these other

28

elements are. But in fairness, we believe that their potential stature in the overall formula will deserve exploration by scholars, even as we argue for the fuller investigation of minding over time. Sexual or erotic passion, for example, certainly deserves attention as an element which may lead to powerful relationship bonds. The relationship literature (e.g., Hatfield & Rapson, 1993) has indicated that sexual passion is essential early in the course of a relationship but that its essential character may not be as important over time. Nonetheless, passion deserves careful study as part of the composite set of factors influencing long-term closeness and satisfaction.

A second cautionary note is that we are representing an evaluative position about relationships that may be, at least in part, culturally based. Our minding theory essentially says that if a couple does and is able to continue to do certain things, they will be and continue to be happy as a couple. This necessarily implies that "happy couples" are those that achieve the close, very personal bonds that minding advocates, largely through sharing and knowledge about each other. Some readers may object to this characterization of relationship satisfaction. For instance, some may come from families in which their parents were not very self-expressive or did not show clearly much respect and acceptance. Yet these parents may have indicated throughout their marriage that they were very happy. We do essentially contend that people can be expressive in different ways – ways that children may not begin to perceive. Verbal signals represent only part of the continuum of communicative signals humans use. Still, we respect the possibility that there are many "traditional" couples and couples in other cultures who are happy for the long run and who apparently do not show much minding. Happiness for these couples may be based more on security or on upholding cultural values or fulfilling traditional roles rather than on the emotional closeness emphasized by minding.

We also argue, however, that if a new couple in the twenty-first century wishes to succeed and work hard for lasting success, there is more to be learned from couples who show the minding activity pattern well. Why? Because knowing and learning how to mind can ideally create a flexibility in relating that can succeed in a variety of relationship situations and a variety of cultural contexts. It can be adapted to include social and cultural variations on partnership in a way that some traditional relationship roles and expectations cannot. What can we learn from "nonminding" couples that has the same probability for such a satisfying payoff?

CHAPTER 3

Knowing and Being Known by One's Partner

We are, all of us, molded and remolded by those who have loved us, and though that love may pass, we remain none the less *their* work – a work that very likely they do not recognize, and which is never exactly what they intended.

François Mauriac, *The Desert of Love*

Perhaps there is no act more endearing than a partner's attempt to diligently, over time, get to know you and use that knowledge toward the enhancement of the relationship. This activity of questing to know another makes that other feel special, treasured, and cared about. Unfortunately, many of us may live out our lives having few if any experiences with others who made us feel this way. The most transcending thesis of this book is that minding offers just such experiences.

Thus, at the heart of the minding process is the quest to know one's partner. At the outset of dating or casual relating, people seek this knowledge about one another for the purpose of determining how close they want to become to new acquaintances, or to gauge whether there is a possibility that they might eventually have the basis for a commitment. When a relationship involves minding, both partners continue to share this quest beyond the initial information gathering; they pursue it vigorously past the point of commitment and throughout the entire span of the relationship.

In this chapter, we discuss why this knowing activity is a key part of minding and how it is carried out. To create a well-minded relationship, couples must first cognitively recognize the *value* of knowing each other intimately and well. They then need to act on this value with behaviors designed to share and seek out this knowledge. We also link knowing to self-disclosure and social penetration, foundation concepts in the development of close relationships. As we describe the knowing activity, it is vital not only to the development but also to the maintenance of a close relationship.

We begin by examining some literature involving self-disclosure. One of the most common ways of sharing knowledge about oneself is through self-disclosure – the process of revealing information about oneself to another. Self-disclosure is most often studied as a verbal behavior, such as talking or writing about oneself, but on occasion it has also been considered nonverbal as well. Eliciting self-disclosure is one of the major methods people use for gaining information about others in social interaction.

SELF-DISCLOSURE, SOCIAL PENETRATION, AND MINDING

Self-Disclosure

As social beings, people are constantly revealing information about themselves. They do so with what they say, how they say it, the clothes they wear, the way they walk, everything from the most outlandish of self-presentations to the most minute nuances of conduct and presence. Why is this disclosure activity so prevalent and important?

In an analysis of self-disclosure in close relationships, Derlega, Metts, Petronio, and Margulis (1993) define self-disclosure as "what individuals verbally reveal about themselves to others (including thoughts, feelings, and experiences)" (p. 1). We believe that in close relationships people self-disclose frequently in nonverbal ways too. Both verbal and nonverbal self-disclosure are crucial to minding.

The late clinical psychologist Sidney Jourard (1971) was one of the first psychologists to call for greater attention to be given to the importance of self-disclosure. Jourard believed self-disclosure was conducive to health and essential to achieving closeness in human relationships. He argued that many positive consequences ensue from honestly revealing the self to another. He contended that such revelations help people: (1) to learn the extent to which they are different from one another; (2) to understand and support one another's needs; and (3) to learn the extent to which they hold common values and standards for behavior. These outcomes would allow a greater understanding of oneself and one's immediate community of friends and family.

Jourard also recognized, however, the courage involved in the decision to self-disclose to another. Disclosing not only presents an opportunity to increase understanding and closeness; it also presents the possible risk inherent in letting another know one's inner self: rejection. He described this dialectical dilemma of self-disclosure:

> Self-disclosure follows an attitude of love and trust. If I love someone, not only do I strive to know him: I *also display my love by letting him know me* [emphasis added]. At the same time, by so doing, I permit him to love me. . . . Loving is scary, because when you permit yourself to be known, you expose yourself not only to a lover's balm, but also to a hater's bombs. When he knows you, he knows just where to plant them for maximum effect. (p. 5)

In a later discussion, Jourard amplifies his views on the impact of self-disclosure in close relationships:

> A loving man (or woman) opens all his senses, drops his defenses, in order to be maximally affected by his loved one. This is why he can also be hurt by her more than by anyone else. . . . He does not hold back, but is instead transparent during his transactions with his loved one. (p. 62)

What Jourard calls the "transparency" of disclosure is an integral part of how the minding process establishes closeness in a relationship. Revealing oneself allows connections to be made with another. It implies there is at least an initial commitment to explore the possibility of closeness by letting down the guards and becoming "transparent" to one another. It indicates a cognitive set or belief that knowing each other is a valuable and worthwhile goal in relationships.

But "minding" a relationship does not just mean permission to express all of one's feelings and expect unconditional and unvarying attention. The focus in minding is on eliciting disclosure from one's partner and on the value placed on the information gained. Thus, when minding, partners recognize the necessity of reciprocal self-disclosure, of give and take in the personal exchange. Thus, partners will disclose, encourage their partners to disclose, and be willing for their partners to seek to know them through disclosure processes.

Reis and Shaver (1988) have suggested that intimacy between two people is created by a similar process of escalating reciprocity of self-disclosure. One person discloses at a relatively low level, which is followed by the second's disclosure at the same or slightly more intimate level. The first person again reciprocates, and the process continues. The key is that in each round of disclosures, each person feels his or her innermost self is validated, understood, or cared for by the partner.

Chelune, Robinson, and Kommor (1984) argue that the association between self-disclosure and intimacy is one of mutual influence. Self-disclosure helps to create a feeling of intimacy, and intimacy promotes honest disclosures. One almost surely has an impact on the other. In the same way, not only does minding emphasize the encouragement of self-disclosure, but self-disclosure itself is conducive to minding.

Aron and Aron (1986) describe a concept of love as self-expansion. According to self-expansion theory, when we establish close relationships with others, we do so in order to learn and to grow beyond our current limits. When we know another person intimately we can add their unique attributes to our own; we can thus expand our own reach and our own abilities. This self-expansion is hypothesized to be highly satisfying, and to occur through close connection with another.

Aron and Aron (1996) argue that this process mainly involves an escalation of self-disclosure (citing Reis & Shaver, 1988). They state that "when people first fall in love there is often a rapid, exhilarating expansion of self. People stay up all night talking, sharing, just doing everything they can to merge selves" (1996, p. 340). We argue that minding involves just such sharing and associations between knowing one's partner and feelings of intimacy and closeness.

Confiding Our Troubles to a Close Other

James Pennebaker (1990) has produced an important theory and research about the importance of self-disclosure for health. He and his colleagues have conducted several research studies in which students have written disclosures of past traumas in diaries. Throughout the following weeks, these students' reported health problems were compared with those of another group of students who had been instructed to write only about trivial events in their diaries. The students who disclosed traumas reported fewer health problems and made fewer visits to student health services than did the students who wrote about trivia (Pennebaker & Beall, 1986).

This work has suggested that people who confide their troubled experiences, whether in a diary, to a spouse or friend, or in religious confession, are relieved of the stress caused by the trauma. At least one of Pennebaker's studies has also found differences in immune function between disclosers and nondisclosers, with disclosers appearing to be more resistant to common illnesses (Pennebaker, Kiecolt-Glaser, & Glaser, 1988).

Pennebaker has also studied the reactions of persons orally recounting such traumas as the Vietnam war, rape, and the Holocaust. His results indicate that for many people, while making the disclosure can itself be upsetting, being able to verbally share their traumatic experiences appears to improve their health over the long term. Much of this type of research has been done with persons disclosing less dramatic problems, however, with similar results.

Harvey and his colleagues have done considerable work in the area of research devoted to "accounts." Accounts are the stories we create about our own experiences, to tell to others and to record as memories for ourselves. In work on the verbal accounts, or personal stories, that people share with each other in relationships, Harvey and colleagues (e.g., Harvey et al., 1990) have also reported that telling stories of loss to close confidants has value for health. Their work emphasizes how critical it is that the reaction of the confidant be appropriate and encouraging. When confidants react with empathy to expressed concerns or stories of humiliation and great loss, people indicate that they have been greatly comforted. When confidants do not show empathy, however, people report not only that they felt worse than before the disclosure, but that they also became less willing to discuss the loss with others in the future (Harvey, Orbuch, Chwalisz, & Garwood, 1991).

Thus, having a trusted partner in which to confide one's hopes, fears, and disappointments may be more than emotionally satisfying. It may also be important to physical and mental health. In addition, as important as the revelation itself may be the quality of response – the support and comfort received. One outcome of minding is to give partners this "safe" place to reveal themselves in a way that may create not only a healthy relationship, but also healthier people.

Self-Disclosure and Knowing via Story-Telling

The importance of the knowing and revealing component of minding is clearly seen in the ways people use the stories they have shared about the present and past with their partners. Pennington and Hastie (1991) have argued that people often develop judgments about specific situations by piecing together meaningful stories from observed and inferred data bases. Rather than adding or subtracting pieces of evidence to come to a conclusion about someone, we instead put those pieces in a story-like order and complete the blanks according to how we believe the story would most likely go. For example, if after several dates a new partner invites you home to meet his mother, you might assume with little other objective evidence that he is intending to try to move the relationship to a more committed level, because this is how our "stories" of relationships work. Meeting the parents is the next "step" to commitment.

These social judgments have great impact on how we view our

world and our relationships. Sharing our own stories with a partner and hearing his or her stories is a way to ensure a good "match" and also to avoid misunderstandings based on conflicting templates of stories. Going back to our previous example, the woman in this case may be less inclined to presume commitment if she has heard beforehand his stories of the many previous girlfriends who have come to dinner; she knows then that, for this man, meeting his mother does not necessarily indicate a serious relationship. Therefore, when partners tell us their stories of past experiences, this self-disclosure facilitates our formation of social judgments. This, in turn, affects our thoughts and emotions regarding the social context of the disclosure and of the relationship (Harvey et al., 1990; Bochner, Ellis, & Tillman, 1997).

This sharing involves stories of who we are, where we have been, with whom we have been close, and what we have become as a consequence of those experiences. It has been hypothesized that we all create and hold in memory "accounts" or stories of our own lives. In the larger account that encompasses one's life as a whole, each individual event that is experienced could be considered a "subaccount." This is one way in which we connect with others – by trading and sharing subaccounts about events we may have in common. According to the logic of interpersonal accounts (Harvey et al., 1990), people have as many subaccounts as they have had important experiences. Harvey and colleagues refer to the compilation of those subaccounts as the "master account."

When we share these subaccounts with others, are we accurate in reporting the details of our stories? Do we tell our stories the way they "really" happened? Or do we edit them to reflect our views and self-interests? It is often frustrating, usually bewildering, and sometimes amusing to be faced with a situation where each person who experiences an event may recount it quite differently, with contradictory details.

For example, imagine a couple the day after a first date. Each recounts very different descriptions of the evening to friends, although they both shared the same events. The man recalls a quiet dinner with good conversation and indicates a willingness to go out again. The woman recalls a dull evening with a man who just wanted to "sit and talk about himself." Who is right? Perhaps neither, perhaps both.

Regardless of accuracy, when we tell our stories we still communicate meaningful points. All our details may not be historically, objectively "true," but the points we make have a narrative truth. They tell about who we are and why we act as we do (Spence, 1982; Ellis, 1996). Each member of the couple described above reveals, in describing the date, something about the qualities he or she values in a new partner. When they tell this story to friends, or perhaps to other potential partners, their listeners learn something about their values and preferences. Who was "right" about the date is not, in this sense, important.

There is in fact a good deal of research indicating that people may often distort part of their histories either purposefully or unintentionally in their reports about past events (Loftus, 1993; Conway, 1995). The psychological mechanism underlying this type of distortion is still unclear, but there are several possible explanations. People may be less accurate about past events because of social cues in the immediate environment, strategic self-presentational issues, or the self-relevance of the shared information itself. Using our couple as an example, the woman may be prompted to be overly critical of her date because of a romantic movie she has just seen (environmental cue) inviting comparisons to her favorite male actor. The man may describe their date as overly successful in order to present an image of himself to his buddies as being socially popular (self-presentation). Or each may simply date so often and be so unconcerned about finding long-term partners that describing the details of any one date seems unimportant (relevance).

For a variety of reasons, therefore, including fear of revealing unpleasant truths about ourselves (Goffman, 1959), we may never communicate all of our specific stories, or even the full details of any one story. In close relationships, though, we may gradually reveal a great number of subaccounts to our partner. It is perhaps only after a lengthy relationship that we may reveal much of our overall master account – our synthesized view of our experiences.

Below is an example of a relationship story that illustrates the complexity of understanding involved in relationships and the nuances of meaning that swirl around as couples discuss vital questions of living and of love. This story was excerpted from the writing of the late Raymond Carver, who wrote with astounding insight about the dynamics and background issues of close relationships. These lines come from the story "What We Talk About When We Talk About Love" (1986). Mel, a middle-aged doctor, is sitting at his kitchen table drinking wine with his wife, Terri, and their friends. During the conversation, Mel begins to philosophize about his past loves:

> It seems to me we're just beginners at love. We say we love each other and we do, I don't doubt it. . . . But sometimes I have a hard time accounting for the fact that I must have loved my first wife too. But I did, I know I did. . . . There was a time when I thought I loved my wife more than life itself. But now I hate her guts. I do. How do you explain that? What happened to that love? What happened to it, is what I'd like to know. . . . And the terrible thing, the terrible thing is, but the good thing too, the saving grace, you might say, is that if something happened to one of us . . . I think the other one, the other person, would grieve for a while, you know, but then the surviving party would go out and love again, have someone else soon enough. All this, all of this love we're talking about, it would be just a memory. (pp. 132-133)

In terms of minding, developing stories and communicating them in storytelling represent an essential means by which we know and are known. It is not that important that some or even many of the details of our stories of past events may be distorted. What matters is the sincere attempt to communicate about one's self and to inform the other, and the other's acceptance and respect for this act. It also matters how the couple agrees to handle stories – how much detail they decide is appropriate, topics that are appropriate, and so on. Mel's story of the vagaries of love may be an instance of minding if it is consistent with understandings he and Terri have developed in discussing past loves, including making public (even to close friends) aspects of their past lives and their feeling and thinking about those lives. It is important that couples develop "ground rules" for disclosure with which both members are comfortable.

Our stories inform others about us, guide our own thoughts, and contribute to interactions in our relationships. This creation of intimacy through stories appears to be common to most people and is certainly one of the most uniquely human capabilities we possess. In fact, the sharing of stories with one another has been referred to as a "bedrock human capacity" (Coles, 1989). Whatever our background or education might be, we always have the capacity to tell our own story, and research described earlier indicates that this telling may be important for our health and well-being.

But simply the ability to tell our stories is not enough. We need to have close others in whom we can confide. That is as much a bedrock need as is the storytelling act a bedrock capacity. A central thesis of minding is that each partner has, in the other, a person who cares – a person who knows a lot about you and wants to know more. Our lives may change, as do our stories, but the need for a confidant never ends as long as we live.

Social Penetration

In 1973, Altman and Taylor proposed a theory called "social penetration." This theory emphasized how people develop relationships and sometimes lose relationships, all via the patterns of self-disclosure over time. Development of a relationship was hypothesized to depend on an increasing level of reciprocal, intimate self-disclosure. The dissolution of a relationship, on the other hand, was expected to be indicated by a gradual decrease in shared disclosure.

Social penetration theory used the analogy of peeling back an onion skin to describe the process by which people "peel back" layers of another's characteristics, moving toward greater degrees of intimacy through increasing levels of information. These layers might include knowledge of one another's body, personality, attitudes, beliefs, and, at a quite deep level, the other's most profound fears and hopes. Through this process, each partner achieves a great depth and breadth of knowledge of the other. Both escalating movement toward greater knowledge, hence greater intimacy, and deescalating movement away from knowledge and intimacy are posited in Altman and Taylor's model. Also, there is an assumption that, for a relationship to progress satisfactorily, members of a couple will reciprocate in their penetration activities. The partners will make revelations, and peel back the layers, at approximately the same rate and in similar amounts.

Our idea of minding borrows part of its essence from social penetration theory. However, we argue that for closeness and satisfaction to continue over the long term, the social penetration process must never end. Aspects of the "layers" being explored change too much over time for the process of knowing another to ever be complete. Our bodies and our psyches both are in flux throughout life. Minding patterns of thought and behavior are essential if a couple is to take these changes into account. We also contend that accompanying attributions about the disclosure process (e.g., that a partner is being honest and sincere in telling about him- or herself) and acts that show respect and acceptance of what is learned form other parts of the scaffolding that support continuing mutual social penetration. And we emphasize that it must be mutual.

It has been suggested that women often are more expressive and self-disclosing about relationship concerns and issues than are men (Berscheid, 1994). For a relationship to be well minded, however, there cannot be a considerable difference in the acts of self-disclosure by either partner. Both men and women must recognize that mutual self-disclosure is vital to a relationship's health, and must act upon this recognition. While some research may indicate that men may have to learn this skill to a greater extent than do women, we have no hesitation in believing that they are capable of doing so.

Some researchers, when surveying people about disclosure, have found that men perceive greater risks related to disclosing personal information than do women (Petronio & Martin, 1986). Other studies have demonstrated that men who disclose "too intimately" are more critically evaluated than are women who do the same (Derlega

& Chaikin, 1976). So, it seems that men have a real social basis for their reluctance to disclose. We would also, therefore, suggest that men who want to build intimacy with a partner may initially reveal more about themselves in nonverbal disclosures. Female partners, in well-minded relationships, may need to learn to recognize these nonverbal cues and be patient in creating a conducive atmosphere for verbal disclosure. Thus, both men and women need to recognize the importance of disclosure and the importance of listening well. The stakes (happiness in their love lives) are too great not to learn!

Revised Version of Social Penetration

A more recent version of social penetration theory is found in Knapp and Vangelisti's (1991) staircase model of relationship stages. As in Altman and Taylor's model, Knapp and Vangelisti propose complementary processes of union and separation. The stages are composed of various steps that highlight the importance of disclosure and shared knowledge in relationships.

In the coming-together stage, Knapp and Vangelisti identify these steps: initiating, experimenting, intensifying, integrating, and bonding. Minding can be conceptually related to all these steps. Initiating and experimenting involve asking questions and gradually moving into topics that are more important to both individuals. Intensifying is defined as a significant enhancement of self-disclosure with the occurrence of sexual relations and/or other acts of commitment. Integrating involves continued movement toward greater breadth and depth in self-disclosure and the accompanying recognition by the individuals' network of friends that they now constitute a couple. Bonding is defined by public commitment acts such as marriage ceremonies, living together, or other acts designed to indicate to others that the pair have formed a close relationship.

Parts of this coming-together sequence are similar to what we propose as ingredients of minding. The sharing of knowledge and self-disclosure are explicit components of the minding process, and the first four steps of Knapp and Vangelisti's model depend heavily on increasing self-disclosure. Bonding corresponds partially to the public, mutual acknowledgment of a close relationship. It is our contention that this bonding commitment emerges because of continued mutual behaviors aimed at knowing and facilitating positive development of the relationship. Minding therefore is a process that stimulates and energizes all of these integrative and bonding experiences.

Knapp and Vangelisti additionally describe a complementary set of coming-apart steps. These include differentiating (psychological separation), circumscribing (avoiding certain topics), stagnating (continued creation of distance), avoiding the other, and termination of the relationship. These steps reflect each partner's deemphasis of the desire for knowledge and understanding of his or her partner and the relationship. Minding processes are being phased out during this period. The cessation of the sharing and seeking of knowledge will lead to an eventual shutdown of the minding process and, we hypothesize, the relationship itself. Whenever a relationship is foundering or in disarray, our theory would presume that a low degree of minding is occurring.

Intimate or Taboo Disclosures: Past Lovers

Taboo topics are defined by Baxter and Wilmot (1985) as topics that a couple determines, either implicitly or explicitly, should be avoided if mutual satisfaction is to be maintained. Their survey research uncovered several topics that students were reluctant to discuss with their current romantic partners. These included the discussion of past romances.

Our own research with this same population provides some evidence that topics considered "taboo" in some circumstances are openly discussed in others, especially topics concerning past relationships (Omarzu, Harvey, & Chavis, 1997). In our surveys, young adults report that discussing past romantic relationships is an important part of developing a new partnership. They also describe a variety of motivations for revealing this information, from the opportunity to share oneself with a partner to the need to give their own version of a possibly ugly past event.

Our research and that of Baxter and Wilmot may not necessarily be incompatible, however. "Taboo topics" may vary depending on the stage of the relationship. Couples may share important details about past romantic experiences at the beginning of a new relationship, but avoid discussing such stories after a time in order to show consideration for the new partner's feelings.

Along with the quest for knowledge, minding emphasizes acceptance, respect, and concern for a partner's welfare. These should be at the center of any interaction involving disclosures, especially those consisting of such delicate, "taboo" types of revelations. Disclosure about past lovers deserves analysis in its own right, as it is a topic so important to most couples.

We have conducted research over the last two years on strategic aspects of self-disclosure about past relationships. In beginning this work, we obtained a number of accounts by people of varying ages regarding their general strategy for disclosures about past lovers, in particular. One very interesting and thought-provoking report was made by a woman in her late twenties who was quite experienced in dating and relating. Here are excerpts from her account about her own strategies. First, on whether she would want to hear this type of information from a new partner:

> I have asked men about their numbers of past lovers. . . . I ask for this information because it indirectly gives me an idea about how he felt about sex, like if he gets emotionally attached. I can translate it into the present. I can track his progression by knowing what phases he has gone through and what phase he is in. I can see how his idea of sex has changed. I can see how he feels now as we talk about it, rather than just asking him how he feels about sex. Gives me a time line.

Next, what she herself tells new male partners:

> I would not tell him how many partners I had previously. I wouldn't offer the number, but if he asked I would revise the number. For me it would be in the past, behind me, but for him it would always be something in the present, something he would be conscious of. In ten out of ten men, I would revise the number. . . . Men, they can't

handle all that information and put it behind them. They can't stand the thought of you with somebody else. If you were going to tell them about all those people, that's a lot of "somebody elses."

We should note that this response does not necessarily reflect all, or even most, women's views about this kind of disclosure. However, this woman's position on what men "cannot handle" about a woman's past love life does resonate with a well-known and sometimes considered controversial theory about gender differences in dating and mating. David Buss (1994) suggests that as an evolutionary development, in general men seek sexual relationships with as many women as possible, while women prefer monogamous relationships with men who are good providers. In this way, presumably, men increase their chances of passing on their genes through reproduction by creating as many children as possible. Women are more selective in order to increase their chances of obtaining quality care and nurturing for their children, thus increasing their odds for genetic survival.

A derivative of Buss's logic is that men should be most troubled by the possibility of their partners being involved sexually with other men. Sexual infidelity on the part of their female partners makes it more difficult for men to be certain theirs are the genes that are passed on to any offspring. On the other hand, women are hypothesized to be more upset by the possibility of their partners being intensely involved emotionally with other women. Other emotional involvements threaten the woman's reliance on her partner for support and assistance during childbirth and the early years of raising children. Our respondent's experience that men are uncomfortable hearing about her many "somebody elses," while she uses such information about her partners primarily to gauge their emotional involvement, coincides with Buss's theory.

What does minding theory have to say about this respondent's strategic disclosure of information about past lovers to potential new male partners? Minding would suggest that revising one's history should be based less on gaining approval from a potential partner than on simple discretion. In early stages of a relationship, as the partners begin to disclose and to know one another, each most likely will want to find out about the principles of relating and sexuality that characterize the other. Why would a man who wants to make predictions about his possible partners desire this information any less than would a female? In fact, our survey research indicates that there is no gender difference in how important this type of information is perceived to be.

In early relating, partners may send up "trial balloons" (Kelly & McKillop, 1996) to test a new partner's reaction to such information. Thus each may be selective about what is revealed until he or she is more certain that the relationship is worth pursuing seriously and that the new partner will be accepting of honest revelation. Each partner may reveal some information about past loves and "lovers" strategically so as to check out how the other feels about such divulging and to elicit such information from the other.

An interesting finding in our work on self-disclosure early in relating was that both men and women emphasized honesty in presenting specific information, especially regarding past sexual relationships as they might pertain to sexual diseases. They said they tried to be honest and wanted honesty in others. Whether our respondents are in reality this honest with others was not a matter we could assess in this research; the respondents may have been simply espousing honesty as a principle.

In summary, we suggest that taboo or difficult topics are a matter of social and relationship context. After a relationship has stabilized through the process of minding, people in long-term relationships may have dealt with the "whats" and "whys" of their private lives and may have few areas in which taboo topics exist. Or taboo topics might continue to exist for such a couple in a well-minded relationship because after a period of exploration, the partners may agree that further discussion about certain areas would not be in the best interests of the relationship. A couple who is minding the relationship well will make mutual decisions about "off-limit" areas for discussion and will be concerned that both partners understand and accept the reasons for such decisions.

Overall, however, we believe that taboo topics arise less frequently in well-minded relationships. Minding makes available for exploration potentially delicate topics, because partners make positive attributions about each other's revelations and reactions. Minding emphasizes acceptance and respect for one another and sincerity in broaching such topics. This creates a safe and stable atmosphere for confiding even potentially troubling thoughts or experiences. Partners' positive attributions, sincerity, and respect may open up many aspects of their history, fears, disappointments, or personality features for mutual exploration and constructive attention. The overriding concern in well-minded relationships is that the acquisition of knowledge about the other will be as complete as possible while still enhancing to the relationship.

NONVERBAL KNOWING

As noted at the outset of this chapter, in presenting themselves to others people are always self-disclosing. Up to this point in our discussion, we have focused on verbal disclosure, but individuals disclose information about themselves even when they are not speaking. This nonverbal behavior has been called "irrepressible," meaning that it is impossible to repress such behavior completely. Even if one remains completely "poker-faced" and physically still, observers are likely to assume this behavior discloses inhibition or withdrawal (DePaulo, 1992).

Nonverbal scholars suggest that people "leak" cues, intentionally or unintentionally, regarding how they are feeling and thinking. These cues are displayed in appearance, tone of voice, stance, walking patterns, and so on (Knapp, 1978). People can sometimes strategically use such behaviors as part of their presentations to others, but some research has demonstrated that individuals are often mistaken about how their nonverbal behaviors are interpreted by others around them (DePaulo, 1992). An important skill in minding behavior is the "reading" of nonverbal messages (Manusov, Floyd, & Kerssen-Griep, 1997).

One of the most prevalent forms of nonverbal disclosure is contained in our facial expressions. Social psychologists studying nonverbal behavior have discovered that it is often difficult to read nonverbal cues and to correctly infer what the cues reveal about the actors. Facial expression, however, is a relatively rare example of a nonverbal behavior that often is easily read, is difficult to control, and conveys considerable information about what a person is feeling. Most of us learn to read others' facial expressions fairly well, usually early in life. It may be how well we then use this skill to infer others' emotions or thoughts that indicates how capable we are at minding our close relationships.

Proxemic cues, or distancing behavior, is another form of nonverbal behavior that is relevant to minding. People who are very close emotionally tend to touch a lot and stay quite close physically as well. Conversely, a couple's lack of emotional closeness may be reflected in a decrease in their physical closeness. For example, when there is great turmoil in the relationship, a couple may sleep in the same bed without touching, and in essence feel as if they are on separate continents despite the few inches separating their bodies. Minding a relationship well may lead one partner to challenge the other's physical withdrawal in an effort to bring a problem into the open; or, alternatively, minding may promote the sensitivity that allows partners to recognize another's need for "space" or time alone to work something out.

Tone of voice and "code word" exchanges also appear to be frequently significant in the dynamics of close relationships. Verbal statements may send implicit, hidden messages, which are quite different from what was literally said. People in close relationships learn quickly how to interpret these differences in the tone of voice of their partners. For example, they may learn to recognize the tone of a partner's suppressed anger. On the other hand, there may be great ambiguity associated with exactly what can be inferred from tone, diction, code words, and emotional expression. Much may depend on the social circumstances. It may take many years to learn a partner's varied and numerous quirks of nonverbal expression.

This discussion of nonverbal behavior is of vital importance to the minding conception. Nonverbal behavior is complex and may be misleading. It is therefore imperative that a couple make meanings as clear as possible in any interaction that may be significant to the relationship. They need to know, and will know if they are minding well, that there is much ambiguity in the world of nonverbal behavior. Even when we make every effort to communicate as clearly as possible on all levels, there will still be miscommunication. However, like other forms of minding behavior, it is crucial that a couple continue to try to make intimate contact via all of the means of communication at their disposal.

Beyond the importance of nonverbal behavior to clarity of communication, it is inherent in minding that communications are not simply delivered and forgotten. Messages given quickly and thoughtlessly may nevertheless have long-term and often unexpected impact. For instance, a spouse may interrupt his partner while she is engrossed in difficult work; she may with little thought yell something insulting at him out of frustration and annoyance. This may damage the relationship far beyond the interrupted partner's intention. Or, in a different example, imagine a woman offhandedly mentioning an anniversary date to her partner. The comment may seem casual, as if not much importance was attached to it. However, if her partner disregards the underlying reminder without stopping to question, assuming that she must not care much about the anniversary after all, again much unintentional hurt can result.

The foundation of knowledge, acceptance, and positive attributions that minding lays down in a relationship should enable couples to identify and review these types of misleading or harmful messages or patterns of communication. It should also help to prevent misunderstandings from festering, unresolved, for great lengths of time. (Imagine our hypothetical couple above arguing perhaps years after the initial incident, "And there was that anniversary I specifically reminded you about and you didn't do anything!" "But you were so casual about it! I thought you didn't really want a big celebration!")

Nonverbal behaviors may also be used to acknowledge or extend previous disclosures and discussions. To act on a loved one's expressed wish, to give a comforting hug after listening to a partner's frustrations, to literally stand behind or near the other during a stressful situation – all these are acts of minding based on shared knowledge. They are methods of affirming that disclosed information has been received and is valued.

Minding improves the ability of both partners to address difficulties in communication because they will be more confident that their efforts will be met with approval and reciprocal efforts. Minding takes the inherent ambiguity of nonverbal behavior and works with this ambiguity to enhance created meaning and make explicit the implications of such behavior. Minding allows partners to use and acknowledge what they have learned about each other in acts that are constructive and supportive of the relationship.

PERSONALITY AND SELF-DISCLOSURE

Is self-disclosure a skill learned through relating, or is it primarily related to individual differences? One individual difference associated with relationships is that of attachment style. Bowlby's (1969) attachment theory proposes that people's relationships throughout their lives are affected by the quality of the relationships they had as infants with their parents. This early parental relationship leads to a person's "attachment style," which they then carry on into most of their relationships, even as adults.

There are three specific attachment styles: secure, avoidant, and anxious/ambivalent. Hazan and Shaver (1987) found that people who exhibit a secure attachment style (involving feelings of security and safety with loved ones) report high degrees of trust, acceptance, and felt friendship for their primary love partner. Persons who appeared to have an avoidant attachment style reported fear of closeness. Individuals who revealed an anxious/ambivalent attachment style reported falling in love too quickly, without good results, and being obsessed with finding the right close relationship.

Hazan and Shaver's research on these attachment styles in adults can be associated with possible differences in self-disclosure. There is evidence that self-disclosure is intimately connected to developing secure, trusting relationships. Therefore, it might be inferred from

Hazan and Shaver's work that individuals with secure attachment styles are also most likely to be comfortable with self-disclosure. This is not, however, a very solid link between personality and disclosure. Attachment styles may be more related to familial experiences, and thus may be less "personality" characteristics than learned patterns of behavior.

Another individual difference characteristic related to differences in disclosure is McAdams's (1989) intimacy motivation. The concept of intimacy motivation assumes that some individuals are more driven than others to strive for a condition of intimacy with other human beings. Thus, one could be "high" or "low" in intimacy motivation.

McAdams generally defines intimacy as "sharing innermost thoughts and feelings [with another] . . . but that also recognizes one another's individuality" (1989, p. 46). The intimacy motive is defined as a recurrent desire for warm, close, and sharing interaction with other human beings. McAdams argues that people high in intimacy motivation are described by their friends and acquaintances as especially loving, natural, and appreciative. Over the course of a day, persons high in intimacy motivation are reported to spend more time thinking about other people and their relationships with them, engaging in more conversations with other people, and experiencing high levels of joy and happiness in the presence of other people, as compared with persons low in intimacy motivation. Further, the high-intimacy person tends to smile and laugh more and to be more direct in eye contact than does the low-intimacy person. Again, it can be inferred from this evidence that high-intimacy individuals may be more likely, or more able, to disclose personal information and to receive disclosures from others.

McAdams has developed a projective personality technique for assessing intimacy motivation, based on the Thematic Apperception Test. People view pictures and write or describe stories about the pictures. Their responses are scored for different "motives." The intimacy motive is one of several that can be elicited using this test.

Similar to Pennebaker's findings regarding confiding problems, McAdams indicates that there is a variety of evidence available to support the value of high-intimacy style for health, adjustment, and maturity in life. He reports data from a seventeen-year longitudinal study following individuals from their college years to mid-life, showing that men who are high in intimacy motivation are more satisfied in their marriages and careers than are men who are low in intimacy motivation.

It is to be expected that other personality characteristics, such as extroversion, might be associated with different levels of self-disclosure activity. There is to date, however, little evidence indicating that personality variables are primarily responsible for differing levels of intimacy or disclosure in close relationships. It appears, as of now, that disclosure, and thus minding, is a skill that can be learned.

SEXUALITY, SELF-DISCLOSURE, AND MINDING

How does sexuality enter into the formulation of self-disclosure and minding proposed in this chapter? Sexual acts may be acts of self-disclosure and of minding. Certainly they may reveal information about our bodies, attitudes, and feelings, and even our stamina.

It is also possible to engage in sexual acts that are not indicative of self-disclosure or of a desire to know one's partner. Couples who have known one another for short or long periods of time are capable of sexual acts that constitute "limited emotional involvements." In discussing people's sexuality in a liberated sexual world, Rollo May in *Love and Will* (1969) suggested that the "sexual revolution" may not play well for some people. For them, sex may become machine-like, with passion and pleasure diminishing, and sexuality itself may be put on the shelf and avoided. May quotes T. S. Eliot's verses in "The Waste Land": After the "lovely woman stoops to folly, and the carbuncular clerk who seduced her at tea leaves,

> She turns and looks a moment in the glass,
> Hardly aware of her departed lover;
> Her brain allows one half-formed thought to pass:
> "Well now that's done: and I'm glad it's over."
> (III: 249-253, quoted in May, 1969, pp. 58-59)

In a caring and well-minded relationship, sexual acts communicate commitment. Caring behavior and minding provide a context that surrounds the act with meaning. Without that meaning, sexual acts remain open to a wide range of possible interpretations. A common interpretation, often occurring early in a relationship, is that one partner has merely "used" the other in the sex act. When minding increases in a relationship, the concept of "being used" becomes irrelevant. In well-minded relationships, sexual acts are exchanges that have a natural place in the spectrum of exchanges that the couple enjoys and whereby they affirm their relationship.

De Villers (1997) sums up advice about sexuality that the couple who is minding their relationship very likely has learned well:

> Sex doesn't begin under the sheets . . . it's important to realize that a lot of the attitudes and feelings that occur during love making result from the interactions between you and your lover all evening, all day, all week. (p. 22)

A couple needs to know one another well and accept and respect that knowledge. Part of that knowledge is sexual knowledge. It is knowing about a partner's sexual inclinations and how experience has shaped those inclinations; it is knowing how a partner finds pleasure in sexual activity.

Another reason minding is so vital to the sexual relationship is that individuals possess different boundaries and definitions for sexual activity and what this activity means to the relationship. Couples have to develop their own comfort zones for defining these concepts. For many people, especially young people, this area is replete with uncertainty and confusion. Minding, through reciprocal knowledge and respect, establishes the relationship as a place of safety in which to explore and define one's sexuality.

Rubin (1985) has argued that sexuality transforms people's friendships. He suggested that people who move from the status of close friends to the status of lovers, via sexual relations, will never be the same. If they discontinue their physical intimacy, Rubin believes that they may become friends again, but only if they are able to work out new, different conditions of what their friendship means.

Minding is a process that can assist couples moving between the roles of "friends" and "lovers." It is in fact one of the only process vehicles proposed in the relationship literature by which people may make these transformations without a lot of pain being experienced. This may be especially true if the couple changes first from friends to lovers, and then tries to move back to friends. Minding helps with this transition because it emphasizes the continuity of mutual self-disclosure, consistency in attitudes and behavior, and constructiveness in relating. All of these elements are necessary if a couple is to make these transitions and maintain either type of relationship. A couple may make mistakes in moving back and forth across what they perceive to be the friend–lover border. But minding will help them restore their relationship and eventually achieve a stable one.

HOW DO PEOPLE LEARN AND DEVELOP KNOWING AND LISTENING SKILLS?

Answering this question will help us understand how and whether people can purposely develop what we define as well-minded close relationships. While this question has been the subject of considerable theory and research, there is not as yet a strong, unequivocal set of findings and base of knowledge about developing relationship skills. This is particularly true with regard to highly intricate combinations of skills, as is the minding group of skills.

Knowing by the Very Young

While growing up, most of us learn relationship skills and knowledge often incidentally and vicariously by observing our parents, caretakers, the media, peers, and others in our environment. Research suggests that indications of the skills involved in later minding activity begin to develop very early. By age four, children show a remarkable breadth of interest in their social world and a coherent grasp of the bases of human action in terms of beliefs, intentions, and desires. They can and do talk about intentions, motivation, and false beliefs (Dunn, 1988). They distinguish intended acts from mistakes, and judge accurately how someone will act given mistaken beliefs. Children also learn at a very young age the rules of social exchange in self-disclosure. As early as eight years of age, children are likely to tell personal things about themselves only to other children who have themselves previously disclosed something intimate (Cohn & Strassberg, 1983).

Further, as reviewed by Dunn (1988), children have been found to be able to grasp psychological causality of actions in terms of the goals and beliefs of storybook characters. They pursue with persistence their inquiries into why people act the way they do. Dunn suggests that beginning about age two, narrative activity by parents is particularly powerful in teaching children about their social environment and about how people operate psychologically. At the same time, children are learning about their own psychological operations and landscape.

While this area of work regarding young children's learning of their social environments holds considerable promise, there are daunting questions that have not been well studied. For example, within the same families, young people often show different capacities to understand others (Rutter & Rutter, 1993). Why? Have they received differential inputs from parents and other significant agents of socialization? Also, we know too little about how the causes of turmoil in families, such as divorce and death of siblings or parents, affect the way children learn about others and the early skills they acquire for developing closeness with others.

Filters of Learning Intimacy: Teens and Twenties

Burleson (1995) argues that people gradually develop relationship skills. For each phase of relationship development, individuals must develop the prerequisite skill in order to pass through a "filter" and thus be available for further, more intimate development. If they fail to develop the prerequisite skill for a certain passage, their relationships will be stunted in terms of growth and intimacy. They will not progress beyond a certain point, no matter how old they are or how many relationships they initiate. Until they learn the necessary skills to pass through the next "filter," they will remain "stuck" at their current level of relating and their relationships may not be fully developed or mature.

We believe that this type of skill development involves experimenting with and exploring the minding process early in a person's life. In early friendships, a child or young adult who minds well begins to pass through these relationship filters of opportunity into closer, more intimate associations. This person will be reinforced for his or her minding by this increase in intimacy, and will also learn more of the nuances of minding/relating. As we have discussed in this chapter, these skills include: careful observation of others, listening with care and compassion to others, self-disclosure and making oneself available as a confidant to others for their self-disclosure, care in attributing qualities to others or understanding them in general, and care in planning acts relevant to the relationship that are considerate of others' needs and interests. Even relatively young children can show these nuanced skills of quasi-minding behavior.

In the teenaged years when close relationships have tremendous salience and importance, it is important that these skills be honed and refined. In a well-minded relationship, even this early in a person's life, people learn to solicit self-disclosures with care. They learn about the implications for future interaction that may emerge from such disclosures. For example, young people may learn to pick up cues about a new date's previous lovers, and can use this information to recognize potential partners who may be "on the rebound" from a previous relationship. Or teenagers may learn from information about a new partner's family how to make inferences about possible future relationship problems, based on family patterns of relating. A young girl, for instance, may thus consider disengaging from a relationship with someone who has observed his mother being physically or emotionally abused. Akeret (1992) suggests that this disclosure might be facilitated by couples going through their picture albums together. Such information may be of general value to the present relationship.

The way such information is disclosed and then approached is a delicate matter that teens and adults, too, must work hard to learn. Is the partner ready to disclose this information? How does one respond to the information after receiving it? How does the discloser feel afterward? People who learn to mind relationships learn how to carry out these calculations in the midst of the stream of interaction. Certainly, this type of learning is advanced and complicated. Individuals are better off when they begin learning minding skills early and continue refining this knowledge constantly through experience and observation throughout their lives.

In our culture we have witnessed the development of a phenomenon termed the "starter marriage." This is a short marriage of people in their twenties involving no children and ending in an easy divorce without elaborate legal negotiations (Riley, 1991). This concept has become popular among sociologists as a way of understanding the high divorce rate, especially among people in their late teens and twenties. Like a "starter home," people are thought to try out marriage, make lots of mistakes, and move on – learning from their mistakes, it is hoped, for the next marriage. We would argue that more care in learning minding skills and in recognizing these skills will help people in their twenties learn how to have constructive close relationships well before they move into marriages that may be short-lived.

Learning Empathy and Empathic Accuracy

As people mature, they learn that listening and observational skills are gifts that facilitate understanding one's world as well as oneself. Despite the obvious relevance of these skills to all that humans do, there has been little research on the development of listening and observational skills. Existing work suggests that these skills are important components of empathy (Kleinke, 1978; Davis, 1993).

Empathy is the ability to imagine one's own consciousness in another person and to perceive the world as she or he perceives it. To feel empathy or to be empathetic, we must learn to observe and understand how environmental factors influence others, as well as ourselves. This is a daunting proposition, but one that is essential to close relationship satisfaction.

One of the few research programs concentrating on the study of empathy and its development is being implemented by social-personality psychologist William Ickes and colleagues (e.g., see Ickes, 1996). These scholars suggest that empathic accuracy should be measured as pioneering psychologist Carl Rogers (1975) contended was necessary: by someone's ability to infer the specific content of another's successive thoughts and feelings during the course of an ongoing interaction. Thus Ickes and his colleagues have done a series of studies in which one person (the perceiver) observes another person (the target) acting or interacting. The perceiver then must describe what the target was thinking or feeling during that time. Empathic accuracy is determined by how well the perceiver's judgments match the target's actual thoughts or feelings. This paradigm allows the isolation and examination of a variety of factors that may increase empathy or the development of empathy.

Among the tasks they have begun in this program, Ickes and his colleagues are endeavoring to develop an understanding of whether people can be taught to be more empathetic in their interactions with others. They have found, for example, that repeating exposures to another person may increase accuracy. Giving a perceiver immediate and truthful feedback about a target's thoughts and feelings may also "teach" the perceiver to become more empathically accurate.

Thus it appears that empathy may possibly be a learned social skill, although some people may be temperamentally predisposed to acquire it earlier and more easily than others. In this way, it is similar to what we hypothesize minding to be: a learned combination of behaviors and thinking patterns that enables one to establish richer and more fulfilling relationships with others.

SUMMARY AND CONCLUSIONS

In this chapter, we have revealed some of the problems related to the quest for knowledge as it applies to gaining closeness with another and to the minding process. We discussed how this quest is often implemented through self-disclosure and what has been termed social penetration. We described the special role of stories and storytelling in the self-disclosure and knowing enterprises.

Included in the self-disclosure literature is the hypothesis that couples may treat some topics as taboo and are reluctant to discuss them. We suggested that when close relationships are well minded, there may be fewer taboo topics than when the relationships are not well minded. Couples in well-minded relationships will develop rules of dialogue about such taboo topics.

We discussed learning about the other and disclosing about one-self through nonverbal behaviors. We pointed out the inherent ambiguity of meaning in much nonverbal behavior, the differences between what the perceiver sees and what the actor believes he or she is displaying, and the essential step of explicit clarification of meaning that is a part of well-minded relationships. We referred to the role of nonverbal behavior as a method of acknowledging and validating information previously shared verbally.

We discussed sexuality in the context of self-disclosure and minding, noting that sexual behaviors can also be a form of self-disclosure and may be acts representative of minding. The invaluable role of minding was stressed in forming a context for sexuality, which then contributes to greater satisfaction in the relationship. We also described the blurred boundary that may exist between friends and lovers and how minding may help people make transitions between these roles without losing their relationship altogether.

We addressed the topic of how individuals develop knowing and empathy skills. Apparently, very young children begin to develop sophisticated understandings of their social environments. With practice and feedback, people appear to be able to learn to a considerable degree empathic accuracy in understanding others' true thoughts and feelings.

There is an iceberg of information regarding the knowing and disclosing activity. We have only revealed the tip of this iceberg. Such is true of psychology and the social and behavioral sciences in general. Cognitive science is one of the "hot" areas of modern science, but it has had much too little to say about the building of human knowledge applied to developing and maintaining close relationships. Nor has it sufficiently explored the skills necessary to develop and maintain them.

There have been strands of very important and relevant research, as partially discussed here. Nonetheless, adequate statements of problems and adequate theoretical conceptualizations are essential steps in the discovery process. In the area of close relationship research, these steps are still embryonic in implementation.

One of the goals of this book is to at least describe the problems of knowing and being known in a new way, a way that may facilitate work on the "cognitive science" of close relationships. Such a science cannot be narrow and must embrace knowledge of emotion and behavior, just as it builds on what is known about social cognition and social learning processes. Such a science cannot be decontextualized from the events of life that impact individuals and families, and hence that have impact on the development of thinking and feeling about closeness. Such a science cannot disregard the possible background, family, cultural, and ethnic differences that may accompany our understanding of our social worlds.

CHAPTER 4

Attributions in Close Relationships

The mind is not a vessel to be filled, but a fire to be lighted.

Plutarch

Knowledge about one's partner is a necessity to the minding process, but it is not enough to guarantee a relationship's success. What is done with knowledge once it is gained? How do successful relationship partners process and account for conflicting or negative information that may be learned? How does the way in which we think about our partner's behavior affect the way we feel about our partner?

This chapter continues our discussion in Chapter 3 of the quest to know the other, but it emphasizes the conclusions we develop during this quest. These conclusions we come to about our partners, after listening and observing, take the form of attributions and other kinds of inferences.

Attributions are the mental explanations we create in order to understand events or behavior. Why are these attributions of vital significance to minding? Why does it matter to the long-term success of our close relationships what we think caused particular relationship events to occur? Why does it matter what particular traits we attribute to our partner? Why does it matter what evidence we use in inferring causality for relationship events and attributing particular traits to our partner?

These questions are at the heart of the inspiration for the minding theory. They directly address the importance of the use of the mind in relating. The attributional component of minding theory addresses how we cognitively utilize the knowledge structures we have about our partners and about relationships in general. Good relationships are not only based on what we do or on what we know. They are based on how we think.

UNDERSTANDING ATTRIBUTION

Attribution refers to a person's attempts to explain events occurring in his or her life (Heider, 1958). By definition, attribution refers to people's inferences of *causality and responsibility*. In other words, these inferences involve judgments about the causes of observed events: why they happened and who, or what, was responsible. Individuals often make inferences about others in their environment, but they can also make inferences about themselves based on their own behavior.

Simple versus Complex Attributions

There are several different ways to classify or examine attributions. One method of examining attributions is to consider how quickly or deliberately they are made. People can make attributions very quickly, or make them after long deliberation.

We tend to make attributions quickly when events seem simple and clear-cut, and when causes seem obvious or easy to identify. People have a variety of cognitive schemas and expectations about different kinds of situations. These schemas facilitate these nondeliberative types of attributions. When an event occurs that fits easily into one's cognitive schemas or expectations, an attribution is simple to make and is made quickly. Unexpected or unusual events, on the other hand, require more thought and perhaps a reexamination of beliefs or existing schemas.

For example, most of us have fairly well-developed schemas about various types of social situations related to dating and meeting new partners. Imagine a man on a blind date, seeing a woman for the first time. Their meeting place is a rather formal restaurant. If she is beautifully and appropriately dressed he is likely to make a quick (possibly relieved) attribution about her interest in the date. If she is casually or sloppily dressed he is again likely to make a quick attribution that she is uninterested in him, and perhaps was coerced into the date. Our schemas or expectations for appropriate dating attire are probably highly developed.

Now imagine that he arrives at the restaurant to find his blind date dressed as a pirate. What attribution does he make? Is she coming from a costume party? Is she some kind of actress? And what inferences can he make about her enthusiasm for the date, based on this outfit? Clearly this is an unusual situation and our probably very surprised man will likely have to ask questions and observe this woman carefully before making attributions about her behavior with confidence.

Behavior in Relationships Can Be Complex

The temptation to take "cognitive shortcuts" and make fast and simple attributions can sometimes lead to confusion and misunderstanding. Sometimes we may defensively make attributions too quickly or too generally rather than deliberating about other possible explanations: "He's five minutes late, so he must not care about me at all." At other times, we may want to avoid making the obvious attribution because it reflects negatively on our desirability, so we frantically search for others: "She didn't call me because she's lost my number. Or she's been sick. Or maybe her phone service has accidentally been shut off." How carefully and accurately we make attributions in our relationships can have a great effect on our subsequent thoughts and feelings about those relationships.

Attributional Motivation

It has been theorized that there are various motives behind attributional activity (Harvey & Weary, 1984). One is the quest for understanding or knowledge. This is a salient motive in relationships because we are constantly confronted with another person's behavior. We then have the problem of understanding and interpreting it. For example, we may be faced with our partner's anger. We then might try to interpret this angry behavior by asking questions such as: Is this behavior toward me caused by ill will? Is it caused by a history of family abuse? Is it caused by something about me? Is it caused by the rotten weather? One motive for attributional activity is to try and make sense of the events occurring around us.

A second motive for attributional activity is to try and present ourselves in a particular way to other people, or to defend our own self-concepts. We often are guided by our egos in making these types of attributions. We take credit for events that have positive outcomes and try to exonerate ourselves from responsibility for events that have negative outcomes. Thus, in the example of the angry encounter above, most people would resist accepting the "something about me" explanation, in favor of one that placed blame elsewhere. So we can also use attributions to enhance and protect our positive beliefs about ourselves.

Ego-motivated attributions also occur when people try to influence others via their attributional activity. Orvis, Kelley, and Butler (1976) reported that couples used attributions in attempts to persuade their partners about various relationship dynamics. For example, a woman might attribute a husband's interest in frequent trips to see his mother to the controlling nature of his mother. She might use this type of attribution in discussion with him, to influence him to agree that his mother indeed does play this role in his life and that he should change the practice. In the angry partner example, the target partner might confront the furious one with the attribution that job stress is causing such bad temper. This attribution could then be used as a lever to influence the angry partner to think about changing careers or spending less time at work every day.

THEORIES OF ATTRIBUTION

"Common Sense" Psychology

Psychologist Fritz Heider (1944, 1958) provided the seeds for the development of attributional theory in social psychology. Heider analyzed in detail how people perceive and interpret questions such as: "Did she intend to hurt me by that action?" "What is he really like when you get to know him?" Heider referred to his analysis as "common sense" or "naive psychology" because he was concerned with the manner in which people understand and explain everyday events. We should emphasize, however, that in no sense was Heider's analysis itself naive or simple-minded. It is an extremely provocative and perceptive theoretical conception that has stimulated much work in social psychology and that still contains many ideas that await exploration.

Heider believed that people make two basic types of attribution, either to a person and the person's dispositions (e.g., their arrogance or humility, greed or generosity) or to situational forces, which consist of anything outside of the individual. Heider recognized that often people may think that both dispositions and situational forces are involved in the occurrence of any particular event. In close relationships, with their complex patterns and underlying dynamics, it is particularly true that people who are thoughtful about their relationships will conclude that most of their partner's behavior as well as their own are the joint products of personal dispositions and situational factors. In fact, it may be important for people in relationships to learn not to jump to simple conclusions about why a partner did whatever he or she did. It may be important for people to learn the high degree to which complex answers are needed to understand behaviors that have complex determinants.

One of Heider's main contributions was his delineation of conditions involved in the attribution of responsibility. Heider assumed that, when making attributions for someone's behavior, we observe conditions specific to that person and that behavior. The judgments we make about these conditions assist us in making attributions.

The conditions specified by Heider were: (1) observed or apparent causal contribution to an outcome; (2) knowledge of the consequences of the action taken; (3) intention to produce the outcome; (4) degree of volition versus coercion involved in the action; and (5) appreciation of the moral wrongfulness of the action.

To examine these conditions, let's take as an example a couple's argument over financial problems. One partner has loudly begun to complain and berate the other about lack of financial responsibility. This outburst involves a description of all the bills they have and strong accusations about who was responsible for the overspending. At least implicitly, the defending spouse may consider the conditions suggested by Heider in trying to determine the cause of the other's anger and whether this outburst indicates the relationship is in trouble.

Here is how Heider's conditions might overlap with the listener's attributional activity. He or she may ask: (1) What were the partner's overt actions in initiating the outburst? (contribution to outcome) (2) Was the partner able to anticipate what the reaction to the outburst was likely to be? (knowledge of consequences) (3) What were his or her intentions regarding the argument's effect on the relationship? (intentions for outcome) (4) How in control was he or she of this behavior? (degree of volition) (5) Does the partner realize how hurtful such behavior might be? (appreciation of moral effects). The answers to these questions will help the defending partner decide whether to attribute the other's outburst to personality characteristics, stress, real financial collapse, lack of care for the relationship, or other causes.

Do people actually ask each of these questions when deciding whether someone is responsible for a negative outcome? For example, would a spouse really consider these conditions in deciding whether a partner was responsible for a major outburst about how much debt the couple had piled up? As reviewed by Shaver (1985), there is ample evidence that people do use these conditions in attributing responsibility.

In a well-minded relationship, spouses would be careful in making attributions. They would be wary of making them too quickly or too defensively. They would also have great resources of knowledge about their partners to draw on when pondering possible causes. Those in well-minded relationships will most likely make considered attributions about important relationship events, and thus will indeed be equally likely to consider Heider's "conditions" surrounding an event before deciding on causality.

Covariation Principles of Attribution

Harold Kelley (1967) elaborated and refined Heider's ideas about attributional processes. In particular, Kelley's ideas about covariation between events are relevant to attributions and minding. Kelley, like Heider, argued that people operate very much like naive scientists in analyzing situations and inferring causality. We all possess a "common sense" psychology about the actions of other people based on our experiences.

Kelley hypothesized that when we make attributions, we base them not only on the conditions of the current behavior itself, but also on factors outside the behavior. According to Kelley's covariation principle, an event challenges the attributor to determine what factors covaried in time and space with the occurrence of the event – that is, what other things happened or changed. This analysis helps to determine what factors may have caused the event to occur. Three factors which Kelley identified as important to attribution are consistency, consensus, and distinctiveness.

Consistency refers to how often such behavior occurs. In the foregoing argument example, Kelley's logic suggests that the attributing spouse would first evaluate how consistent the angry spouse was in exhibiting such outbursts. If similar outbursts are common occurrences, it becomes logical to interpret them as stemming from the partner's personality or temperament. If the partner does not consistently engage in such outbursts, the spouse would look instead for external or environmental causes for the outburst (e.g., "downsizing" rumors at work that make money matters more salient).

A second type of information the spouse would consider is consensus information. Do other partners engage in such outbursts? The spouse may have such information based on discussions with friends about what happens in their close relationships. If such an outburst is not that common in other relationships, this would make it more likely that the spouse would lean toward seeing the partner, or something about the partner, such as the partner's temper or angry disposition, as the principal causal agent.

Finally, is the behavior distinctive? Is the angry partner's outburst distinctive of his or her behavior in other situations? That is, does the partner exhibit such behavior in other situations and toward other people? If so, confidence in the partner's angry disposition as a key causal factor in the outburst would be increased. If, on the other hand, the partner behaves this way only about money matters or only with the spouse, it could reflect a real financial crisis or a problem within the relationship.

Kelley (1979) imported basic attribution theory to his interdependence analysis of the structures and functions of personal relationships. Interdependence refers to the intertwining of people's lives that is such a defining feature of close relationships. In close relationships, our thoughts, feelings, and behaviors toward our partners affect our partners' thoughts, feelings, and behaviors toward us. Our actions and reactions in a relationship are to some extent determined by the actions and reactions of our partners. Thus, partners are interdependent and the course of the relationship is based on the quality and stability of this interdependence.

Interdependence interacts with general attributional tendencies and impacts our interpretations of other's behavior. Kelley (1979) suggested that people interpret relationship events in terms of their partner's intentions, attitudes, and traits. If a wife does not acknowledge her husband's birthday, for example, he may ask himself: Did she mean to hurt me? (intention) Is this a reflection of her feelings about me? (attitude) Is she just an absent-minded person? (trait).

Correspondent Inference

Jones and Davis (1965) and Jones and McGillis (1976) developed systematic predictions based on Heider's idea that

> it is an important principle of common-sense psychology, as it is of scientific theory in general, that man grasps reality, and can predict and control it, by referring transient and variable behavior and events to relatively unchanging underlying conditions, the so-called dispositional properties of the world. (Heider, 1958, p. 79)

In other words, according to Heider, we often try to make sense of complicated situations by finding stable and predictable explanations for them. This makes us feel more in control of the very unpredictable and uncontrollable world around us. Because of this need for feelings of control and predictability, we tend to attribute events more often to people's temperaments and dispositions rather than to ever-changing situational factors. It is simply *easier* to say to ourselves, "Oh that Mary is such an impatient person," than to think through all the possible situational influences that could lead Mary to snap at us angrily.

According to Jones and colleagues' correspondence inference, we always are searching for the dispositional qualities of others and how they are linked to others' behavior. Presumably, we strive to find these dispositional qualities because they help us achieve a sense of order in our world – even if the order is illusory. It is much easier to identify a person and that person's qualities as the primary cause of an event than it is to comprehend the myriad situational influences that may lead to a behavior.

In theories of correspondence, people use various conditions surrounding another person's behavior to infer whether or not the behavior was caused by the person's dispositions. Correspondent inference is always about the other and not about oneself (i.e., it does not apply to self-attribution). In making correspondent inferences, people examine whether the other's behavior was freely taken, whether it involved intention and foreseeability of outcome, and what the actual outcome was, such as how extreme it was.

If your partner suddenly begins coming home later and later from work, you might ask yourself whether he or she is freely choosing to work late or is being coerced by the employer. Is the partner aware of how this new behavior is disrupting the relationship? Finally, how extreme or different is this behavior from past habits? Answering these questions would help you determine whether or not to attribute your partner's behavior to his or her personal feelings or traits. If you did attribute the behavior to your partner's traits or personality, you would be making a "correspondent inference."

One hypothesis stemming from Jones and colleagues' work is that behaviors leading to more extreme outcomes will yield more correspondent inferences. That is, when an outcome is unusual or extreme, observers will more likely see qualities of the person, such as temper, as critical in producing the event. For example, Jones and colleagues have reported that an event that has an extreme outcome (such as a spouse's feeling betrayed by a partner's telling of a private story at a party) will often lead perceivers to draw inferences about the actor's dispositions (for example, the storyteller is not loyal to his or her partner). Extreme outcomes also make perceivers feel more confident about these inferences.

Correspondent inference is highly relevant to minding. People in well-minded relationships will be especially careful about inclinations to draw negative inferences about a partner's dispositions. They often will discuss their inferences about each other's behaviors and whether the evidence really supports their inferences. If it does, they also will discuss whether the disposition is something that could be changed if it is impairing the relationship.

Orvis and colleagues (1976) reported evidence that people may use attributions to try to influence their partners. For example, a woman may suggest to her partner that he has an arrogant streak. The accuser actually may be trying to persuade her partner not to exhibit a particular type of behavior, and uses this attribution to force the partner to see such behavior in a negative light.

We suggest that minding skills provide a means of bringing such implicit attributions out in the open and allow overt negotiation of attributions about dispositions of ourselves and our partners. Minding may make the relationship climate more open, thus making it easier to state overtly that a particular behavior is simply troubling to one partner, without using correspondent inferences to create another negative context that justifies objections. For instance, a woman in a well-minded relationship may feel free to simply say, "I wish you wouldn't talk about your job so much at parties; I feel left out," rather than hide her feelings behind a negative dispositional inference by saying, "I wish you wouldn't talk about your job so much at parties; it's arrogant of you to show off like that." This first comment allows an opening up of discussion between partners, while the second contains mainly blame and criticism.

Self-Perception

Bem (1965, 1972) has argued that people draw conclusions about their own attitudes and other internal states (e.g., how much they love their partner) after observing their own behavior and the context in which it occurs. This process is called self-persuasion or self-perception. Bem's reasoning about self-persuasive attribution deserves brief mention here. It seems counterintuitive; yet it may apply at times to the problems of couples. For example, if a person observes himself behaving lovingly toward a partner, without recognized ulterior motivation (such as wanting sex), he will examine his own behavior and infer that he must really love his partner. If he is aware of some ulterior motives, however, these may very well stifle the conclusion that a true feeling of love exists in this situation.

Bem's position elicited considerable debate when it first was presented (e.g., see Abelson et al., 1968) because many attitude theorists could not agree that people may not actually know their attitudes until after they act. In our example, for instance, how could the person be so undecided about his commitment to his partner that he would have to examine his own behavior to figure it out? But Bem's ideas do ring true in some contexts of close relationships. Self-persuasion theory may be especially applicable when people are trying to decide how *much* they like and love one another. Self-persuasion may also occur during periods of otherwise highly committed relationships when couples, temporarily uncertain of their devotion, pay extra attention to how they are treating one another for evidence about how they really feel.

We believe that minding has a rippling effect in relationships. The rippling influence of minding in the context of self-persuasion theory is of further benefit to the relationship. Minding leads to behavior that shows care and commitment. Thus, when both persons see themselves engaged in minding behaviors, this observation stimulates their own self-perception of greater commitment.

Self-Fulfilling Interaction Sequences

A final attributional topic that deserves discussion here concerns people's tendency to exhibit self-fulfilling tendencies in their behavior toward others. A self-fulfilling prophecy refers to the process by which someone's expectations about another person or group leads to the fulfillment of those expectations (Franzoi, 1996). It is easy to see the connection between this concept and Kelley's ideas about interdependence in relationships. Our attitudes and behavior are to some extent determined by the behavior and reactions of others, which are in turn influenced by our reactions.

Darley and Fazio (1980, p. 868) analyzed the social interaction process involved in self-fulfilling prophecy patterns in terms of the following six steps in the sequence of interaction between a target and a perceiver:

1. Either because of past observations or because of stereotyped categorization, a perceiver has expectancies about a target person.
2. The perceiver then acts toward the target in a manner consistent with these expectancies.
3. The target interprets the perceiver's actions.
4. The target's response is based on this interpretation.
5. The perceiver interprets the target's action.

6. The target interprets the meaning of his or her own action and incorporates that into his or her self-concept.

While Darley and Fazio acknowledged that this sequence is arbitrary, in that step 1 may itself be a response to a previous step, nonetheless this type of expectancy confirmation sequence is fairly common in social interactions. It is one of the most provocative social tendencies discovered in social psychology.

In a classic study of this phenomenon, Snyder, Tanke, and Berscheid (1977) conducted an experiment to evaluate how positive feedback can bolster social poise and confidence. These researchers first gave college men information about a woman with whom they soon would be having a telephone conversation. Included in the information was a photograph that showed the woman to be either very attractive or much less attractive. Based on considerable work on interpersonal attraction in dating and other situations, Snyder and coworkers assumed that the men would believe that the attractive woman would be more warm, likable, interesting, and outgoing than the unattractive woman. These assumptions were supported in the results.

But there was more to the study. In reality, the women whom the men talked to on the telephone were other naive subjects. They were not the women shown in the photographs. The telephone conversation then was analyzed in terms of how sociable and outgoing both interactants were while talking on the phone. Men who believed that they were talking to an attractive woman were more sociable and outgoing than were men who believed that they were talking to a less attractive woman. The self-fulfilling part of the evidence occurred when the women's telephone responses showed that those who had been associated with an attractive photo were more confident, warm, and animated than were those who had been associated with a less attractive photo. Interestingly, it has been found that this same self-fulfilling pattern may occur for female callers and male targets whose pictures showed them to be attractive or unattractive (Anderson & Bem, 1981).

What do these self-fulfilling prophecy sequences have to do with minding? Minding calls for openness regarding the major expectations we hold for our partners and for our relationships. Partners may not readily accept the expectations that are proposed for them, and having those expectations overtly expressed makes negotiating compromises and mutual goals easier. A well-minded relationship will thus involve explicit discussion and negotiation of expectations that are important to the relationship. This does not imply that people who mind must necessarily completely understand these powerful human tendencies to try to make the world the way we see it. It does imply that taking steps to seek out accurate information about a partner's expectations for a relationship, along with taking care in one's attributions for that partner's behavior, will reduce the likelihood that self-fulfilling expectations will operate negatively in a relationship. Minding makes it less likely that one or both partners will gradually find themselves acting out relationship roles in which they are unhappy or uncomfortable.

Summary of the Theories

Theories of attribution are highly complex and they have built on each other through years of research. To summarize briefly, it is believed that we have a need to make sense of the complex world around us by creating explanations for various events. When these events involve people's behaviors, we attribute the behaviors either to dispositional factors (personality, temperament) or situational factors (outside forces). We evaluate conditions such as a person's knowledge, intentions, and volition to make this attribution (Heider, 1944, 1958). We also examine how consistent, distinctive, and consensual such behavior is when determining an appropriate attribution (Kelley, 1967). Overall, when behavior is extreme or conspicuous, we have a tendency to attribute it to dispositional causes – to make a correspondent inference (Jones & Davis, 1965).

Our attributions are not made in a social vacuum, however. Behavior and attributions for behavior are affected by others in our social environments. In close relationships, a couple's actions and attributions may be interdependent, based to some extent on each other's behavior (Kelley, 1979). The patterns of social interaction and attribution that we engage in can sometimes lead to self-fulfilling sequences, in which we take on the qualities that others believe us to possess (Snyder et al., 1977; Darley & Fazio, 1980). These self-fulfilling sequences may take place in part because we may also observe and make attributions about our own behavior, as well as that of others. When we see ourselves behaving in accordance with others' expectations, we may attribute the same qualities to ourselves that these others have assumed of us (Bem, 1965, 1972).

How does minding relate to these theories? Minding assumes that couples will first have sought to know and understand each other well. It helps to create open lines of communication between couples so that there is much information available to them regarding the conditions and factors used to make attributions. A minding couple has a better chance of clearly understanding each other's intentions, aims, and capabilities. Minding acknowledges and accepts interdependence between partners, considering it a strength of relationships, while also providing the open atmosphere necessary to dispel distorted expectations of partners.

HOW MINDING ATTRIBUTIONS STRENGTHEN RELATIONSHIPS

Minding affects and strengthens attributional activity most powerfully in three ways. First, it promotes a particular type of attributional pattern: relationship-enhancing attributions. Second, it assists couples in avoiding continuous attributional errors and distortions. Finally, it helps to create agreement between partners on the meaning of events so that shared, positive memories of relationship events are cognitively held by the couple.

Relationship-Enhancing Attributions

Minding emphasizes a tendency toward relationship-enhancing attributions. There are certain patterns of attribution that have been linked to distress in marital couples. In general, research shows that,

75

in distressed relationships, each partner tends to be blamed for negative events by the other, and each partner receives little credit for positive events by the other (Fincham, 1985; Bradbury & Fincham, 1990). This does not appear to be because distressed couples are more negative in their attributions in general, or because they do not see other possible causes. They simply view their partners as being responsible for negative relationship events (Fincham, 1985). Distressed couples also appear to be more likely to believe that their partners' negative behaviors reflect their true attitudes toward the relationship (Fincham, 1985). These negative or "maladaptive" attributions also seem to lead to poor problem-solving and negotiating behavior (e.g., hostility, rejection, refusal to accept responsibility, abandonment of possible solutions) between partners (Bradbury & Fincham, 1992). Kayser (1993) has additionally suggested that among distressed or disaffected spouses, this blaming the partner for negative events plays a self-serving role. It can help alleviate personal guilt or responsibility for marital problems. These findings apply equally to both men and women.

In nondistressed, positive relationships, Fincham, Bradbury, and colleagues (e.g., Fincham & Bradbury, 1992) have found that partners tend to make attributions that give partners credit for positive events and that excuse them from responsibility for negative events. Manusov, Floyd, and Kerssen-Griep (1997) provided evidence about how people use nonverbal behaviors to make such enhancing attributions for their partner's behavior. This enhancement tendency is what would be generally expected in well-minded relationships and is what we term a "relationship-enhancing" attributional pattern. Along with the open discussion of problems, minding thus assumes that partners will tend to give each other the "benefit of the doubt."

This relationship-enhancing pattern does not imply, however, that partners should gloss over personal culpability for negative events. Rather, they should raise attributional questions relating to responsibility for negative events that focus on ensuring that such events do not occur again, or on solving miscommunication problems. Attributions with the sole intent of placing blame, however, in no sense will characterize the attributional activity of couples in such relationships. For example, if a couple's financial troubles stem from one partner's spending habits, it would truly be detrimental for them to refuse to acknowledge this. However, rather than the thriftier partner making an attribution placing all blame on the spendthrift (i.e., "You're a weak and greedy person. We'd never have money problems if it wasn't for you!"), a relationship-enhancing attribution can be made which still places responsibility (i.e., "We're overdrawn because you spent too much money last month. It must have been those gifts you needed to buy for your family. How can we save money next month?"). In this second attribution, it is still clear who has spent too much money, but an external reason is acknowledged for the behavior and a constructive, problem-solving discussion is initiated.

By the time people in close relationships begin to use attributions to blame one another in a regular manner for their relationship problems, it is clear that minding has been absent from the relationship for some time. Consistent attributions of blame directed toward a spouse often occur late in a disaffection process. It is possible that, at this point, there may not be any will for minding to begin occurring in the future of the relationship. To begin to heal, the couple must resume a dialogue about the relationship, which includes discussion of the validity of these attributions and recognition of the harm of constant negative dispositional attributions about each other. Otherwise, their attributions may simply serve as a barometer of the imminent demise of the relationship.

Combating Attributional Distortions

As suggested by Kelley (1967), illusions, errors, and distortions are common in attributional activity. Kelley, amplifying Heider's (1958) analysis, explicitly linked these imperfections in the attribution process to the problems of close relationships in his 1979 treatment of processes and structures in close relationships. Four types of distortions relevant to relationships are distortions based on overlooking interdependence, overwhelming social context, taking cognitive shortcuts, and reliance on positive illusions.

One common attributional error involves the interdependence of relationship behaviors. People often misinterpret the role of their own behavior in influencing their partner's. They fail to take into account how their own actions may precipitate, or in some measure cause, their partner's reactions. In our earlier example about the missed birthday, for instance, the aggrieved husband may have discounted the effects of his own behavior on his wife's apparent neglect. Perhaps he has verbally complained about his upcoming birthday or reacted negatively to celebrations in past years. He may have failed to significantly recognize his wife's birthdays. Any or all of these behaviors may have led, at least partially, to the wife's lack of enthusiasm. Yet the husband may fail to analyze his own contributing behavior, focusing all his attributional energy on the intentions, attitudes, and traits of his wife.

Other distortions in attributions may arise due to social contexts or individual differences. Heider (1958) theorized that behavior sometimes engulfs the perceiver's field. In other words, we may focus only on very salient or vivid events while ignoring others, even when those others may provide important background detail to understanding the "main" event. Kelley, using this idea, noted that people also may weigh certain salient or vivid kinds of behaviors inappropriately in making inferences about a partner's feelings and dispositions. The context of a situation may lead someone to view a behavior as more or less distinctive than it actually is. Or partners may cling to dispositional inferences in the context of behavior that regularly contradicts such inferences.

Take our forgotten birthday example again. Imagine this is not just any birthday for the husband, but perhaps one he perceives as important, his thirtieth or his fiftieth, for example. The couple in question may have agreed implicitly to not "make a big deal" out of birthdays and so the wife may be acting in what she believes to be an appropriate manner. To the husband, however, the importance or salience of this particular day overwhelms past history. He views her behavior in a different context. *This* birthday, he feels, should be different. What is more, his wife should *see* that it is different. The emotional power of this particular event has engulfed the background "field" of their previous relationship patterns.

Now let's consider how minding would relate to the attributional interpretation problems discussed by Kelley. First, a couple needs to take particular care in making attributions about the event. In general, when minding is involved, a couple should be active in discussing the whys and wherefores of their behavior. They will be open to trying to explain why they are angry, upset, hostile, feeling neglected, slighted, and so on. These explanations may include pointing out the behaviors of *both* partners that led to the problem (highlighting interdependence). It may also bring out discussion of behavior that may have been overlooked or ignored by one or the other, preventing distortions arising from an overwhelming context. These overt explanations make it less likely that these types of attributional distortions or errors will persist. While this type of dialogue may not occur immediately after an event, it should occur in a timely manner so as to negate the uncertainties and misunderstandings that otherwise might arise from ensuing hurtful remarks that may be made by one or both partners.

A third type of attributional error is related to our tendency to take "cognitive shortcuts." In the area of social cognition, there is a strong assumption that people are cognitive "misers" in how they deal with social information (Taylor, 1981). People want to save cognitive energy, and so often do not take the time to analyze information carefully or to make decisions cautiously based on such analysis. It is not that people are lazy or ill-intentioned in how they carry out their attributional activity in close relationships; rather, they are naturally biased toward cognitive shortcuts. Kelley's logic is consistent with this work in social cognition, implying that couples need to be cognitively vigilant lest they fall victim to these shortcuts in their daily interactions. It is this implication that we emphasize as a crucial justification of minding.

Minding first creates a cognitive "set" that provides cognitive shortcuts that are constructive to the relationship: Positive events are attributed to a partner's disposition, negative events are attributed to external factors. Second, minding's quest to know the other produces a climate that promotes open discussion of the thoughts, feelings, and behaviors surrounding events. This sharing of knowledge may make misattribution and distortion less likely. Finally, a couple who is minding places overt importance on their relationship and thus can justify the cognitive time and energy it takes to avoid the shortcuts that can lead to errors and misunderstandings.

A final type of attributional distortion is that of positive illusions. Holmes, Murray, and colleagues recently have produced interesting work on the role of these illusions in the maintenance of close relationships. Murray and Holmes (1993) propose and provide evidence to indicate that relationship satisfaction is associated with idealistic, rather than realistic, perceptions of one's partner. People may develop storylike representations of their romantic partners that quell feelings of doubt engendered by their partners' faults. For example, if a married man spends a lot of time going to visit his mother, a wife may choose not to view this in a negative way, as evidence of his neglect of his spouse. She may instead view it as an indication of the man's disposition to be devoted to family – even if it is his family of origin instead of his current family.

Murray and Holmes showed that dating couples can be so flexible in their construal activity regarding their partner that they transform the meaning of negativity in their stories: They see faults as virtues! Hence, dating partners may entertain positive representations of a partner, not in spite of the partner's faults, but because imperfections have been construed to fit into positive overall meanings. Murray, Holmes, and Griffin (1996) replicated and extended these findings by focusing on both dating and married couples and found similar types of results for both groups.

This research is quite compatible with minding's premise of relationship-enhancing attributions. Although some of the evidence on positive illusions would seem to contradict our notion that minding leads to more knowledge about each other's behavior, we do not contend that minding must always lead to perfectly rational processing of this knowledge. Minding implies rational direction in its focus on continuing exploration and seeking for more information, but how this information is subsequently used is critical to the minding process. Information may be used by a couple to protect themselves from having to mutually recognize certain faults. This type of illusion may eventually cave in owing to its self-deluding basis, or it is conceivable that a couple may spend a lifetime "covering" for one another's faults and deficits. More research is needed on the long-term implications of such illusions. We suspect any and all such possibilities exist in the world of couples.

In a well-minded relationship, however, error in attribution and perception should be redressed over time because of the diligence involved in the partners' pursuit of knowledge about one another and the relationship. Partners may not always be correct in their deductions and understandings, but will be open to working on them. Further, this very work will be taken by couples as evidence that they care for one another, as would be predicted by the self-persuasion or self-perception mechanisms (Bem, 1972) described above. A well-minded relationship will not involve a long-term "covering" for one another's deficits without explicit recognition, at some point, that such qualities exist – perhaps also with explicit agreement that they are unimportant to the larger goals of the relationship. Minding a relationship may involve a quest to try to correct those deficits, or it may involve a recognition that they exist and the decision that, in the interests of the relationship, correcting them is not possible or desirable.

Reconstructing Relationship Memory

The area of reconstructed memory represents another facet of attributional activity that may be related to minding. It has been contended that people rely on personal theories of change in the reconstruction of memories (Ross, 1989). Ross provided data and arguments to the effect that memories of the past are shaped by people's assessment of the present, and their implicit theories about how any changes have occurred. If, for example, a couple is currently feeling quite satisfied with their relationship, they may recall past periods in the relationship, which may actually have involved relatively high degrees of conflict, as being similarly satisfying and without major problems.

Holmberg and Veroff (1996) used Ross's work as a foundation to suggest that reconstructed memories are one means by which a couple attempts to see their present in a positive light. If a couple is presently functioning well, they may reconstruct their memories of the past to emphasize and reflect their growth toward the present happy state. They persist in this reconstruction even when outside observers disagree that such growth occurred. This research also is compatible with the view that attributions and explanations are made by partners in well-minded relationships in such a way that they enhance the relationship or put it in a positive light, regardless of what those outside the relationship might view as the "reality" of the relationship.

What is also critical to minding theory is the reciprocity of the reconstructive memory patterns, even when they involve degrees of illusion that accommodate the present and misrepresent the past. If both members of the couple are "on the same page" regarding their key attributions and recall, they may prosper even if the attributions and memory are quite disparate with reality. If one member, however, begins to doubt the validity of such attributions and recall, that development may lead to a crumbling of the edifice of illusion that has propped up the relationship.

SUMMARY AND CONCLUSIONS

Attributional activity is relevant to minding in that people engage in it in order to interpret and understand knowledge about their partners, themselves, their relationships, and the factors that influence relationship development. People also use attributions to protect their own egos after threatening events. Minding implies that partners make attributions that facilitate and enhance the relationship as well as their own psychological well-being. This means that they protect themselves *and* their views of their partners when making attributions. There is a continuing tendency in well-minded relationships to attribute positive events to self or partner and negative events to outside agencies.

Sometimes the knowledge and motivational aims of attributional activity may be in conflict. For example, increasing one's knowledge about a person may lead to the discovery of unpleasant truths about the partner or relationship (e.g., that the partner had an abortion prior to the current relationship). How then can the attributions be enhancing to the partner or the relationship? In a well-minded relationship, the couple will work toward solutions to any problems that emerge during the knowledge quest. In committed relationships, they will have established a process of problem-solving that should help them cope and find solutions, even to quite unpleasant discoveries.

In this chapter, we have described the attributional component of minding. We characterized this component as both knowledge acquisition and imputation of qualities to the other that are constructive to growth. We discussed major attribution theories and their relevance to minding. We also focused on attributional tendencies such as those involved in illusion, error, and distortion. We noted that minding involves a redress of these tendencies over time, such that a couple who is minding their relationship may decide to change an overly positive illusion regarding their well-being, or may decide to recognize its illusory quality, but let it alone if it has no capacity to impair the relationship.

Key features of minding that interface with this attribution literature include recognition and negotiation of cognitive sets, stereotypes, and expectations that each partner may have regarding the other and how the other will behave. Such features ensure that classic patterns such as those involved in expectation confirmation and self-fulfilling prophecies do not go unnoticed and unchallenged in the relationship. We believe that minding a relationship allows partners to build a pattern of relationship-enhancing attributions, avoid the common attributional distortions that lead to couple misunderstandings, and create a shared positive view of their relationship and their life together. This is the type of "positive thinking" that we think will benefit relationships and promote the feelings of stability and closeness that so many people strive to attain.

CHAPTER 5

Acceptance, Respect, Reciprocity, and Continuity

Chains do not hold a marriage together. It is threads, hundreds of tiny threads which sew people together through the years. That is what makes a marriage last.

Simone Signoret, *Daily Mail*, July 4, 1978

So far, we have discussed the importance of seeking to know and understand a partner. We have described the ways in which attributions and explanations for relationship-oriented behavior can improve or harm those relationships. But knowing a lot about a partner and/or using relationship-enhancing attributional patterns is not enough to ensure a smooth relationship. There are other key components to the minding theory that, in combination with the knowledge and attributional elements, can help stabilize and transform relating.

First, it is necessary to respect and accept the information gained in the process of discovering one's partner. Second, there needs to be reciprocal minding behavior on the part of both partners. One partner can initiate minding, but cannot "carry" a relationship successfully alone, at least not for long periods of time. Both partners need to participate in minding. Last, there is a need for continuity in minding a relationship. People and relationships change over time. To keep "up to date" with a partner, and to keep the relationship thriving, partners must continue the minding behaviors throughout the life of the relationship. Seeking knowledge, verifying attributions, displaying acceptance, and striving for reciprocal bal-

a friend with a problem . . .''). Thus, in a new relationship, partners may begin by disclosing superficial facts about themselves and watching to see how they are received. If the acceptance is there, the disclosure may continue at a deeper level. If rejection or lack of acceptance is indicated, disclosure may cease. This may lead to the dissolution of the relationship, or may simply hamper partners' attempts to become close, resulting in an unstable, nonminded relationship.

A personality measure, the "opener" scale, attempts to assess skill at eliciting self-disclosure from others (Miller, Berg, & Archer, 1983). The very existence of this scale implies that all confidants are not created equal. Individuals seem most willing to disclose to those who are good listeners, are discreet, can take another's perspective, and can provide insight. All of these attributes are indicative of respect for another's confidence and another's point of view.

A climate of acceptance not only increases disclosure, it also reduces fears of overall rejection in partners. Fearing or perceiving rejection by a partner can lead to feelings of insecurity and unhappiness in a relationship. People who are more sensitive to rejection seem to have less committed relationships and to feel less secure and satisfied with their relationships. They also appear to undermine relationships, by displaying more hostility, jealousy, and controlling behavior (Downey & Feldman, 1996). While these findings pertain to people who are more generally sensitive to rejection, it can be inferred that anyone who feels rejected may respond in this destructive way. When a relationship does not contain acceptance, both partners may suffer from these rejection fears, and their interactions may deteriorate rapidly into defensiveness and control attempts.

Acceptance also implies trustworthiness and discretion. We begin by attributing positive qualities such as sincerity to our partners, and we check their behavior over time to verify whether such dispositional traits apply to them. Of course, our partners make the same type of checks about our dispositional traits. We may come to different conclusions regarding a partner's trustworthiness. If, for example, a person belies this trust by making public the contents of intimate knowledge so as to embarrass or denigrate a partner, this is an act of bad faith that is not in keeping with the minding of a relationship.

One of the key benefits of minding is that the emphasis on seeking knowledge about a partner helps to uncover negative information early, before commitment is made. Nevertheless, sometimes secrets may come out late in relationships. It is conceivable that a partner might have originally withheld the information because it was embarrassing or because it did not seem relevant to the current relationship. Or perhaps a couple's relationship was not well minded in the past but the couple is seeking to improve, and it is through the new minding behaviors that this information finally comes out. For example, what if, after having been married five years, you discover that your husband had committed a serious crime? What are the limits of acceptance in such a case?

Such a revelation in a well-established relationship may lead to some serious discussion about why the information was withheld, and possibly to some reevaluation of the attributions previously made about the partner. But it need not be "fatal" to the relationship because of the restorative value of such discussion and the acceptance and respect both accorded and attributed by the partners to one another. Continuance of the relationship will be facilitated if there is a history of trust and positive attributions developed through the minding process.

Are there realistic limits to acceptance, or is it all-encompassing? How would minding theory recommend dealing with negative information about a partner or a potential partner? Obviously, acceptance is not intended to be absolute. It is built into minding that as much as possible is discovered as early as possible so that potentially disastrous relationships can be avoided altogether. But even after a commitment has been made, some behaviors will be unacceptable to the continuation of a relationship. Certainly a partner who causes physical or emotional harm to the other and refuses to desist in such behavior cannot be accepted. Refusing to participate equally in a relationship or in the spirit of the minding process of relating may be a choice that is too destructive for another partner to accept. Overt dishonesty about past events that have direct impact on a current relationship may also cause insurmountable changes in a couple's thoughts and feelings about each other. But problems from the past, personality quirks, or differences of opinion that cause no direct damage to the other or to the relationship are aspects of a partner that most likely can be accepted and respected, even when learned about years later.

The ability to accept and respect each other is crucial to the success of the complete minding process. Over time, minding leads to feelings of deep intimacy as each person recognizes the high amounts of sincerity, effort, and care being exhibited by both partners. Acceptance is necessary for this feeling of closeness and intimacy to be created.

RECIPROCITY IN MINDING

As noted in Chapter 1, minding cannot long involve just one member of a couple engaged in the requisite behavioral patterns we have outlined. There needs to be a sense of equity in relationships, such that each partner receives benefits from the relationship roughly equal to the amount he or she contributes to the relationship. When a person gives more than he or she receives, this could lead to a sense of being underappreciated or "used." Conversely, someone who gives little to a relationship but receives much from the other may conceivably develop equally uncomfortable feelings of guilt or obligation. An inequitable relationship situation can thus affect long-term relationship stability and satisfaction.

There are challenges to this view. Communal relationship theory hypothesizes that in some kinds of relationships, people are willing to give and contribute freely without requiring any "return" on their investment or effort. The ability of individuals to give communally is believed to be adaptive for families, when parents, for example, give unconditionally to children. Communal relationship theory may indeed be applicable to relationships in which the participants differ greatly in terms of power or resources, and where these differences are dictated by outside circumstances (age, serious illness, etc.). Most romantic relationships involve people who are at least possible equals.

Some studies have documented that, at least for American couples, a sense of equality is connected to higher relationship satisfaction. People in relationships where they feel either "underbenefited" or "overbenefited" express less satisfaction than when they believe they are equitably treated by their partners (VanYperen & Buunk, 1991).

This idea of equity is translated in minding theory into the idea of reciprocity: each partner's active participation and involvement in relationship-enhancing thoughts and behaviors. One partner may stimulate, or trigger, the other partner's involvement, but that reciprocity must not be long delayed, lest the more constructively active partner feel betrayed and lose interest in preserving the relationship. Both partners will be involved in the process, even if part of the time their representative behaviors are carried out in a scripted manner (Schank & Abelson, 1995).

Scripts are preplanned "programs" for behavior that are carried out on a routine basis. Scripts can save people time and cognitive energy because they can be relied on and acted on with little thought or discussion. Couples often rely on scripts in their daily lives to simplify necessary decisions that must be made on a continuing basis. For example, a couple may decide just once who picks up the children after school or who buys groceries, and then that person continues to follow that "script" regularly without further daily discussion.

Scripts can help people cope with time and energy pressures. If they help to divide work in a reciprocal fashion or assist in the couple's achievement of relationship goals, they are not incompatible with minding. But both partners must be wary about the potential power of scripts to replace the process that produced the comfort of closeness. It can be easy to fall back on scripts, even when they are no longer satisfactory, and allow communication and connection in a relationship to stagnate. Minding a relationship permits scripts to be included in a couple's life, but only if they have been created based on the knowledge, enhancing attribution, and mutual respect that minding has helped a couple to achieve.

Is one gender at a disadvantage when considering the reciprocal element of minding? Acitelli and colleagues (e.g., Acitelli & Holmberg, 1993) have found women to be generally more aware of relationship patterns than are men. While we do not necessarily posit that this gender difference is found overall in minding activity, we do believe that minding requires a high level of relationship awareness and communication about troubling matters on the part of both partners.

Berscheid (1994) suggests that women may possess more highly developed relationship schemas because they appear to spend more time in social interaction and in talking about relationships than do men. We would suggest that men who have learned well their lessons of relating will be responsive to the "We need to talk" requests sometimes made by women (Tannen, 1990). If they are not, they risk the development of possible secondary issues, including women's attributions that they do not have the motivation or ability to engage in dialogue about relationship problems. Women, in turn, may become more attuned to a male partner's nonverbal expressions of relationship commitment through use of the minding process. Minding does not insist that men become aware of relationships in the same way as are women, but it does insist that partners in an individual relationship strive for equal awareness of each other and each other's needs.

In part, what people are doing in minding is learning about the other's attributions regarding relationship patterns and making adjustments according to what they learn. The adjustments may involve challenges of these attributions or accepting and taking these attributions into account. Berley and Jacobson (1984) describe such a procedure for using attributions in relationship therapy, which will be discussed in Chapter 11, on minding and counseling couples. Reciprocity and mutuality are features of minding that cannot end if the relationship is to be close and satisfying.

CONTINUITY AND MINDING

This component relates to a criterion for closeness articulated by Kelley and colleagues in a 1983 book: "... the close relationship is one of strong, frequent, and diverse interdependence that lasts over a considerable period of time" (p. 38). Since people and situations change, the knowledge gained about a partner through minding cannot remain static. This is a point that Kelley (1967) also made about attributions mirroring the data appropriately, accurately reflecting the behavior or situation. Each and every person represents an intricate set of experiences, personal qualities, dispositions, hopes, plans, and potential reactions to environmental stimuli. Being and staying close to any person over an extended period requires personal planning and action aimed at acquiring and updating knowledge on a regular basis.

We agree that the amount of time a couple has been together does not necessarily correlate to how well that couple is minding. One couple may be minding well after knowing each other a few weeks, while another couple may fail to achieve a high state of minding after thirty years. Because of the complex nature of relationships, however, a relatively complex process is necessary to understand and describe them. Minding is such a process and, perforce, will take some time to fully mature in a relationship. We also emphasize that minding is a *process* that leads to closeness and satisfaction, not an ultimate destination: Process implies time and continuity. That is a reality that cannot be overlooked by the couple who wishes to be close.

This line of reasoning is consistent with the classic treatment of mind and the structure of behavior by Miller, Galanter, and Pribram (1960). These theorists discussed the interaction of plans with behaviors designed to test those plans. Such sequences take periods of time to unfold. Miller and colleagues proposed sequences of "tests–operations–tests–exits" in which plans are checked out against real world circumstances. This type of sequence can be followed in the minding process as well.

People develop plans to become closer to others. As has been suggested in the minding sequence, people thus come to know and be known by, to attribute qualities to, and to accept and respect their partner over some period of time. Throughout this process, individuals are constantly "testing" their thoughts and beliefs about their partners, as well as their overall level of closeness and satisfaction with their relationships. When the tests detect a problem or discrepancy, a new "minding operation" can be directed at correcting it. All of this involves the checking of the "plan to be close" with which each partner starts.

We do not believe that our focus on time is trivial. As implied by Miller and colleagues (1960), the planning–testing parts of the process of minding and the structure of behavior for highly intricate social behavior are learned over lengthy spans of our lives. We need experience. We need to do a lot of observing and checking to obtain that experience. Knowledge is also imperative to plans to stay close and execute related forms of behavior. But knowledge, too, is acquired over considerable time, and time is required to fully integrate that knowledge into a repertoire of behaviors and attributions regarding a partner or a relationship.

Given the complexity of each person, it stands to reason that the minding process will require a similarly extensive period of time to become well established. How long? That probably varies across people and couples. Skill at the minding process develops along with care and thoughtfulness regarding how one carries out one's life as it intersects with the life of another person with whom one aspires to a long and close bond.

SUMMARY AND CONCLUSIONS

This chapter discussed the minding components of acceptance and respect, reciprocity, and continuity over time. Acceptance and respect are both attributed and implemented qualities of a well-minded relationship. One partner shows them in her or his behavior toward the other. The other recognizes this display and attributes it to the behaving partner's disposition to be loving and caring. The process goes back and forth in this fashion.

Reciprocity or mutuality in thought, feeling, and behavior is essential to minding. A relationship will not be close long if only one partner is constructively engaged in the search for closeness. Minding also requires time to be established in a close relationship. People and situations are too complex for quick implementation of this process.

Over time, the power of reconstructed memory (referred to in Chapter 4) involves the couple's mutual sharing of memories and perspectives on the past and how the past is relevant to their interactions in the present. This activity of recalling a shared past becomes endearing because it is contextualized within a framework of long-term knowledge, behavior consistent with the knowledge, acceptance, and respect for what has become known. In minding the relationship, the reciprocal conveyance of respect, acceptance, and attribution of constructive intentions and motivations go hand in hand with acts of sharing. Each of these lines of behavior builds in momentum over time. Such development becomes, in time, part of the relationship synergy described in Chapter 1. It is, in effect, becoming more complex in meaning and more complete than partners could have anticipated when they made their initial commitments to one another.

CHAPTER 6

Beginnings and Endings

I love you. I've loved you since the first moment I saw you. I guess maybe I even loved you even before I saw you.

> Montgomery Clift to Elizabeth Taylor in the
> movie *A Place in the Sun*

To live in hearts we left behind is not to die.

> Anonymous

ARE LOVE AND ROMANCE ENOUGH?

Aaron Beck argues, in *Love Is Never Enough* (1988), that many elements are necessary for long-term happiness in a relationship, in addition to love. This chapter echoes that message and applies it to the processes of beginning and ending relationships. It is too bad that love is not always as mystical and fated as is suggested by Montgomery Clift's character in *A Place in the Sun*. But most of the time, lasting love and closeness emerge only over time and a process of mutual activity by the partners. The process of getting to know another human for potential closeness embodies many small representations of the minding process that we believe operates most completely and effectively in long-term, committed relationships.

The anonymous quote that opens this chapter suggests the importance of the abiding mental presence of past lovers in our lives. Over the course of a "relationship career," as it has been called in family sociology, people usually make a number of starts and endings at romantic close relationships. Some of these involve marriage; many do not. But all leave some impression on us that carries over into our beliefs and expectations about future relationships.

This chapter considers both the initiation and the termination processes in relationships. As we embark on this discussion, it should be remembered that minding was created as a concept that relates primarily to people *already involved in a committed, close relationship*, and to whether or not they will achieve abiding closeness and satisfaction. Thus, the present suggestions for minding-like activities at the beginning and ending of relationships should not be confused with the larger theory about process in ongoing relationships.

"FALLING" IN LOVE

Dante wrote that love "swiftly seizes the gentle heart" and "spares no one from loving." Before beginning a discussion of the possible logical progression of minding acts in beginnings and endings, we wish to consider whether people readily fall in love and, if so, how falling in love may relate to minding.

Italian sociologist Francesco Alberoni wrote a book entitled *Falling in Love* (1983), in which he argues that people very definitely "fall" in love and that this act represents an intense affective experience of desire for the other – beyond just physical desire. He points to a mysterious and very strong spiritual affinity as central to the falling-in-love phenomenon. Alberoni writes:

> This spiritual affinity, however, did not exist before; it came into being when the lovers encountered each other. Before they met, they spoke two different languages; now they speak the same language. With the nascent state [that of falling in love], the profound structure of their way of thinking – what transcends their individual personalities – has become the same. The fact that every experience of the nascent state has the same distinctive structure ensures that even two people who speak such different languages as French and German and know little of each other's language can fall in love and understand each other. (p. 63)

Alberoni goes on to say that although we usually associate falling in love with being young, people can fall in love at any age. He contends that the specific steps involved in falling in love involve a series of tests. These are "proofs of truth." When we fall in love, often we become "sated" (filled up) with the other person. Falling in love, to Alberoni, is a resistance to love, an unwillingness to yield to the existential risk of putting ourselves completely in the other person's hands. Thus, he says, we search the beloved, but we do not want to do without the beloved. People who are falling in love presumably can abandon themselves totally only because they think that this time of falling in love will be the last time. After a separation from the beloved, the person notices that the desire returns – the love continues and the person needs another "last time." Hence, the last time becomes a new beginning and the necessity for a new beginning. Alberoni believes that with every "last time," people fall in love again. It is a struggle against ourselves that we lose and must surrender.

Other scholars have attempted to define or classify feelings of love. Hendrick and Hendrick (1986, 1989) have identified six different love "styles" or types: eros, ludus, storge, mania, pragma, and agape. Eros is a romantic, passionate love. Ludus is described as "game-playing" love. This love style regards the forming and dissolution of relationships as a playful, strategic game. Storge is a love based on friendship and companionship. Mania is possessive and dependent; pragma is a practical love; and agape is selfless and giving.

Minding theory would emphasize that while eros may be a large component of attraction, incorporating at least some elements of the storgic and the agape love styles would be beneficial to long-term relationships. Minding promotes relationships based on knowing, accepting, and respecting a partner. These are patterns of thinking and behaving that reflect close companionship, sharing, and giving. The strategic games of ludus and the dependence of mania are probably not conducive to a true minding approach to relationships. Indeed, the Hendricks' (1986) research has found that individuals

99

who are high in ludus tend to have many relationships, rather than one or two stable ones. Those low in eros or agape report low rates of ever feeling "in love" with anyone. This study seems to indicate that those people who have at least some eros and agape in their personal love style are more likely to "fall" in love. We would argue that those two, combined with the comfortable companionate love of storge may form a good base for starting and developing well-minded relationships.

Another approach to defining what "love" means is presented by Aron and Westbay (1996). They hypothesize that we know when we are "in love" by comparing our own feelings and situation to our personal prototype of the experience of love. Aron and Westbay surveyed people about "love" and they analyzed the structure of their participants' responses. They found that people's descriptions of love broke into three basic parts: passion, intimacy, and commitment. This, they theorize, is our culture's prototype of love. When in a relationship with another person, each of us examines the interactions that occur. If we find these three characteristics (passion, intimacy, commitment), we have a "match" to the prototype of love, and we therefore conclude that we must be "in love."

The three components of this prototype overlap nicely with the eros, storge, and agape styles described by the Hendricks. Love could be said to consist of passion and romance, combined with the intimacy of a close friendship, topped off by some selfless commitment to another. Minding relates to how intimacy is developed and how commitments are woven from a base of trust and acceptance. While minding seems to have less ability to explain passion – the "love at first sight" sexual attraction – we contend that there is a passion that may be longer lasting which is also based on the trust and intimacy created through minding. We also maintain that minding strategies can balance and deepen the experience of love, from the very beginning of a relationship.

BEGINNINGS

The Process of Initial Attraction

Scholars who investigate close relationships have long known that people tend to be attracted to familiarity, similarity, and proximity in romantic partners (Hatfield & Rapson, 1993). In other words, we gravitate toward those others who are somewhat like us and who are around us much of the time. While there certainly are ways in which opposites may attract, most of us prefer the boy or girl next door – someone in many ways like ourselves in background, opinions, and even level of physical attractiveness.

It is easy to see how minding fits into this theory of attraction. Trust, acceptance, and comfort with disclosure are all more quickly established with someone similar to us than with someone radically different in experience or behavior. The understanding of the other that is inherent in minding is simpler to attain when the other is much like ourselves in background and beliefs.

Minding-Like Detective Work

Minding-like activities in getting to know another person for potential closeness are reminiscent of a detective who is systematically evaluating clues regarding some mystery. We suggest that there is a variety of actions people can take when trying to determine what another person is like and whether movement toward closeness should occur. In going over the following list of possible actions, consider also that the prospective partner is doing her or his own detective work at the same time.

1. Asking questions about a person's background, love history, beliefs, hopes, and fears based on past love experiences.
2. Meeting the person's family and friends and hearing their opinions of her or him. How does the person treat his close others? (With considerable acumen, women sometimes say that they can predict how a man will treat them by observing how he

treats his mother.) Are they people whom you would want to be your family or friends?

3. Studying a person's albums and memorabilia, especially those that pertain to experiences and people that the person describes as most important in her or his life.

4. Finding out about the person's medical history and family medical history and how well the person takes care of herself or himself.

5. Determining how the person behaves under more stressful conditions, such as in traffic jams, when major difficulties arise at work or school, and in interpersonal conflicts.

6. Learning what the person's future plans are, especially what kinds of plans she or he has about a family and how to balance work and family life.

7. Determining whether or not the person keeps her or his word, and is reliable in behavior (i.e., keeps appointments, follows through on agreements).

8. Observing whether this person does small things that are meaningful to the relationship (e.g., being helpful to a partner when the partner is sick and laid up in bed). More generally, does the person do a lot of small acts that are positive for both parties?

9. Does the person spontaneously remember meaningful dates and show that recognition in thoughtful ways?

10. Does the person call or write notes to you, or in other ways stay in touch, reflecting caring and interest?

In this list of possible activities, we see that the rudiments of minding will begin to emerge and operate if the relationship proceeds. Throughout this period of detection, attributions about the person's intentions and deeper dispositions to act in certain ways are being made. If these attributions do not paint a "pretty picture" of the person, other acts by the person designed to be positive for the relationship will not matter, because they will not be attributed to positive motives. For example, if A perceives a pattern of dishonesty and irresponsibility in B's behavior, even B's most caring gesture may be attributed by A to selfish ulterior motives, rather than to genuine concern for the relationship. Conversely, if R consistently observes S in loving, solid relationships with other friends, even an outwardly selfish act by S may be attributed by R as a one-time occurrence, not reflective of S's true involvement. To advance a new relationship, each decision maker most likely needs to attribute positive intentions and dispositions to the behavior of a prospective partner.

Along with the development of a positive attributional pattern will be the emergence of acceptance for what is discovered about the person and respect for the person. Knowledge about the other that is not easily accepted may lead to an early termination of the relationship. Regardless, though, of what is learned, constant reevaluation of the relationship should be occurring, based on the new information being uncovered through the detective work.

The detecting activities described above have been presented in fairly abstract form. At the more concrete, day-to-day level there will be much verbal and nonverbal behavior that produces these meanings and understandings. Scholars have analyzed some of these types of interaction behaviors. Knapp (1984) has proposed that there are stages of interaction in relationships, and offers some typical verbal statements ("interaction lines") that go along with these stages. For example, in a stage where one person is trying to intensify the relationship, he or she may say, "I love you." If that "interaction line" is reciprocated, the relationship is intensified.

At the stage of bonding beyond early intensification, Knapp suggests that people may then propose marriage or become engaged. Partners may say, "I feel so much a part of you," or "I want to be with you forever or for a very long time." On the other hand, if a relationship is moving away from intensification or bonding, lines such as "I just don't understand you" may serve to differentiate partners. These kinds of interactions are perhaps indicative of serious divisions. Significant steps toward termination would be suggested in lines such as, "What's there to talk about?" or "I'm too busy to talk to you – I'm not sure when I'll be able to." Of course, people may also include sarcasm or hostility in their lines of departure.

"Getting to Know You": Social Penetration

Dear Dr. Laura: I am a 26-year-old female who was sexually as-
saulted four years ago. I have been dating a guy now for more than
a year, and we are contemplating marriage. I am struggling with
whether I would be lying if I said I was a virgin.
[Dr. Laura]: If you really can't talk to your man about important
feelings, thoughts and experiences, then marriage ought not be a
consideration. Marriage is not simply advanced going steady. (Excerpt from letter to Dr. Laura Schlessinger, *Chicago Tribune*, December 21, 1997)

The above excerpt from a letter to advice columnist "Dr. Laura"
probably reflects a reality that exists in many romantic relationships.
Partners sometimes do not know critically important facts about one
another. They may think that to disclose would be to damage or
even destroy the relationship. But silence (or, worse, deception) may
be much more perilous for most close relationships in the long run.

How much should we tell about our relationship histories? When
should we begin to disclose such information? The minding position
suggests a relatively open posture regarding disclosure. It also suggests tact in how disclosing is done – not too soon, but not too late
either, as was the case for the letter-writer who has allowed her
partner to think that she is a virgin for a year-long relationship. Both
her lack of virginity and the sexual assault are matters that deserved
discussion much earlier in the relationship. We believe that Dr.
Schlessinger's response about this woman's dilemma reflects the
logic of minding.

When beginning a relationship, two people first concentrate on
finding out about each other. Social penetration theory (Altman &
Taylor, 1973) is a model for social interaction that proposes that
people establish "close" relationships by revealing increasingly
more about themselves to each other. Like "peeling back layers of
an onion" we come nearer to the heart of another person and share
our inner selves in turn. With this increasing disclosure comes a
feeling of intimacy and of closeness to another person.

Disclosure is also associated with liking another person. Many studies into human interaction have demonstrated that, within limits, the more someone shares with us about him- or herself, the more we like them. This phenomenon also works in reverse; after we disclose to another, we like the listener more (Collins & Miller, 1994).

As discussed in Chapter 3 on knowing a partner, Sidney Jourard (1971) was a pioneer in the field of self-disclosure research. He proposed that this relationship between liking and disclosure is actually curvilinear in nature. When we meet someone, we like them most if they disclose moderate amounts to us. Those who disclose very little or those who disclose inappropriate amounts are not liked as well. As we become more intimate with someone, however, we expect the level of disclosure to increase. We also expect the types of information disclosed to increase in personal intimacy.

When a couple begins a relationship, they will most likely begin with general disclosures about opinions, preferences, general past experiences. If one partner is unwilling or unable to disclose this type of information, the other's attraction or liking for this person may fade. Conversely, if one member of the couple discloses too much prematurely, perhaps giving graphic details of past love affairs, this may also cool the other's initial liking.

We surveyed college undergraduates about when and how they told new potential partners about their past romantic experiences. They overwhelmingly expressed the importance of this type of disclosure but also described how delicate the timing of such confession must be. Their reasons for telling these stories to new partners included wanting to share themselves and their experiences with the new partner, to avoid future misunderstandings, and to demonstrate a commitment to the new relationship (Omarzu et al., 1997).

These three reasons most likely explain most of the disclosures that take place in beginning relationships. People disclose so that they learn about each other, so that they know what to expect in the future, and so they can demonstrate their desire to become closer. Disclosures alone, however, do not guarantee that a relationship will succeed. As a relationship begins, the minding process needs to begin as well.

Fundamental Minding Questions

Disclosure is essential in a beginning relationship, primarily so that the partners can decide if they want the relationship to continue. But what happens once you have heard enough about someone to evaluate their potential as a relationship partner? We propose that people should ask themselves four questions relevant to the minding process. These are the larger questions that encompass the specific types of minding activity suggested earlier in the chapter. For example, the first question about trust is being asked over and over as we observe a potential partner's life and history.

1. *Do I believe in this person?* This question addresses the heart of the attributional component of minding. Do I believe that what he or she says or does is in the best interest of this relationship? Do I believe that this person is demonstrating a commitment to me and to our partnership?

The attributions or explanations we make about a person's behavior directly impact our opinions and our feelings of intimacy. A well-minded relationship should be easiest to create when it begins with positive attributions about behavior. Answering "yes" to this question should mean that you believe that your potential partner's actions and words are sincere and well-intentioned, that you are able to give him or her the benefit of the doubt in ambiguous circumstances, and that you believe his or her interest in you is genuine.

2. *Can I respect and accept this person?* After a couple has disclosed personal information to each other, it is likely that some things will be revealed that are unpleasant or unexpected. As a new relationship progresses, differences between the partners will naturally arise. If a relationship is to succeed, from a minding standpoint, the partners must respect each other's differences and accept limitations.

Along with acceptance and respect goes the willingness to demonstrate these feelings. A minded relationship should not involve implicit plans to somehow change the other partner once a commitment has been made, but should involve verbal or active acknowledgment of a partner's preferences and opinions. This component requires the honest evaluation of one's own desires in a partner.

Felmlee (1995) describes what she calls "fatal attraction": when the very quality that draws one to a prospective partner eventually drives one away. For example, the wild spontaneity of mood and behavior you found exciting in an occasional dating partner may seem irritating and irresponsible in the day-to-day activities of a spouse. Fatal attraction may stem, in part, from an unwillingness on the part of individuals to seriously consider whether they can or cannot accept a partner's unique attributes over the long term. The ability to accept both the positive and negative implications of a partner's idiosyncrasies is inherent in the acceptance and respect component of minding. Creating this stability of feeling is essential to the long-term continuation of the minded relationship.

3. *Do we share equal levels of commitment?* This query speaks directly to the reciprocity element of minding. The fundamental basis of the minding process is that both partners are equally and reciprocally engaged in the purposeful continuation of the relationship. This requires that both be involved in all the elements of that process: disclosure, trust, and acceptance.

When beginning a new relationship, all doubts and negative considerations may at first be subsumed by physical attraction and the novelty of sharing with a new person. As the relationship develops, the partners gradually determine whether or not they can fully accept and respect what they learn about each other. They examine each other's behaviors and attribute positive or negative motives. Each partner must decide whether the other is trustworthy and whether his or her behaviors and eccentricities are acceptable over the long term. Even if the answer to both of these questions is "yes," a well-minded relationship will not exist unless both partners commit equally to it.

Early in a relationship, trust is established only when people's behaviors are consistent with their reported attitudes and beliefs. If one partner professes commitment, but then flirts with others regularly at parties, the verbal commitment may mean little to the other partner. She or he may confront the partner who flirts: "Did you know you were flirting? If so, how do you think that makes me feel in light of our committed relationship? If not, don't you think you should be more careful regarding what you say and do toward others that may cast doubt on our commitment?" From an early minding position, these are legitimate questions to put on the table. Anything less will lead to uncertainty about trust and whether the flirting partner is telling the truth about his or her commitment.

Often, we may meet someone who appears to be our ideal partner. Certainly it is worthwhile to investigate the possibility of a long-term relationship with such a person; however, to pursue someone who shows little willingness to commit to the minding process may prove to be a futile quest. Answering this minding question depends heavily on one's willingness to face, to understand, and to accept the other's feelings. It may take time for a couple to make the determination of whether or not there is reciprocal intent. By that time in a relationship, one partner may be too heavily invested emotionally to be able to evaluate the other's intent dispassionately. This fundamental minding question may thus be the most difficult to answer definitively and may cause the most anguish.

4. *Is this relationship progressing over time?* The nature of well-minded relationships is to grow and deepen with time. The minding process is a process of interrelating and knowing another person. Because people change with time, minding must help partners cope and understand that change.

Even in the early stages of a relationship, events occur that alter the balance of power, affection, or commitment between partners. Minding will help a couple adjust a relationship to these events. A partnership that appears to be static, in which disruptions of routine cause disruptions of affection or satisfaction, is most likely not well-minded and not destined for permanence.

Answering this question with a "yes" indicates that partners have committed to each other, that trust and acceptance is present, and that enough knowledge has been shared to enable partners to assist each other in or even predict rough spots or probable crises that will require substantial change in the relationship.

108

Predictions of Permanence

Once new partners have disclosed important information about each other and have answered affirmatively the fundamental minding questions, what guarantee do they have that their relationship will be one of relative permanence and stability? Given the constant change inherent in human societies and interactions, this is difficult to predict. We propose, however, that couples who continue with the minding process over time have a high likelihood of long-term satisfaction and stability in their relationships.

So often, people report that their partners' decision to end the relationship came "out of the blue" and was totally unexpected. Well-minded relationships should not encounter such fates. Indeed, through the knowledge and perspective gained in minding, people can make reasonably accurate predictions about their partners and the course of the relationship.

Implied in this reasoning is that when minding-like activities are a part of courtship, a lot of work has already been done. A lot of knowledge has been gained. This knowledge allows us to make firm predictions about how we may relate with others over a period of time. Well before the commitment, people should know a lot about their partners' plans, hopes, and fears. Well before the commitment, they should know a lot about how their partners act in different situations, about their history of behavior in close relationships, and about their relationships with family and friends. Well before the commitment, they should know a lot about their partners' behavioral patterns both within the relationship and with other people. Each partner should be gathering this information in preparation for commitment decisions. So from a minding perspective, aside from temporary insanity, there is little room for "out of the blue" decisions by a partner.

Of course, people sometimes make commitments, including marriage, after brief courtships without engaging in much work or these minding-like activities. These couples may sometimes have long and happy relationships. We would argue that in order to achieve such a blessed state over a long period of time, the whirlwind courtship couples must have done this minding-like and detective work *after* the marriage or committed relationship commenced. We believe that, for most people, it is less expensive and less hazardous to do the work before making the commitment. In any case, our thesis is simple: At some time during the relationship, the work has to be done for long-term happiness.

ENDINGS

If a relationship must end, minding-like behavior helps a couple emphasize constructive, honorable outcomes for each person. Therapists and mediators usually try to influence couples to engage in such behavior when their relationships are headed toward dissolution. In the Western world, divorce has been rampant for more than two decades, with one out of two new marriages ending in divorce since the mid-'70s. Minding-like behavior emphasizes rationality and care for the parties concerned, including the children involved when relationships end.

In an important book entitled *The Good Divorce* (1994), family therapist and theorist Constance Ahrons argues for a much more rational approach to divorce in which parents put the needs of the children first when the breakup occurs. Her recommendations are very like those of the minding process:

> Slow down the process – children need time to adjust. Accept that your child needs – and has a right to – both parents. Cooperate with your ex if only for the sake of your children. Establish a limited partnership agreement with clear rules. Accept that your child's family will expand to include nonbiological kin. (p. 252)

Many couples, some seemingly perfectly happy together, decide eventually to dissolve their partnership. Why and how does this happen in relation to the minding process? We propose that there are three ways in which minding, or lack of minding, can predict the failure of a romantic relationship.

The Never-Minded Relationship

The first way in which relationships may break down is through the lack of minding from the beginning. The "never-minded" relationship is one in which partners are drawn together through circumstance or physical attraction, but at some level never carefully consider the questions of minding. They may make a commitment to each other because of loneliness, sexual satisfaction, or social pressures, without really knowing each other. They may even get married. As implied above regarding the work necessary to know another person before marriage, the world is filled with marriages inhabited by ill-suited mates. They may not be long for marriage. But while there, they represent the large group of people who would readily agree with the conclusion: "We should never have gotten married in the first place!"

As the relationship progresses, and more is discovered about the other, at some point the partners are forced to examine the questions of trust, acceptance, equality, and change. They may find that the answers to these questions are unsatisfactory. Typical of this type of breakup would be feelings of confusion and of "not knowing" who one's partner "really" was. One partner may feel taken advantage of or abused, owing to lack of reciprocal feeling or behavior. Partners may ask themselves why they ever made the commitment initially, and the events that led to their meeting and falling in love may seem hazy or disjointed in their memories.

An interesting example of a marriage that apparently was never minded very well at the start was presented in the December 21, 1997, *Chicago Tribune* column "Tales from the Front," written by Cheryl Lavin. Since its start in the 1980s, this column has dealt with myriad relationship dilemmas people face in starting, maintaining, and ending close relationships. This particular column concerned the quest to find a mate "in a hurry and get married no matter what." Women in our society may be especially susceptible to this type of urgency, motivated by personal or societal emphasis on "biological clocks." Such pressures by themselves are not enough to necessarily doom a relationship from the start, but with too little preliminary minding of the relationship prior to commitment, the combination of time pressure and mindlessness in relating probably is enough to predetermine a negative outcome.

In her column Lavin describes these pressures in the story of Melanie and Dennis. Melanie and Dennis met in 1989, and they dated for two years. By the end of 1991 Melanie was tired of just being a guest at weddings, and felt it was time for them to get married, despite Dennis's apparent "no rush" attitude. She began "campaigns" before her birthday and Thanksgiving, neither of which resulted in engagement rings. Melanie described how she really applied the pressure before Christmas. At last, Dennis came through and "surprised" her with a ring. She said that she will never forget how "sincere" and "romantic" Dennis sounded as he got down on his knees, placed the ring on her finger, and asked her to marry him.

Melanie then described the next eight months as a whirlwind of registering for gifts, attending showers, and taking care of wedding details. She was having the time of her life. Dennis, though, had not continued his enthusiasm for the event. Melanie said that at the actual wedding, Dennis's hands were cold and clammy and that he was obviously quite nervous and unsure of himself.

Lavin suggested that at that point, this couple could have predicted themselves that the marriage would not work out. But usually, even if they surmise as much, couples become so committed to going through with the whole, expensive wedding ritual – and not "letting down" their families and friends – that stopping that wedding train barreling down its track is rarely considered.

By Christmas of 1994, two years later, the distance between Dennis and Melanie was great. As Melanie was drifting off to sleep on Christmas night, Dennis said: "There's one more thing. I want a divorce." Melanie described being shocked, not because Dennis wanted out, but because he had never been willing to see a marriage counselor. Why not? What Melanie had difficulty seeing was that Dennis had been diffident throughout the entire relationship. Melanie had pushed him through the engagement and wedding, but she couldn't continue to push him through years of an unsatisfactory marriage.

Melanie's story is an example of a couple who used little if any preliminary minding as part of the process leading to the decision to marry. It may be possible for a couple in this situation to salvage their relationship by "starting over" and going through the entire minding process as if they were making the initial decisions about a relationship. They may find that there *is* a basis for a long-term commitment, or they may not. Even if unsuccessful in reuniting the couple, instituting the minding process might allay some of the confusion or feelings of betrayal, and help both partners more fully understand the course and dynamics of the relationship. Of course, both partners must be willing to engage in the hard work of questioning and answering if even a "successful" dissolution is to occur.

Crisis-Driven Breakups

A second type of relationship failure may stem from a sudden life crisis that pulls partners apart. This type of crisis will be given more attention in later chapters during our comparisons of minding with other major conceptions of relationship closeness. Wallerstein and Blakeslee's (1995) argument suggests that in order to get to the point where couples have established "a good marriage," they will have to learn how to master crises that are inevitable in life (e.g., deaths of loved ones). These crises may lead to considerable individual grieving and psychological difficulties that create major obstacles to communication and the sharing of love within the primary relationship.

Even a couple who has been engaged in a satisfactory, minded relationship may be thrown off track by illness, unemployment, or family tragedy. It takes real courage and commitment to continue disclosing, trusting, and respecting one's partner while also dealing with severe physical or emotional pain. When both members of a partnership are suffering it is doubly difficult.

Obviously, the more immersed partners have previously been in the minding process, the easier it will be for them to continue it, to lean on it, and to allow the process to help them through the crisis, relationship intact. Dealing with personal crisis entails many of the skills inherent in minding: disclosing one's feelings, knowing whom to trust and ask for assistance, acceptance of what one cannot change, positive belief about the future, and acts of commitment. Partners who are aware of the process they have used in the past to create a healthy and trusting relationship may be more likely to consciously use that process again in a crisis. These couples may find that, paradoxically, their relationship becomes stronger through facing their fears and pain together.

Couples who have not been consciously aware of their relating process or whose minding has worn down to a comfortable but low base line over time may be surprised into defensiveness by crises. These couples may turn away from each other and minding may cease altogether. Alternatively, a crisis may point out a crack in their minding armor that they had not detected before, and this may cause them to stop trusting the relationship and to lose their belief in minding as a way to heal.

Typical of this type of breakup might be feelings of shock or surprise and feelings of great pain, combined with a feeling of inevitability. One or both partners may come to believe that the breakup was only a matter of time, anyway. There may be bitterness here if one partner feels he or she has "suffered" more than the other, or that the other "doesn't care about" or "doesn't understand" the importance or the weight of the crisis.

The difficulty in repairing this type of relationship breakdown is that partners must deal with both the critical event that precipitated the breakup and the problems in the relationship itself. Minding can assist with both of these issues, but again, it will be used more easily by couples who have consciously engaged in the process before. Couples who have not given much conscious thought to their relationship will find it more difficult to learn now, while also being forced to deal with the emotions of loss or crisis.

Winding Down

The third type of relationship ending is one in which minding simply winds down to a stop. The prototypical example of this might be the middle-aged or even retirement-aged couple who decides to divorce after many years of an apparently satisfactory marriage. Couples who gradually stop minding after years of togetherness may drift apart until finally they enter a spiral of separation (Gottman, 1995), in which they pursue unshared interests and virtually separate lives. The erosion may have occurred early in the relationship. Then the couple, because of the desire to "stay together for the children's sake," or some other reason, may have hung on in a pro forma marriage for many years. Gottman suggests that negative attributions including disrespect and contempt for one's partner, as well as hostile and defensive behaviors toward the partner, often characterize these relationships. Such relationships are in their dying stage, regardless of how long they have lasted.

Both partners may look across a table at each other one day and realize that they are unfamiliar with each other and, more, do not have much desire to relearn about each other. Alternatively, one partner may reach this realization before the other and experience great anxiety over what to do, possibly leading to infidelities in an attempt to recapture a lost sense of intimacy. This type of relationship dissolution may be a slow, long-term process, in a sense imitating the winding-down process itself.

Typical of this experience might be emotions of sadness at the ending of something that had once been so precious to both partners, but there may also be a sense of new beginnings and opportunities. Alternatively, a partner in this type of relationship who is "left" by the other may feel great betrayal, as if his or her loyalty had not been worth much. If the relationship has been of long standing, others who are affected (such as children or other family members) may complicate and suffer through this type of breakup more than the partners themselves.

Salvaging a Dissolving Relationship

All three of the relationship endings described can possibly be avoided through use of the minding process. First, couples must make a decision to institute or reinstitute the process. They probably never have used the process very fully. Thus, there must be a willingness to engage in the work and effort required even to begin minding again via small steps that may proceed to more significant steps over time.

There must be fresh disclosure, perhaps catching up over years or filling in blanks that had never been filled in before. The couple must examine the attributions they had been making about the other's behavior and determine whether they are able to substitute positive ones for any negative or relationship-disrupting attributions they have become used to making. Both partners must practice behaviors of acceptance and respect – even if at first they are only "acts," scheduled and planned out in advance. Finally, they must honestly examine the reciprocity and equality of their relationship and be willing to at least consider making a commitment to the future.

Chapter 11 discusses minding in couples' therapy and counseling. We should point out here, however, that the minding components are all vital to the work that often is done in couples' joint sessions with counselors. As Berley and Jacobson (1984) suggest, contributing to the distress may be the couples' negative dispositional attributions about one another. In therapy, these attributions may be discussed and challenged.

For example, a husband may blame his wife's weight gain for their loss of affection in the marriage. The wife may blame the husband's earlier disinterest in her weight gain. The therapist may ask the couple to discuss the validity of these attributions and others that contribute to their difficulties. The therapist may offer different interpretations and encourage the couple to recognize the importance of attribution in affecting their behavior. The emphasis in the new attributions encouraged by the therapist may be toward mutual responsibility for all of the major ills of the relationship: "We both contribute to what is wrong. Now, what can we do to contribute to a remedy?" This is the type of constructive attributional stance that the therapist may try to implement in the couples' day-to-day interactions.

In a useful analysis of why close relationships end, Karen Kayser (1994) suggests that repairing a love relationship is much more feasible early in the process of disaffection. During the beginning phase of disaffection, people may be still be hopeful that changes can be made. They may be most open then to seeking outside help. Kayser indicates that at this point, a therapist may be most effective in challenging the couple to engage in minding-type behavior that likely was involved when they were happiest in the relationship. Later, however, as hope dwindles, it is more difficult to gain cooperation for such work since one or both partners may not foresee any positive outcome associated with their effort. They likely will see the continuation of difficulties over a long period as evidence that the other partner is not interested in making the relationship work.

Essentially, the couple must return to the preliminary minding behaviors we recommended for the beginning of a relationship. They must ask themselves the minding questions they perhaps never asked thoroughly enough. They must learn, or learn over again, to understand and appreciate each other. Minding can be the tool that allows them to accomplish this, that brings the relationship full circle, back to the beginning, and assists a couple to plan a new future together.

SUMMARY AND CONCLUSIONS

In this chapter, we have dealt with minding-like processes at the beginnings and endings of close relationships. By definition, these relationships are too early to be committed relationships, or they are at the point at which the commitment has ended. Essentially, they may display semblances of the minding process we define for well-established, time-tested, committed relationships. We presented a list of possible minding-like activities that may occur in courtship as a couple attempts to discern the "real self" of the person whom they are considering for a long-term relationship. Critical to the process of establishing a close relationship is the act of disclosure of important aspects of each partner's relationship history. During disclosure, couples often are fraught with concern about whether they will damage or enhance the current relationship. To put off disclosing important matters, though, jeopardizes the relationship's future. Very likely, the relevant historical events will come out. Thus, sometime not too long after a couple begins dating, honesty regarding at least the "big picture" of one's past relationships is an integral part of the minding position on necessary steps for long-term closeness.

Each partner is operating very much like a detective searching for clues as to what the other person is like and whether a committed relationship with him or her would be wise. We noted that these activities involve asking questions, observing behavior, looking at parts of another person's life such as his or her family and friends, and discussing future plans and hopes with the person. All along, the decision maker is making attributions about the other person. All along, behavior is evaluated. Is it thoughtful? How does the other act under stress? Acceptance and respect for what is learned begin to emerge. Overall, such activities constitute a lot of work in courtship. If long-term satisfaction in a relationship is desired, there is no good option to such work. If it is not done during the courtship, it very likely will have to be done during the marriage or after the commitment is made.

Couples either will move forward to a point in commitment in which minding is more clearly a part of their relationship, or they may never reach such a point. If they are ending relationships, minding likely will be exceedingly fragmented in the couple's interactions. In this situation, we mentioned the important work of Ahrons (1994) on the "good divorce." This work argues that rational, constructive actions are imperative for couples who are splitting, especially when others such as children may be adversely affected by their dissolution.

This chapter has addressed general minding-type questions that couples face at the beginnings and endings of relationships. These are questions that the couple may not be approaching as a unit, and operating as a unit is a sine qua non of a well-minded relationship. However, because they lack the commitment of a well-minded relationship, each partner must do the individual cognitive and emotional work to decide about her or his interest in the future of the relationship.

These issues include: Do we have enough of what we mutually want in this relationship to try to take it to another level of commitment and involvement? Do we have enough commitment to work on problems that we have identified so as to make the relationship stronger? Do we have enough invested in the relationship and enough hope for it that we can resurrect or repair it despite any major problems that have occurred?

CHAPTER 7

Minding in the Close Relationship Literature

In this chapter, we examine contemporary, mainstream concepts in the close relationship literature that link well with or provide questions about the idea of minding. We pay special attention to general analyses of intimacy, attachment, and love. For example, the concept of intimacy, as posited by major theorists, has considerable similarity to minding. We argue that minding is a process that couples can use to attain intimacy.

A bridge between minding and the literature on love is a natural step given the centrality of love in the conception of what it takes to succeed in a close relationship for a long period of time. Love often has been conceived in terms of styles of loving behavior that are part of an individual's personality. Further, love often is analyzed as if it were a stable type of trait or style, without the same emphasis on process that we provide in minding theory. We contend that through minding activities, couples may change one another's loving styles. They may, for example, go from a style of dominant passion or eroticism to one of more dominant friendship.

Overall, we repeat the claim that minding is a major vehicle whereby couples achieve states such as intimacy and different types of love. We believe that some of the key features of minding – reciprocity, self-disclosure, behavior involving knowing and being known, attribution, acceptance and respect, and continuity – have been given short shrift in the many writings and theoretical works on intimacy and love. Moreover, the idea that these features need to work together in synchrony over an extended period is nowhere to be found in this literature.

INTIMACY AND ATTACHMENT

The concepts of intimacy and attachment, as they have been articulated in theoretical analyses, may be conceived of as products of the minding process. Intimacy especially has received considerable attention in recent years (Reis & Shaver, 1988; Prager, 1995; Reis & Patrick, 1996) and is discussed at length here. Prager lists more than a dozen different conceptions of intimacy in the literature. In no way can we comprehensively deal with all of these varied conceptions of intimacy in this discussion. Our objective is to relate minding to the models of intimacy with which it seems to have the most overlap.

Reis and Shaver offer this definition of intimacy and intimate relationships:

> Intimacy is an interpersonal process within which two interaction partners experience and express feelings, communicate verbally and nonverbally, satisfy social motives, augment or reduce social fears, talk and learn about themselves and their unique characteristics, and become "close" (psychologically and often physically: touching, using intimate names and tones of voice, perhaps having sex). Under certain conditions, repeated interactions characterized by this process develop into intimate relationships. . . . If the frequency and quality of intimate interactions decline below some level which is probably unique to different couples and individuals, the relationship will no longer feel and be perceived as intimate by one or both partners. (pp. 387-388)

Reis and Patrick (1996) refine the earlier analysis of intimacy by Reis and Shaver, and in so doing differentiate between intimacy and attachment. They define attachment "as an affective bond in which partners feel close and emotionally connected to each other" (p. 525). They further articulate common components of attachment and intimacy as follows:

> (1) Both processes involve emotion and both describe the regulation of emotion through interpersonal means. . . . (2) Both processes emphasize the importance of having responsive interaction partners. . . . (3) Both processes highlight the influence that experiences in significant prior relationships may have on current relationship be-

liefs, emotions, and behavior. In both domains, the vehicle for such influence is a highly complex network of interconnected mental models, or representations, of self and self-in-relation-to others that guides expectations, perceptions, and feelings about relationships and particular partners (both potential and actual). (p. 525)

Prager (1995) also offers a multilayered conception of intimacy. She differentiates intimate interactions (e.g., communicative exchanges) from intimate relationships in which people have a history and anticipated future of intimate interaction. Although she offers many possibilities for identifying the various components of intimacy, she argues that "intimacy [is] a superordinate concept and . . . , as a concept, cannot be defined precisely enough for research purposes. Rather, basic intimacy concepts, within a clearly delineated superordinate structure, can be defined with more precision and are therefore more likely to be serviceable for the study of intimacy" (p. 26).

Prager then suggests that the two basic intimacy concepts that are addressed in her analysis are intimate behavior and intimate experience. "The former is any behavior in which partners share that which is personal and/or private with each other. Intimate experience is the positive affect and perceived understanding that partners experience along with or as a result of their intimate behavior" (p. 26).

Comparison of Intimacy Analyses and Minding

Our analysis of minding is conceptually similar to the intimacy model offered by Reis and colleagues, but it is our contention that we extend Reis and colleagues' logic in an important way. The major difference is that we posit that the experience of intimacy derives from the package of perceptions, feelings, and behaviors that we refer to as minding. Minding is the overall vehicle that is necessary to achieve the components of the intimacy process. Reis and colleagues' analyses do emphasize mutually escalating self-disclosure as central to the development of intimacy, but are less explicit about the types of behavior, related perception, and attributions that also may be necessary to achieve intimacy.

Our focus on the importance of minding continuing as a process over a substantial period of time also represents a difference from the Reis position. Reis and colleagues' discussion of interaction patterning and responsiveness in interaction hints at the roles of continuity over time, but it does not squarely come to grips with the notion that the complex process that moves people along cannot stop if intimacy is to be preserved. A final apparent difference with the Reis conception of intimacy concerns minding's emphasis on attributional processes. We believe that this emphasis extends Reis and colleagues' logic in an important way.

The elements of mutual understanding and shared meaning, reciprocity, self-disclosure, respect, and acceptance appear to be common to both analyses. Consistent with minding, Reis and Patrick (1996) emphasize responsiveness and shared meaning systems as central to the experience of intimacy. They also suggest that the understanding so imperative to intimacy need not imply agreement. This is a position that is congenial to minding. The process of working to act in accord with shared meanings is critical to minding, but in no sense must partners who are minding effectively become clones in thought and feeling. They can agree to disagree, but respect and accept other's position, as well as attribute good will and honest differences in position to their partner. Thus our minding model is essentially in agreement with Reis and colleagues' position on intimacy; it is our contention that minding is a more extended and broader look at the processes of close relationships.

Our analysis differs from Prager's concept of intimacy in that we do not believe that minding is not amenable to precise definition, including operational definition and empirical study. Certainly it is a complex model and components may be studied separately, but the concept comes as a whole and at least theoretically should be keep intact if it is to be of value in describing fully the process of relating.

LOVE AND SELF-EXPANSION

The Hendricks' Concept of Love Styles

How does our conception relate to some of the major ideas about love in the literature? Minding has the clearest connections with theories about love that involve a significant component of mutuality in thoughts, feelings, and behavior. One of the most useful analyses of love is presented by Hendrick and Hendrick (1986, 1992). Their theory emphasizes that styles of love may not be mutual in a relationship and may involve little ongoing thought on the part of the interacting parties. However, in general, they posit that the phenomenology of love may involve both a sense of "lived time together" and "bestowal" (1992, pp. 111-113).

"Lived time together" is conceived of as a combination of feeling close and having access to the other. Both of these qualities may exist most often when a couple is minding their relationship. The continuity of sharing knowledge about each other across all circumstances can make people feel that they are in a sense living together and have access to one another even if they are physically separated.

The concept of bestowal may be even closer to the idea of minding. Bestowal is seen as giving to one's partner in a way that makes the partner feel valued and worthwhile. Such giving probably involves inquiring and learning about the other and behaving in a way that reflects what is learned, with each partner aware that this activity is going on. It also seems likely that for bestowal to create a feeling that someone is special over time, it will most often occur in the context of reciprocity between partners and mutually attributed effort and sincerity.

The Hendricks also mention a concept of giving that almost seems divine, suggestive of what they call an "agape love style," which involves selfless giving to one's partner. Such an idea also is relevant to Clark and Mills's (1979) notion of "communal love," which pertains to giving based on a partner's needs and good intentions toward the giver, whether or not reciprocal giving occurs. Their analysis appears to be cogent mainly with regard to familial relationships. Family members may feel communal love despite what appear to be vast inequities in contributions to the relationship. It is not clear, however, whether communal love is not somehow reciprocal in nature, even if the reciprocity is one of expectancy rather than immediacy. One may fulfill a family member's or partner's needs seemingly without reciprocation if one believes that at a future time of need, these others will then provide support and assistance.

The dynamics of communal love are complex and deserve further research. Partly because of this, we have chosen to emphasize romantic close relationships and possibly very close friendships in our analysis of minding. These types of relationships appear more reliably related to reciprocal giving. For minding to contribute to closeness and satisfaction, it must be reciprocated. In these types of relationships, promissory notes of giving very likely will not be acceptable in the long run. While minding may be felt as divine among those privileged enough to experience it over the course of a relationship, our view is that it is one of the most pragmatic of human potentials.

The Arons' Concept of Love as Self-Expansion

Another important model of love that relates to minding has been developed by Aron and Aron (1986, 1996). The Arons propose that in close relationships, elements of the two people's cognitive structures overlap; the closer they are, the greater the overlap. This overlap is integrated into each person's set of cognitions, thus "expanding" their existing cognitive structure. The Arons term this process "self-expansion" and propose that this experience is inherently positive: "[W]e have argued at length that self-expansion is a fundamental human motivation. Self-expansion is the desire for enhanced potential efficacy – greater material, social, and information resources. Such self-expansion leads both to the greater ability to achieve whatever else one desires (i.e., both to survival and to specific rewards), as well as to an enhanced sense of efficacy . . ." (1996, p. 334).

How does this self-expansion occur in close relationships? Aron and Aron describe self-expansion as produced mainly through the process of reciprocal self-disclosure. We contend that the most effective long-term approach to expansion of selves is through the more complex process we have termed minding. Minding involves more than the early merging activities described by the Arons and thus will enable self-expansion activity to continue well beyond the stages of early relationship formation.

Aron and Aron acknowledge that after a rapid period of early expansion and disclosure, people sometimes "get used to one another," leading to a diminution in expansion and interest. Consistent with our argument about how minding brings new, important elements to bear on how people achieve intimacy, we argue that a person's feeling of the other being "included in the self" and related self-expansion activities are mediated over time by processes more intricate than escalating self-disclosure. Without minding, after a period of time there will be a contraction rather than expansion of selves within the relationship.

RELATIONSHIP SCHEMAS AND SCRIPTS

Planalp (1987) introduced the term "relationship schema" to reflect the expectations and cognitive sets people form regarding their interactions in close relationships. This term is similar to the term "script" (Schank & Abelson, 1977, 1995), which is defined as an event schema comprised of the expected temporal ordering of events in a situation. It has been suggested that scripts help people in relationships almost automatically perform and unconsciously process relationship information in ways that may facilitate interaction (Fiske & Taylor, 1991). It also has been argued that couples in times of potential relationship difficulty may fall back on scripts about what relationships such as theirs are supposed to be like (Surra & Bohman, 1991).

From our position, a couple who minds their relationship will be alert to the power of scripts to influence their relationship in undesirable ways. Returning to Surra and Bohman's (1991) point about scripts, we suggest that when major stressors occur, couples in well-minded relationships recognize the importance of their own actions and dialogue in addressing the issues, rather than rely on conventional scripts for such situations.

Scripts in some areas of relating (e.g., who picks up the groceries) may simplify domestic problem-solving for time-pressed couples. In more important areas of action and decision, however, relying on scripts may be highly problematical. For example, many couples would not want scripted decisions about parenting to prevail unless the matter has first been subjected to thoughtful discussion. Even when couples agree on major scripts in their relationship, the minding process will help them recognize the need for reexamination of scripts, in order to ensure their continued viability and to verify continued mutual agreement.

For example, one or both members of a couple may adopt the script of buying flowers on special occasions. The minding logic suggests that it is not the script of buying flowers per se that contributes to long-term feelings of good will associated with the act. Rather, it is the attribution about the intention and motivation behind this and similar acts – a determination to which couples in well-minded relationships will give regular, conscious consideration and acknowledgment. If this script should be disrupted, a couple minding their relationship will be able to substitute a related activity more easily than will a couple not minding their relationship. The couple minding their relationship will more readily recognize both the import of the original behavior and accept a new behavior that demonstrates the same caring as the flower buying formerly did. This ease of script substitution and lack of reliance on static, rigid scripts is aided by the foundation of relationship-enhancing attributions, acceptance, and sharing that is built up through minding.

Our argument about how couples should be alert regarding scripts is similar to Beck's (1988) contention that couples need to be careful to avoid automatic negative thoughts that are detrimental to the relationship (e.g., "He started this discussion of calories to hurt me because he knows I am ashamed of my weight"). As is true in our conception of minding, Beck emphasizes the importance of careful interpretation of our partner's acts and of the expectation that our partner will likewise be careful in making attributions about our acts. The knowledge component of minding facilitates accurate interpretation and its positive attributional component helps prevent automatic negative thinking. Accurate and positive attributions assist couples in avoiding the destructive loop of negative scripts.

SOCIAL CONSTRUCTION

Schonbach (1992) and Gergen and Gergen (1987) have emphasized what has been referred to as a social constructionist position regarding the nature and development of close relationships. Our interactions with others and our own individual perceptions of the world combine to "construct" our own view of our relationships that may or may not be the same as the views of our relationship partners. This constructive process may involve projection and characterization that goes far beyond the knowledge one has learned about the other via observation and the other's self-disclosure.

To the extent that such a construction of one's partner is consistent with what one learns about the partner (as attested to by the partner), the social constructionist position bears a lot of similarity to our minding argument. Indeed, we might suggest that the minding position is only "social" to the degree that there is agreement. If, however, one's construction is at great odds with what a partner would say about herself or himself, then the minding process has not been well done. In such a case, the construction of the other is a private construction, based more on one's own beliefs, prejudices, and individual experiences, than it is a social construction that could be confirmed by the other.

The social constructionist proposition that relationships are creations of a relational process occurring over time, however, is congenial to our analysis. By definition, minding is an interactive relational process that requires active involvement by both partners. Like social construction, minding is a process of negotiating meaning, including identities.

Also similar to what the social constructionist position might

128

argue, there is no assumption about accurate or inaccurate processing in the minding argument. A couple who is minding their relationship will evaluate and negotiate divergent interpretations of "facts" and events pertinent to the relationship. Thus, a person who was minding a relationship would not incorporate an event into a private construction of the relationship without weighing both the expressed view of the partner and any mutual discussion of the event's influence on the relationship.

SWANN AND COLLEAGUES' WORK ON SELF-VERIFICATION

Another body of evidence relevant to minding is Swann and colleagues' work on self-verification effects in close relationships (see Swann, 1996, for a general summary). The major argument of self-verification theory is that people desire feedback from others, especially close others, that verifies or affirms their view of themselves. If they believe themselves to be relatively unattractive to others, for example, they will like most those close others who do not kid them about how attractive they are, but who appear to share their own opinion.

This fascinating argument has been subjected to considerable investigation by Swann and associates. A finding by Swann, De La Ronde, and Hixon (1994), which differentiated effects for dating versus married couples, showed that dating partners were happier when their partners flattered or idealized them. Married couples, on the other hand, appeared to resist such flattery and were happier when their partners viewed them as they viewed themselves.

Swann (1996) suggests that happily married couples come to grips with and redress any perceptual and behavioral tendencies to delude the self or the other (in attempts to conform to the "romantic ideal" which may characterize dating for many couples). He writes:

> Why doesn't the romantic ideal cause the majority of people with negative self-views to end up in relationships with the adoring dating partners whom it urges them to seek? Some may discover that

their desire for self-verification makes them think twice about their inclination to embrace a favorable partner, thus dissuading them from choosing such a partner. Others may seek favorable partners but find that such persons become disappointed and either develop negative evaluations of them or leave the relationship entirely. (p. 119)

The minding position on this latter evidence and argument is that we would expect that on the average, happily married couples will have engaged in more minding activity and thus show more convergence in self- and other perceptions for important personality qualities than will dating couples. This logic would seem to confirm that of Swann and colleagues.

If a person in a close relationship has been maintaining a constellation of highly negative self-views about qualities that presumably can be improved, effective minding would suggest that the couple could jointly acknowledge and constructively address these qualities over time and try to change them in a more positive direction, and that this would be a desirable situation for both partners. It also suggests that partners would accept and respect qualities in each other that are less amenable to change. When change in traits is mutually deemed possible and desirable, the reciprocal attribution of effort on the part of the individual working toward change is vital in this progression, as is the individual's belief that a partner will not forsake him or her if a desired result is not attained.

This idea complements self-verification theory in that partners are assumed to prefer an honest and respectful acknowledgment of their true qualities and capabilities. Thus, the minding process would not be quiescent about personal qualities that both partners view as negative and open to change. Minding indicates the efforts to implement these changes will be made and recognized by the couple. This does not negate the importance of positive attributions, however. Partners may be honestly perceived to possess potentially negative qualities (such as unattractiveness), but may still be consistently positively evaluated regarding the relationship or behaviors that are viewed as working toward improvement of negative qualities or weaknesses.

COMMITMENT, INVESTMENT, RESOURCE EXCHANGE, AND TRUST

Commitment, investment, resource exchange, and trust have also all been described as vital to relationship satisfaction (Rusbult, 1980; Brehm, 1992). Each of these is involved in the minding process. Acts of minding are committing, investing acts. They demonstrate through behaviors the desire to know and to respect the other. Acts of minding are resource exchanges. They require considerable effort, whether it is mental or physical. Acts of minding are acts of trust. They embody faith in a partner's motivation to enhance a relationship and respect one's disclosures.

No gift exchange can rival the act of showing consideration of and empathy with another person in both words and deeds. It has been suggested in various conceptions of resource exchange that attributions about the nature of exchanges mediate subsequent feelings and behavior (e.g., Foa & Foa, 1974; Mills & Clark, 1982). This reasoning is consistent with our emphasis both upon self-disclosure and attribution in the minding sequence as mediators of subsequent behavior and ultimate satisfaction in the relationship.

Trust as defined by Deutsch (1973) and Holmes and Rempel (1989) requires the type of correspondent inference process that was described as a central aspect of the attribution within minding activity. These scholars suggest that trust is "confidence that one will find what is desired from other, rather than what is feared" (Holmes & Rempel, p. 188). Yet, without a history of minding, attributions about a partner's behavior and its meaning will be seriously limited and based more on faith and hope than knowledge. That may be necessary early in a relationship. Later, if the relationship is well minded, the validity of attributions should improve as should the ability to predict the other's feelings and behavior toward oneself or any object in the other's environment. Trust, then, builds over time through the process of minding. Trust, like respect and acceptance, becomes a major resource of the relationship that is well minded.

ATTENTION

Is minding mainly an attentional process and hence subject to the literature suggesting that people are "cognitive misers" (Taylor, 1981) in their capacity to process information? To some degree, "yes" is the answer to both parts of this question. To achieve long-term closeness and satisfaction, people need to *stay focused* on major relationship issues and events (e.g., whether or not time together and time for intimacy are perceived to be sufficient). In this vein, they also need to pay close attention to their partners and their changing psychological landscapes.

It is not clear, however, that this type of attentional activity is the same as that highlighted in social cognition research in which persons are primed in particular test situations to attend to certain social stimuli, and whose responses presumably reveal various cognitive-encoding and -accessibility processes. Minding involves many more instances of attention to a diversity of stimuli over a long period of time and probably permits considerable trial and error, not unlike the planning sequences for complex behavior suggested by Miller et al. (1960) and described in Chapter 5. Mistakes in perception no doubt are numerous, but the minding logic suggests that couples will learn to regularly have dialogue about and check their perceptions on matters of moment to the relationship.

Related to this idea of cognitive error is the research differentiating the performance of experts from that of novices. People who are experts in an area have been found to be more focused on the "nuts and bolts" of their performance than are those who are novices (Wicklund & Gollwitzer, 1982). If minding is, as we consider it, in part a set of skills to be learned, this difference should also be seen in behaviors of relating. People learn and implement the identity of "good partner" through continued focus, effort, and learning from their mistakes. Experts at close relationships, then, should be expected to be able to maintain a continuing focus on the process of their relationship "performance" – exactly what we would predict for those adept at minding.

LOVE AND MEANING

At various points in this book, we have suggested that minding is related to the meanings created by a couple in interaction over time. There is little that we do as human beings that is not imbued with meaning. Certainly, the same is true in couples. In fact, couples often share idiosyncratic histories and hence idiosyncratic meanings for events. They may reveal this shared constellation of meaning in memories and stories that they report together and collaborate in retelling (Wegner, 1986). We have described this reconstructive style of storytelling earlier in this book.

One of the most interesting treatments of meaning in the social and behavioral sciences was provided by Viktor Frankl in his classic work *Man's Search for Meaning* (1959), based partially on his imprisonment in a Nazi concentration camp during World War II. This work has great value for our understanding of how humans can relate with compassion to other humans. Many of Frankl's ideas were developed in the concentration camp as he fantasized about reuniting with his wife. Only after he was released did he learn that the Nazis had killed her. She had remained real to him in his mind, and his thinking about her had been a powerful motive to survive. To Frankl, their relationship had continued to have existence and meaning, although his wife was already dead.

Frankl developed a type of psychotherapy based on his experiences and analyses of the importance of people's search for meaning. This form of therapy is referred to as logotherapy (for the development of logotherapy, see Fabry, Bulka, and Sahakian, 1979).

To Frankl, love is "the ultimate and highest goal to which man can aspire." It presupposes the ability of the lover to attain what Frankl calls self-transcendence, which enables the lover to concentrate on values and being outside of the self instead of yearning for self-expression, self-gratification, self-realization, and the like. Thus, to Frankl, love requires going beyond self, or transcendence. He said about a person who has achieved this state:

> Man is never concerned primarily with himself but, by virtue of his self-transcendent quality, he endeavors to serve a cause higher than

himself, or to love another person. Loving and serving a cause are the principal manifestations of this self-transcendent quality of human existence that has been totally neglected by closed-system concepts such as the homeostatic principle. (p. 44)

In Frankl's view, love facilitates the mutual self-transcendence of both partners. It opens up a new world of values and gives to the partners a heightened receptiveness to these values. Love contains its greatest meaning in this context, for it opens up the world of possibility to the couple and stimulates that world's actualization. Frankl argues that by making the beloved partner aware of the inherent potential, the lover helps the beloved make these potentialities come to fruition.

Frankl contends that love triggers an upward spiral that causes both partners to attain heights otherwise unreachable. The loved one wants to be worthy of the lover, to grow more and more in the image the lover holds. In a good relationship, the partners "bring out the best in each other," just as in a bad relationship they bring out the worst. We would argue that minding produces just such an upward spiral.

Frankl emphasizes that although love can give meaning to life, a life without love is not meaningless. Meaning is unconditional, and love is an effective means to meaning – just as it gave Frankl meaning and hope in the grimmest moments of his imprisonment. But other avenues, too, may lead to meaning fulfillment. Meaning is realized not merely through what is given or denied, but rather through the attitude and approach taken.

One may be defiant and courageous against formidable opposition and odds. That is an attitude that may ultimately prove successful, however imposing are the odds. For example, a woman who battles breast cancer with great hope and spirit may achieve personal triumphs and inspire others, even though her ultimate end is to die from the disease. Frankl believes that an unhappy love experience can start a process of self-investigation leading to true fulfillment. Meaning is never anticipated. Rather, it is recognized retroactively through the quality ones sees in each situation one has experienced.

Frankl analyzed sexuality within close relationships in this same vein. Sex is not an end in itself: "For the real lover the physical, sexual relationship remains a mode of expression for the spiritual relationship which his love really is" (1965, pp. 112-113). Thus, again, the fulfillment of personal meaning by giving to the other is the quest of the couple in a strong close relationship. It is not sex that brings love, but love that may involve sex as one form of loving expression or language.

Frankl also suggests that when sex is anything less than the expression of a deeply rooted communication to a partner, the partner is reduced to a mechanistic source for personal satisfaction. Within this framework, a love relationship does not necessarily disintegrate when sexual relations are impossible. The minding position would agree with this view, in that it relies on the mutual and reciprocal sharing, acceptance, and agreements between partners in order to make a relationship thrive. If a couple's sexual activity must be suspended for a time, or perhaps indefinitely, minding can assist them in finding other means of expressing and acknowledging affection and meaning in the relationship.

MEANING AND MINDING

Frankl's conception of love and sex may seem to be highly idealistic. However, from the minding position, there is much that is practical about his conception. There also is considerable overlap between Frankl's position and minding. Minding is an activity that if well done for an extended period of time will produce transcendence in a couple. We contend that minding leads to a product that is more than the sum of the individual contributions. It leads to a gestalt of meaning that is unique to the couple and that defines and stimulates the couple as an action unit.

Aside from this overall meaning that couples achieve and revise over time, they also develop countless other mutual meanings for events and entities in their collaborative life. They may, for example, create endearments such as nicknames for parts of one another's bodies. They may have "code" words or signals. They may develop shared ways of viewing portions of their past (e.g., the "rough years," the "second honeymoon"). These are unique understandings that may facilitate bonding and feelings that the relationship is special.

The type of love espoused in Frankl's approach is similar to the bestowal concept in the Hendricks' analysis of love. It essentially is selfless. While minding is not totally a selfless activity (e.g., one may be aware that minding activities lead to good personal outcomes), it nonetheless has as its primary goals enhancement of another person's outcomes and the close relationship. With such goals, we contend that self-enhancement also is likely to occur.

Similarly, from the minding position, sexual relations can express reciprocity, acceptance and respect, knowing and being known behavior, and attribution. They are all there, particularly in a strong close relationship. For example, we attribute qualities to our mate that make sexuality more exciting and enjoyable. We learn about the other in sexuality and let the other know ourselves. In sexual relations, we give to one another tangible offerings (the contact of our bodies, cuddling, kissing, intercourse), knowledge of our bodies and psyches, and feelings that may enhance the overall feeling of love in the relationship.

Even the way the sexual act is carried out can reflect minding. Reciprocity is essential. We each care about our partner's sensitivities, needs, and desires. We each learn, accept, and respect these aspects of our partner. We apply this learning in sexual as well as other arenas. Although in a well-minded relationship every instance of sexuality may not represent an epiphany, it will be meaningful and enhancing to the union.

One of the most potent points to make about minding and meaning is that they go hand in hand. One cannot mind well unless one has meaning – in this case to love and cherish another person leading to a strong, long-lasting relationship. Likewise, strong, positive meaning cannot be very well attained in a close relationship unless the minding process is ongoing.

CHAPTER 8

Minding and Other Major Concepts of Closeness

Passion always troubles the clear depths of sincerity, except when it is perfectly in order. And passion is almost never perfectly in order, even in the souls of the saints.

Thomas Merton

In this chapter, we compare minding to other global conceptions of relationship closeness. We have selected these conceptions because they represent influential positions on how people may achieve and maintain closeness and satisfaction in their close relationships. In teaching a course on close relationships, the first author has found the first three conceptions discussed to be quite cogent to students. The ideas in these analyses speak clearly to individuals about many of their relationship dilemmas. They offer thoughtful, timely, original responses to queries that defy easy solutions. For example, the merit of Merton's quote which opens this chapter is quite apparent in the logic of Beck (1988), who believes that passion can lead to trouble if not accompanied by care in thought and interpretation of behavior.

As we explain, these positions also have elements in common with the minding model. They do not reflect all of the possible relationship theories with which minding could be compared. They do, however, reflect representative lines of reasoning that pervade the contemporary relationship literature on closeness. These treatments include: Beck's (1988) contention that "love is never enough" to achieve and maintain closeness, Schwartz's (1994) description of the relationship of the '90s called *The Peer Marriage*, Wallerstein and Blakeslee's (1995) depiction of *The Good Marriage*, and Glasser's (1995) analysis of what he calls "control theory" in his book *Staying Together*.

"LOVE IS NEVER ENOUGH"

Psychiatrist and pioneering cognitive therapist Aaron Beck proclaimed in a well-known 1988 book that indeed "love is never enough." In this book, Beck uses his cognitive therapy approach, developed in part with depressed patients, to address common problems that couples encounter. His focus is on the process whereby each member of a couple cognitively controls his or her behavior in order to work toward a state of closeness and satisfaction. His book is filled with elements that the minding approach endorses, including: overall positivity in how we think and feel about our partner, flexibility in thinking and understanding, frequent discussion and checking of interpretations and expectations to see how they compare with those of our partner, and active engagement of issues, rather than avoidance or putting off address of them.

Specifically, what does Beck suggest is necessary for achieving durable closeness? Beck argues that warm feelings, heartfelt promises, and strong family ties – in addition to the feeling of mutual love – are not enough for long-term closeness. In other words, emotional commitments are not enough. He argues that being and staying close necessitates development of relationship abilities. Specifically, he emphasizes the skills of competent communication and interpretation of behavior. Interestingly, Beck suggests that these skills lead to respect for the other and that such respect then nurtures and preserves love over the long run. These ideas correspond extremely well to the attributional and acceptance components of minding.

According to Beck, the aims for an ideal marriage are: (1) Strive for a solid foundation of trust, loyalty, respect, and security. (2) Cultivate the tender, loving part of the relationship: sensitivity, consideration, understanding, and demonstrations of affection and caring. Regard each other as confidant and friend. (3) Strengthen the partnership. Develop a sense of cooperation, consideration, and compromise. Sharpen communication skills for practical issues and decision making.

Further, Beck suggests that misinterpretation and attributing undesirable motives to the other are at the center of many problems couples experience. He says that couples usually are not in the habit of checking out their interpretations. For example, a woman undressing in front of her partner may detect disapproval in his nonverbal expressions. She may interpret his feeling and thinking as dislike for her breasts. She may have thought this previously, and it is possible that her partner has said something that encourages such an attribution.

Beck calls this interpretation "negative automatic thought." He proposes that this type of thinking gets couples in trouble in a hurry. Similar to our minding approach, Beck contends that couples need to discuss their interpretations. In our example, for instance, the woman in the example should find out whether her partner truly dislikes her breasts or whether she is instead automatically misinterpreting his behavior and expression. She should not simply continue to silently engage in this type of negative attribution.

Beck also believes that each partner should take full responsibility for improving the relationship. They can help themselves, each other, and the relationship if they adopt a "no fault, no blame" attitude. This will allow them to focus on the real problems. Beck argues that actions by a partner that get blamed on malevolent traits such as selfishness may be more accurately explained in terms of benign motives such as protectiveness or attempts to prevent being abandoned.

Again, this recommendation to take responsibility is consistent with minding theory. It may be, however, that one partner will honestly believe that the other deserves the bulk of blame for a negative event. As was discussed in Chapter 4 on attribution, the key to the whole potential dilemma is discussion and negotiation of interpretation. It may be that a mutual interpretation is impossible.

But minding will ensure regular, mutual examination of interpretation in relationship events. This type of examination will give partners the reassurances that the other cares and that his or her voice is heard, whether or not there is total agreement on the matter.

In the earlier example, however, imagine such discussion takes place and the man discloses that he does dislike the size of his partner's breasts. Such a negative admission could be problematic, especially if it involves an issue that means a lot to both of the partners. Beck suggests that feelings and interpretations following such information may include secret doubts about what the other feels, believes, or is doing (such as the woman's possible thought: "He doesn't think I'm good enough for him"). Is the relationship doomed when these interpretations and feelings arise? According to Beck, not necessarily. Usually, there are many complex and interrelated issues involved in close relationships, and one problematic revelation will not be enough to destroy them. There is more to a relationship, for example, than our perceptions of our partner's body parts!

At the same time, this is a situation that could involve great hurt for the woman and may touch off a spiraling sequence of hurtful remarks and feelings. There may be a lot more involved than just the overtly expressed feelings about the woman's physical attractiveness. There may have been a growing number of issues leading up to this particular confrontation that have deserved discussion for some time.

This is a type of situation that a couple minding their relationship will be alert to in order to give both parties the opportunity to voice their positions and examine possible background issues. Couples may use a variety of strategies, such as humor, in such situations to alleviate tension or hurt feelings. They may rely on memories of previous conflict resolutions to help them through this one. They may reassure themselves privately with positive thoughts about the other and the relationship. But if they wish to preserve the closeness they have achieved, they will not avoid discussing issues when a hurtful exchange has occurred.

Beck also believes that positive changes in one partner may produce remarkable changes in the other. If one member of a couple begins to correct previous automatic negativity and act with consistency in respect for the partner, the other will begin to follow suit. This cycle continues until the entire relationship may be revitalized and changed. Our own position on this idea is implied in our discussion of the need for reciprocity. Certainly, one partner's work on behalf of the relationship may trigger the other's similar engagement, but one-sided behavior cannot last long if the relationship is to be close. Our perspective is that this type of relationship change is accomplished most reliably when both partners negotiate on at least minor behavioral changes, and preferably when both overtly acknowledge commitment to change.

Obviously, this is an area in which we would take issue with Beck's logic. We cannot force our partners to be "good minders." Either they believe in the types of values and steps needed for positive relating, performing in accord with them, or they do not. We may be able to accomplish minor change by modeling minding behavior in a relationship in the hope that the other will automatically reciprocate, but the minding approach would emphasize explicit, rather than implicit, efforts. In some cases, one partner may not be willing to learn minding and/or execute it in the relationship. This attitude on the part of one makes conscientious efforts on the part of the other futile at best, emotionally exhausting and destructive at worst.

Our concluding view on Beck is that his position is quite compelling but does not emphasize enough elements such as reciprocity and continuity over time as vital to achieving and maintaining closeness. Also, we believe that minding is more parsimonious than the several strands of logic Beck advances under the general heading of "adaptive cognition for close relationships." Minding better specifies the links among the knowing behavior, attribution, acceptance, and respect elements versus the more general statement of cognitive therapy applied to relationships. We believe, in sum, that very strong feelings of love develop through the process of minding, and in turn solidify the minding activity as a means whereby the love never ends. While love alone may never be enough for lasting closeness, the reach and depth of love grows in well-minded relationships. In this latter situation, love becomes a powerful bonding element in relationships.

PEER MARRIAGE OR PEER CLOSE RELATIONSHIP

Sociologist and close relationship scholar Pepper Schwartz wrote an interesting book on equality in relationships titled *Peer Marriage* (1994). Some of Schwartz's ideas are based on interviews with married persons living in various large U.S. cities. Schwartz relates her study of peer marriage to her earlier classic study with Philip Blumstein called "The American Couples Study" (Blumstein & Schwartz, 1983). This earlier study compared how married, cohabiting, and lesbian and gay couples function in their relationships.

Schwartz noted that among these couples in the American Couples Study were several (mainly same-sex couples) who were engaged in *egalitarian* relationships. An egalitarian relationship is one in which each partner is treated as equal; roles, major relationship decisions, and duties are mutually agreed on via negotiation and regular discussion. This became the definition of "peer marriage" that Schwartz sought to depict as having come to full fruition in many Western countries during the 1990s. Equality is the centerpiece of this type of relationship.

Schwartz noted that same-sex couples probably were pioneers in developing egalitarian or peer relationships because they did not have to surmount the more traditional scripts for how men and women relate. She also believes that many heterosexual couples are becoming committed to peer relationships. These couples are not always young in chronological age, but they nonetheless are "new" in their creation of customized family scripts and in throwing out old gender-driven scripts. She says that the people in these couples, who probably now number in the millions, are not ideologues. They construct peer relationships simply because they find them more rewarding than "traditional relationships."

Our definition of "traditional relationships" in general is that they are based on what people believe they should do in relationships, given particular understandings of men's and women's different roles in society, with little or no consideration of the practicality or desirability of those roles in relation to their individual marriages or partnerships. A traditional relationship, for example, may involve a scenario where the male is the provider and the female is the home-maker, but is defined as traditional only when these roles are ac-cepted because "that's the way it's done," without overt mutual agreement or even questioning by the partners. The expectations inherent in traditional relationship scripts may create situations in which people are required to balance two different roles: one dic-tated by tradition, the other by the realities of personal or family needs.

Hochschild (1989) contends that women who are in "new tradi-tional relationships" may be doing a second shift in their domestic life, after having put in a full day at work. These women not only have jobs (often necessitated by the money it takes to pay the bills in many families), but also do most of the household responsibilities such as meal preparation and child raising. People in the inequitable relationships discussed by Hochschild may have aspired to more peer-like relationships at some point in their history, but their at-tempts failed.

From the minding position, people in highly inequitable relation-ships will feel neither close nor satisfied with their relationships over time. Usually in the situation described by Hochschild, it is the woman who becomes so dissatisfied that she eventually decides to leave the relationship, or she may force the man to make the move out of the relationship. This situation of major inequity is similar to the one described by sociologist Jessie Bernard in her classic book, *The Future of Marriage* (1982). In this work, Bernard suggested that from the early part of this century through the early 1980s, marriage frequently made women sick both psychologically and physically because it was so regularly filled with inequities for them. In no small measure, the movement toward peer marriages derived from women's experiences in the decades before the 1980s and 1990s when they felt unfulfilled either in marriage or professionally, and sometimes in both areas. Bernard's work was instrumental in this movement toward equity and equality in close relationships.

Peer marriages do not have the type of inequity involved in the "second shift" marriage. Their participants vigilantly see themselves as equals and work to put that equality into practice. Many of them have experienced a previous traditional marriage or have witnessed that of their parents, and did not like what they experienced or witnessed. They see peer marriage as the only way to achieve the type of respect and dignity that they believe humans in close relationships should maintain.

Schwartz reports some intriguing information about the couples in her peer marriage study. There were about thirty couples in the age range of late twenties to forties; she also compared them with friends whom they identified as being involved in traditional relationships. One datum from the peer couples is that they reported that they generally adhere to at least a sixty–forty split of household chores and child raising. Thus, both partners must be significantly involved, though one may be involved at 60 percent in one activity and 40 in the other, and vice versa. Second, each partner believed that each person in the couple had equal influence over important and disputed decisions.

Another finding was that each partner believed that she or he had equal control over the family economy and reasonably equal access to discretionary funds. Regardless of who made more money, there was a feeling of shared wealth and shared power to make monetary decisions. A related finding was that each person's work was given equal weight in the couple's overall plans. The person who had the less "prestigious" or less financially rewarding occupation did not have to sacrifice unduly to follow the one whose occupation was loftier in status or that paid more.

At the heart of peer relationships is friendship. Peer couples very often identify their partner as their best friend. As Rabin (1996) suggests, the qualities of friendship can survive only in an atmosphere of equality, as friendship implies lack of domination, mutual concern, and respect. But how do couples go about creating this friendship? As you might expect, our answer is that friendship derives from the constellation of actions found in minding. Very good friends, and especially friends in a partnership, inhabit shared worlds. They are frequent confidants about significant and minor concerns. In such partnerships, men and women share worries about their progress or lack of it in many areas, including financial, child-raising, health, and career issues. To a high degree, they share information and perspectives (attributions, understandings, opinions, and feelings). In both public and private acts and in both small and large ways, their relationship-oriented activities are designed to facilitate the partnership. As in minding, acceptance and respect of the partner's qualities and revelations are embraced in very good friendships.

Couples who are not good friends show the opposite of these types of activities (Rabin, 1996). They often follow scripted approaches to their relationship with little overlap and intercommunication. For example, the woman does the child raising, and the man the money making. They may share information about each partner's sphere of activity, but their sharing is not aimed at mutual involvement. Rabin (1996) argues that when close relationships drift away from peer relating, friendship suffers. Women, in particular, may become ambivalent or bitter about this drift away from peer relating. For them, such a drift may mean that they will have more "second shift" responsibilities or that their partner does not respect them as an equal.

Schwartz suggests that in practice, many couples may not be able to reach or to sustain a peer marriage, even if they mutually desire one. Economic and child-raising realities may lead to much more scripted role behavior than these couples believe to be ultimately desirable. In society in general, women still lag behind men in salaries. Child raising may be complicated by blended families after earlier divorces. Mixes of teenage and younger children may be in the home, and each parent may not be equally effective in interacting with these different children and young adults. Schwartz argues, however, that if couples can eliminate a scripted approach to major areas such as earning money and child raising, they will have more creative possibilities available to address these dilemmas. Most important, if they will stay focused overall on the peer concept, they will have set the foundation for achieving a sense of equality as a primary basis for intense and highly nurturing friendship and love.

What are some of the disadvantages of peer marriage? From the perspective of minding, there are no disadvantages that cannot be overcome. Schwartz, though, points to a set of possible issues that emerged from her discussions with couples striving to have peer marriages. They included the following.

1. Who takes the lead in stimulating sexual or passionate activity may be unclear. Most of the old "tricks" of seduction may have been discarded by these couples. Hence, they are reliant on regular communication and action relevant to sexuality. This is not easy if both are involved in child raising, careers, and other activities or hobbies. It is not easy given how most of us still are educated to communicate about sexuality. Too often, our education reflects elements such as parental euphemistic talk about sex, peer gossip and innuendo, and media hype. Couples who are minding their relationships will recognize that all important acts relevant to their relationship, including sexuality, need to be given high priority. They need to organize their priorities, including personal and career responsibilities, so that this recognition is given its due.

2. Peer couples sometimes may compete regarding career advancement or success. Yet, again, if they are minding their relationship, they will realize that career advancement is meaningful only if they maintain a strong close relationship; additionally, if they do not maintain a strong close relationship, that itself may greatly impair their working lives. Hence, it is career-smart to mind a relationship and to make it a higher priority in attitudes and behavior.

3. Perhaps the most challenging aspect of peer marriage is all the constant work involved. This is synonymous with minding in that the behavioral stream of well-conceived, thoughtful acts on behalf of the relationship cannot include big breaks. A couple committed to peer marriage cannot just revert back into traditional roles when the going gets tough. They have to be always flexible and always vigilant to outside influences that may push them away from equal-

ity. Schwartz suggests that parents' input and traditional value systems regarding the nature of the family may represent two of the dissident influences against which couples in peer marriage must hold their own in order to succeed. They will have to be always active in protecting "peerness" in areas that count most to the couple. Compromising and negotiating difficult issues will require a lot of effort on top of the everyday obligations of busy people. Especially when considering the unique problems of a blended family, one can imagine the scope of regular "pow wows" and truce-talks that may be necessary in a large household. As is true with minding, these delicate social interactions require a high degree of work on a regular basis. Just like minding, the payoff can be immense – for the children as well as the parents. And, just like minding, many couples may abandon peer relationships because of the degree of regular work involved.

Schwartz concludes her book with a summary and an eloquent statement on behalf of the future of peer relationships:

> There are no rules on how to construct a peer marriage. For the couples interviewed for this book, the impetus usually came from a rejection of past experience – a woman who demanded equality of her spouse, or a man who was searching to make his wife and children the center of his life. . . . Age seems to tame men's preoccupation with work and control, and it gives women more courage, self-confidence, and direction. Some couples will develop peer marriages only in the senior segment of their lives.
>
> But there is no need for anyone to wait. Peer marriage respects the potential of each person and gives men and women a chance to overcome the biology and sociology that separate them. Future generations might be renewed by a powerful new phase of marriage: two people who can create a strong and durable family because their relationship is secured by a commitment to equality that is underwritten by a deep and abiding friendship. (p. 196)

The minding theory obviously has a lot in common with ideas central to peer marriage. Minding, we contend, is the way in which couples attain peer stature in the relationships. Schwartz describes the activities of several couples in achieving this type of relationship, yet her analysis does not lead to clear-cut principles for maintaining closeness. Adding the peer relationship concept to minding theory gives minding theory greater descriptive breadth in terms of the outcome of minding. Peerness is an ongoing state many couples can work to achieve and maintain. Minding and peer relating are synonymous when broken down to their basics: equity and equality, flexibility, friendship, presentation of self at a deep level, care about and interest in other's most basic qualities, negotiation of difficult relationship dilemmas, and synchrony of behavior and attribution.

"THE GOOD MARRIAGE"

Respected family therapist and scholar Judith Wallerstein and her colleague, writer Sandra Blakeslee (1995), were interested in basically the same question addressed by minding theory: How can we make close relationships work in our time? In an interview Wallerstein described her interest in people's tendency to always worry about the things that are failing. Based on discussions with students, we would agree that this tendency exists. Students often ask: "In light of all the divorce in society, including my own family, how can I make my marriage or close relationship succeed?" Wallerstein suggests that we do not spend enough time considering (or investigating) how people make things work – including marriage.

Wallerstein took on this challenge by interviewing fifty couples who by their own report had achieved lasting, happy marriages. These were people aged from their forties through their sixties. They were California residents, white and generally well off, well educated, and articulate about their relationships. Thus, as Wallerstein recognized, the sample was open to bias on several dimensions. Nevertheless, no one had ever conducted a study like this before, which focused on this aspect of keeping a relationship together. As suggested in Chapter 7 linking minding to the contemporary relationship literature, in general there has been little work on long-term relationships and why they do or do not continue.

Given that the couples defined their marriages as happy ones, Wallerstein was interested in the ingredients that went into that definition for different couples. Were they happy from the start? If not, what events and transformations led to their long-term success? How did they get beyond crises such as the death of a child or a perceived betrayal that so often staggers a couple and makes them highly vulnerable for some time? Indeed, one of the important contributions of Wallerstein's study is the finding that even these highly successful couples all went through crises, and that it is how couples handle crises that may differentiate them in terms of success.

Wallerstein indicates that, overall, she was surprised at how easy it was to find happy couples. She defined these couples as engaged in relationships that were predominantly either "companionate" or "romantic." Companionate relationships emphasize companionship and, like peer relationships, appear to involve conscious efforts to achieve equality or parity for partners. Romantic relationships emphasize a continuation of sexual passion, courtship-type fantasies, and idealization of the partner during the relationship. While Wallerstein did not compare these types of relationships, many of the relationship processes she addresses occur in companionate relationships.

Like Schwartz's sample of peer couples, Wallerstein's couples stressed the high degree of work involved in having a strong marriage and successful family life. Parents often have to sacrifice their own needs for rest or relaxation in order to engage in family activities after spending full days at their work. Regarding parenting young children, Wallerstein made the following comments in an interview about her book:

> If you have young children, there used to be a lot of hands around. Now there aren't. A companionate marriage especially requires a high energy level, because you are combining the workplace, the marriage and the children. And each of those is a full-time job. (*USA Weekend*, May 19-21, 1995)

Wallerstein continued in the same interview to discuss the special place of sex among the couples she interviewed:

> What one couple does, another couple doesn't do. . . . Sex is critical in a good marriage, but sex in a marriage is different than casual sex. It needs time. It needs serenity. You can't have it on the run. It

149

doesn't fill only a physical need; it's central to the marriage, and it has to be treated with dignity. And it is most vulnerable, much more vulnerable than I expected to find among young people.

Similar to Schwartz, Wallerstein does not outline a formula for successful relating. But she does list a set of attributes that tend to be found in most strong marriages: (1) separation from families of origin; (2) togetherness, including both intimacy and autonomy; (3) privacy that is maintained even during the prime of parenthood; (4) staying power, which means bonding intensifies during crises, which occur fairly often in all relationships (see discussion below); (5) the creation of a safe haven that is able to absorb conflict and anger; (6) sex that is protected from the incursions of work and family; (7) laughter, keeping all manner of events in perspective; (8) comfort, which satisfies the need for dependency through the regular encouragement partners offer one another; and (9) memory, which emphasizes the time when the couple fell in love and collectively memoralizes the high moments of the relationship.

One of the most useful aspects of the Wallerstein and Blakeslee book speaks to crises that couples must face together in order to best adapt to their consequences. The loss of a parent to death is one such crisis; even more staggering is the loss of a child. Other types of common crises include severe financial difficulty, sometimes occasioned by loss of a job; major accidents or serious illness; and children's major problems, such as school- or drug-related. Most couples will face multiple such crises during their relationship career. They need to learn how to face them with grace and wisdom.

MINDING AND "THE GOOD MARRIAGE"

In many ways, Wallerstein's study is the kind of research that needs to be done to better evaluate the merit of minding. We need to study people who are happy in long-term close relationships and compare them with those who also have related for a substantial period, but who are not happy. We need to find out about the specific processes articulated by these couples that they believe led to their success or lack thereof. We need, also, to go beyond their self-report and evaluate their possible minding behavior in other ways, such as peer and children reports, their reactions to assessment instruments, and how they interact in solving problems.

A major contribution of Wallerstein and Blakeslee's analysis of the good marriage for minding is that relationships occur in the context of time and events that may play a role in the progression of the relationship. Their idea of couples who succeed in transcending different crises is particularly cogent. Our argument would be that minding is a process that facilitates problem solving, and, hence, it may determine how well a couple does in addressing crises. If they mind well before the crisis, that fact should bode well for them in dealing with the crisis.

The nine attributes of a good marriage according to these analysts suggest the importance of a couples' development of a process to instill these elements into their relationship and at appropriate times. Each of these elements may require a lot of work and skill in relating and negotiating issues. Minding would appear to be one vehicle to help couples continue to be timely in how they handle both external and internal pressures. Minding even implicates sexual activity and humor as acts consistent with knowing the other and knowing what contributes to the success of the relationship.

One of the most penetrating conclusions reached by Wallerstein in her research is that a good marriage is transformative. She says that the prevailing psychological view has been that the central dimensions of personality are fully established in childhood. But based on her evidence, she believes that men and women come to adulthood unfinished. Over the course of a marriage, they change each other profoundly. Further, as men and women in good marriages respond to their partner's emotional and sexual needs and wishes, they grow and influence the other. Ways of thinking, self-image, and values all have the potential for change. As our argument goes, however, we would emphasize that these transformations usually do not occur by magic. They are the products of systematic thought, feeling, and behavior not unlike the constituent activities of minding.

STAYING TOGETHER

In *Staying Together: A Control Theory Guide for Lasting Marriage* (1995), psychiatrist William Glasser presents his ideas about how to achieve lasting relationships via control theory. Briefly, this theory says that we are always making choices, including those about our relationships. According to Glasser, we can make better choices and thus have better relationships. The key to his analysis is what he says about the early decisions we make in getting involved:

> If you are in the beginning stages of a relationship, this is the time to make this assessment. Find out early if you are well matched and also become aware of where there is potential for trouble. Then you can try to deal with some of the differences before you get married and also learn how to deal with any differences that arise after marriage. (p. 53)

Glasser suggests a somewhat intricate way of assessing strength of needs along the dimensions of survival (pertaining to how security-oriented we are), love and belonging, power, freedom, and fun. He recommends that a person considering becoming involved with another person rate each person's needs for these dimensions. Consider using a scale from 1 to 5 with 1 being a very weak need and 5 being a very strong need. For example, if on the need for love and belonging you rate yourself at 2 and the other rates him- or herself at 5, there is a disparity to be analyzed and addressed in some fashion, including possibly terminating the relationship at this early point. If a couple has similar ratings on most dimensions, there is usually not a problem.

Of course, an implication of Glasser's suggestion might be that each party should rate the other as well as the self. Thus, the results may be more complicated than whether the two self-ratings show disparities. What if there are differences in how the other rates a partner's needs versus how the partner rates his or her own needs? There is a lot to think about and/or discuss before going too far with such ratings. Glasser's analysis would be stronger if it dealt more explicitly with the reciprocity aspects of relating. Certainly, in terms of therapeutic implications, both parties need to be involved and to recognize that the interrelationships of their thoughts, feelings, and behavior need regular examination. If that task becomes too labored or technical, the couple likely will grow weary soon.

Glasser also provides input to couples based on his work with needs assessment. He contends, for instance, that it is better for the relationship if the male has a slightly lower power need than does the female, but has a high love need similar to that of the female. Why? Presumably it is because power-oriented men are the worst kind for compromise and negotiation in close relationships. He claims a female is "reserving a place for herself in hell" if she bonds with a male who is very low on love and belonging and very high on power and freedom.

According to Glasser, the need for power is a dimension which can cause other problems in relationships. If both partners have a similar, high need for power, this can also lead to conflicts. He goes on to say that one of the deadliest configurations for a marriage is a same need profile in which both the male and female want power and freedom.

One of the major issues with Glasser's control theory is how to define terms such as freedom and power and the assumption that our needs for these states are relatively unchanging. A person might want power in one sphere of life and yield to others consistently in other spheres. Further, a person may want very specialized power, such as control over the desserts the family has at mealtimes, but not over the entire meal. The same is true for the global concepts of survival and freedom. We may desire freedom in some areas but not others. All shadings of possibility may emerge in human social interaction.

Overall, this challenge suggests the difficulty for the couple of doing any kind of careful needs assessment. They may get a ballpark idea of the differential needs. But this ballpark idea definitely needs to be refined by extensive conversation.

MINDING AND STAYING TOGETHER

Control theory as articulated by Glasser is general and hence may not be helpful to many couples faced with the challenges of making relationships work. The general ideas of the theory are consistent with the minding approach. These ideas include: When we are faced with unsatisfying situations, we act to try to make the situations better. Or we ignore the situations – which is a choice itself, as Glasser argues. Glasser suggests that women often have the onus of raising issues that must be discussed if a relationship is to be satisfying. He notes that men may try to use sex as a cure-all. Glasser's observations about gender differences are similar to Tannen's (1990) arguments that women are in charge of "troubles talk" in relationships, whereas men focus on practical matters. But Glasser's treatment still is quite general about what to do to fix a relationship even if discussion between partners has begun.

Overgeneralizations in this area are dangerous. Men and women increasingly reveal nuances of both similarity and dissimilarity in how they approach relationships. The vast media onslaught about relationships undoubtedly is having an impact in smoothing out major, clear-cut gender differences. But no simplistic pronouncements about men and women and the way they relate is fair to either gender or to the topic.

From the minding position, we do support Glasser's assertion that choices are being made all the time – even when we ignore, avoid, distract ourselves, or otherwise run from a dilemma. Further, we support the idea of being creative in our choices and behavior. That is a necessity in minding and in all of the intricate behaviors that life requires to survive.

Unfortunately, our final perspective on Glasser's analysis is that it is similar to much of the self-help literature on relationships and how to make them work (see the discussion in Chapter 11 of such literature and relationship counseling). The argument presented is too unqualified and too general, and does not capture the complexity of the phenomena under discussion. Glasser's treatment provides interesting and what likely are useful suggestions. But it cannot readily lead to answers for the problems people encounter in trying to preserve closeness.

SUMMARY AND CONCLUSIONS

In this chapter, we compared the minding conception to ideas deriving from some major books on what is necessary to achieve and maintain closeness. We suggested that there is considerable similarity between minding and the arguments presented in the volumes by Beck (1988), Schwartz (1994), and Wallerstein and Blakeslee (1995). There is less similarity with Glasser's (1995) treatment, mainly because of its generality and almost exclusive self-help focus.

Each of the foregoing relationship analyses offers something to the minding position. Beck introduces concepts such as automatic negative thoughts that fit well with the attribution component of minding. People must be more aware of their automatic thoughts in general and be ready to challenge them. Beck's analysis, however, did not emphasize the reciprocity component to the extent that minding suggests is necessary for closeness to be preserved.

We believe that Schwartz's analysis complements the minding position quite well. Peer relationships emphasize equality, friendship, and regular problem solving and negotiation in which both partners share in all major areas of living. We believe that minding is conducive to peer relating. Once peer relating is in effect in a relationship, it should facilitate minding as well. Each approach embraces equality, equity, flexibility, and the use of the mind in relating. While Schwartz does not stress the use of the mind as much as Beck does (with his emphasis on analysis of interpretations and private thoughts), her treatment of peer relating implies that there will be a significant investment of thought and feeling in most of the major relationship decisions a couple must make.

Wallerstein's study of what makes a "good marriage" suggested some of the "nuts and bolts" that are implied by the general principles of minding. Her focus on how couples must learn to deal with inevitable crises such as health problems and death is useful and again suggests the value of minding as a way of dealing with all manner of normal and abnormal events in the lives of a couple. Glasser's emphasis on the constancy of decision making and that we always are making choices also is consistent with minding. We believe, however, that relating takes much more use of the mind than simply this recognition. A detailed knowledge of and experience in how to work with another person toward a cherished goal is really what minding is about. Any overly general statement of this knowledge and experience does not do justice to humans' capacity for closeness and what they must do to achieve it.

We will end with some historical observations. The ideas of peer marriage, minding, and egalitarianism are new ideas in the long history of human relationships and marriage. Only in the last thirty years or so in the West has it been possible to have relationships that strongly embody these qualities. For centuries and well into the twentieth century, hierarchical relationships were powerfully influenced by church and state rules and customs that prescribed roles, with the male being superior in areas of decision making, work, and so on. There truly has been a revolution in close relationships since about the end of the 1960s when equality, freedom of action, and consent began to be viewed as essential to closeness.

Will close relationships of the future across the world be dominated by these peer–minding–equality ideas? We believe that they will as long as people have freedom politically and are able to make a living economically. These ideas have evolved as better ways of relating after decades or even centuries of dissatisfaction with different approaches, such as those involving traditional, male-dominated marriages. When severe stress occurs in the political and/or economic arenas, it perforce affects the way people relate in their intimate lives. In such cases, freedom both as a citizen and as a person with major entitlements in a relationship may be threatened. This reasoning about minding in the larger social context is elaborated in Chapter 10 on international perspectives on minding.

CHAPTER 9

Evidence about Minding in Close Relationships

There are many methodological approaches to researching close relationships. One can interview, observe, or follow real couples over time. One can match up strangers in a laboratory setting, creating artificial relationships and then examining their responses to different factors manipulated in an experiment. One can also survey individuals about their views, experiences, and beliefs about close relationships in general. We believe that all of these approaches (and others besides) can and should be used to investigate and validate a broad theory of close relationships such as the minding theory.

We have only begun to subject our theory to empirical testing. In this chapter we review three of our own studies that have attempted to explore aspects of the minding theory of relationships. We emphasize that this work is rather preliminary in nature, but still presents some evidence about the dynamics of close relationships that we believe to be important.

DO PEOPLE RECOGNIZE WELL-MINDED RELATIONSHIPS?

If our minding theory explains how satisfying and intimate relationships are maintained over time, then people who are in these relationships should display the behaviors we recommend. Minding behaviors should be associated, then, with good relationships. Since most individuals have, at some time or other, observed what seem to be healthy, long-term relationships, they should also have observed some of these behavior patterns and should have come to associate them with good relationships.

We hypothesized, therefore, that individuals in the general population would be more likely to judge a relationship as a good one if they observed one or more of the minding components within it. Conversely, we hypothesized that people who observed a relationship that was conspicuously missing one or more of the minding components would judge that relationship to be troubled. If our hypotheses were supported, this would establish not that the minding theory explained relationship satisfaction, but that at least it had a "common sense" validity.

To examine these hypotheses we conducted a survey of seventy-eight undergraduate students. A team of research assistants wrote vignettes that described incidents in relationships. Each of the vignettes was designed to show a couple utilizing one minding component or neglecting one minding component. Two sample vignettes are below. These illustrate the presence or lack of relationship-enhancing attributions.

> When Karen and Jason moved in together ... from time to time Jason would come home from work in terrible moods and would attack Karen about trivial things in their relationship. This bothers Karen, but she doesn't believe Jason means to attack her. She blames his moods on his stressful job. When Jason arrives home angry, Karen asks him to share his job frustrations with her.

> Sam and Debbie always fight during the holiday season. ... One night Julie tells Sam that the holidays are very difficult for her because it was during this time of year that her father passed away. Sam listens carefully to Julie and understands her grief. Sam still believes, though, that their arguing is not really about the loss. ... He continues to try and determine what the relationship problem is.

The participants in the survey were not told about the minding theory or about the components. They simply read each vignette and scored it on a scale of "terrible" to "ideal." Each participant read and rated twelve vignettes, six written to show "high minding" and six written to show "low minding."

Results were treated as a within-subjects analysis, with each participant's ratings of the high-minded scenarios summed and compared with their summed ratings of the low-minded scenarios. High-minded scenarios had a mean rating of 9.1 and low-minded scenarios a mean rating of 7.6 (out of a possible high rating of 14). There was a significant effect in the expected direction. Participants rated the high-minding scenarios as typifying better overall relationships than the low-minding scenarios ($t = 7.94$, df = 75, $p < .001$).

After establishing this support for our overall hypotheses, we examined the data for possible gender differences. We subtracted each participant's mean score for low-minded scenarios from his or her mean score for high-minded scenarios, giving us a measure of how well each participant perceived the difference in relationship quality between the low- and high-minding couples. We then compared this difference score for male and female participants. There was a marginally significant effect ($t = 1.71$, df = 74, $p < .10$). Women had a slightly higher mean difference score (10.041) than did the men (5.544), indicating that women possibly may be more sensitive to these differences in relationships than are men. We should note, however, that our sample consisted of fifty-eight women and only eighteen men. A sample more evenly distributed in terms of gender would be necessary to establish this effect more securely.

Finally, we wanted to explore other possible experiences that might affect whether or not individuals rated the minded scenarios as higher in quality. We used regression techniques to predict participants' difference scores (their scores for high-minding scenarios minus their scores for low-minding scenarios) from various other factors.

Participants rated themselves on their understanding of close relationships. This was unrelated to their ability to identify minding relationships as better-quality relationships. Their self-reported interest in relationships was also unrelated and so was the number of close relationships they had experienced.

The only factor emerging as a possibly important one in accounting for participants' discrimination between low and high minding was perception of parental relationship success ($p = .11$). Somewhat surprisingly, those participants who reported that their parents had a successful relationship were less able to discriminate between high- and low-quality relationship scenarios (as defined by the presence or absence of minding qualities). In other words, the worse individuals perceived their parents' relationships to be, the more sensitive they appeared to be about rating the quality of others' relationships.

This survey study established that individuals do seem to recognize that the presence of minding components makes healthier and more satisfactory relationships. Thus, not only does our theory fit with existing previous research into close relationships, it also has some validity among laypersons. This may make it especially useful in working with distressed couples, since the minding concept may be easy for them to accept and to believe that it will improve their relationships. A further discussion of minding in relationship counseling appears in Chapter 11.

This study also indicates that there may be possible gender differences in individuals' ability to discriminate between well-minded and nonminded relationships. An alternative is that men and women simply differ on what defines a good relationship, or that they have different priorities regarding relationships. This should be further investigated in our examination of the minding theory.

Last, there is a slight indication that the interactions of parents affect their children's later assessment of the quality of relationships. It appears that observing one troubled relationship in the family may make a person more sensitive to spotting troubles in other relationships. This seems to contradict the idea that having parents with a good relationship teaches children how to have good relationships themselves. However, it is possible that, although observing a poor parental relationship may make one more able to see problems in other interactions, it does not help in creating good relationships for oneself. People in their teens and early twenties whose parents were in well-run successful relationships may simply automatically follow the relationship strategies they saw at home without giving much conscious thought or analysis to how and why relationships do or do not work.

DO REAL COUPLES INTERACT IN WAYS THAT REFLECT MINDING?

The study described above verified only that the minding components are associated with what most people believe to be "good" relationships. Do we actually find these patterns of behavior in real relationships? Are they related to satisfaction with those relationships? A second study (Harvey et al., 1997) was designed to examine these questions.

We recruited forty-nine heterosexual couples and asked them to complete questionnaires regarding their relationships. Each individual completed a questionnaire separately from his or her partner. All of the couples had been together for at least six months prior to completing the questionnaires. Six of the couples were married; twenty were engaged or living together; and the remainder described themselves as being in exclusive dating relationships. The average length of the nonmarried couples' relationships was twenty-six months. The married couples had been together considerably longer. Ages of the participants ranged from seventeen to fifty-six, the majority being college undergraduates in their early to mid-twenties.

Couples completed the Relationship Assessment Satisfaction (RAS) scale (Hendrick, 1988), along with a measure written especially to assess the minding components. This minding assessment included items that asked participants to rate the level of reciprocity, disclosure, and caring in their relationships. Participants also indicated what pleased or troubled them most in the relationships and what types of conflict-solving strategies they had utilized successfully. Finally, participants were asked to make attributions about their partners' general behavior.

Several results support the efficacy of the minding theory. First, those participants who rated the level of reciprocity in their relationships as high reported greater satisfaction on the RAS than those who rated it as low (F (1, 95) = 9.70, $p < .01$). High levels of discussion in the relationship were correlated with greater satisfaction ($r = .31$). Third, generally positive attributions about the partner also were correlated with relationship satisfaction ($r = .34$). There were no significant gender differences found in these patterns. Here is some evidence that at least the disclosure, reciprocity, and attributional components are associated with relationship satisfaction in real couples.

We also recorded written narratives from these couples regarding their relationships. One woman, who had rated her overall relationship satisfaction as quite low, had this to say about her partner:

> He has trouble expressing emotions and feelings about the relationship. I don't like not knowing what's going on inside him. Our biggest problems are misunderstandings. We don't know sometimes whether we can trust one another. Then, if we can't talk openly about it, it gets worse. A few times, this feeling almost has led to the end of the relationship.

Her partner, who also rated his satisfaction as low, reported:

> We don't communicate too well. I know that it often is my fault, but she too quickly assumes I don't care and that I am not interested in improving the relationship.

This couple appears to have low levels of disclosure and of positive attributions. Both rated relationship reciprocity as being very low.

Another couple reported only modest satisfaction with their relationship. They both attested to high levels of reciprocity in their relationship and attempts to disclose and discuss, but indicated trouble with trust and acceptance. The woman stated:

> He loves me but sometimes he doesn't trust me and is very jealous if I am out with my friends. He is too insecure and although he is working on the problem, it still gets in the way of our relationship. Sometimes we just don't seem to be making any progress.

These remarks, contrasted with those of couples who report high satisfaction, point out the importance of the minding components. The next excerpt is from a woman who reported high satisfaction as well as high scores on all the minding component questions. Her partner reported similar scores. Note her own emphasis on the minding components of disclosure, respect, and trust (attributions):

Really, we learned in the first year of our marriage that whenever a problem presents itself, we need to sit down and talk. Either one of us can initiate the discussion. As long as it isn't in the heat of the argument, we feel comfortable in expressing different opinions and that we will be respected for doing so. . . . We have a lot of background differences, but we have learned to trust and respect each other in all areas of our relationship. We are not suspicious of one another when the other is out of town working. . . . We can tell each other almost anything.

The differences between these couples cannot be simply assigned to differences in commitment or in relationship experience. The first, unhappy, couple had been married for ten years. The second, moderately unhappy/happy couple had been living together for two and a half years. And the third, happy couple had been married for five years. There is something else happening or not happening between these partners. We suggest that something is minding.

DOES MINDING MAKE A DIFFERENCE OVER TIME?

Encouraged by these results, we conducted a third study, focusing again on a population of college undergraduates, to which we had easy access. Our objectives in this study were to more completely assess the minding components and also to follow some of our participants over time, to see whether the high-minded relationships also lasted longer. We utilized undergraduate participants because they would be easy for us to track over short periods of time, and we believed that their relationships might be volatile enough for us to observe considerable change within that short period of time.

Fifty-two students from an elementary psychology class volunteered to fill out our survey and to be interviewed for our study. All of these students were in exclusive relationships. We did not attempt to contact the partners of these students, so our observations are limited to one side of their relationships.

Our participants filled out questionnaires that again included the RAS, along with some more comprehensive measures of the minding components. Participants indicated their satisfaction with both their own and their partners' levels of disclosure within the relationship. They reported a typical attribution they might make for both a negative and positive relationship event. They rated the time and energy both they and their partners devoted to the relationship. Finally, they predicted how long they thought the relationship would last.

In rating both their own and their partners' disclosure, participants endorsed one of four possible disclosure descriptions: hardly any, only what is necessary, just right, and too much. "Just right" was considered the ideal amount of disclosure. Those who endorsed "just right" for their own self-disclosure were significantly more satisfied with their relationships, as indicated by their RAS scores, than participants who endorsed any of the other categories ($p =$ .012). When ratings of self- and partner disclosure were both considered, those participants who rated both as "just right" again had the highest RAS scores, significantly higher than any other combination of ratings. As minding theory predicts, levels of disclosure do seem to be important to relationship satisfaction.

Reciprocity was assessed by examining participants' reports of the time and effort they and their partners devoted to their relationships. Participants marked on a scale from 0 to 100 percent how much time and effort they devoted to the relationship, and how much time and effort their partners devoted to the relationship. We subtracted these two scores for a total reciprocity measure. The higher the score, the lower the reciprocity between partners. When we correlated this reciprocity score with the RAS, we found a significant negative correlation, showing that as reciprocity decreased so did relationship satisfaction ($r = .69$, $p < .01$). We then split our participants based on the median RAS score. When we compared the group with the lowest RAS scores with the group with the highest RAS scores, we found a significant difference in their reciprocity scores ($p < .01$). Those with the highest RAS scores reported a mean difference of only 3 percent between their own effort and their partners'. Participants with low RAS scores, however, reported a mean difference of 15 percent in this relationship effort. Reciprocity thus also appears to be important to reports of relationship satisfaction.

To measure participants' perceptions of relationship continuity, we asked them to indicate how long they believed their current relationship would last: less than a year, one to three years, or indefinitely. Participants who foresaw less than a year for their relationships were significantly less happy in them than other participants, according to ANOVA results ($p < .05$). These participants were also more likely to perceive less reciprocity in their relationships than were participants who envisioned a longer future for their partnerships ($p < .05$).

We were less successful in finding a direct relationship between our attributional measures and the RAS scores. Participants were asked to think back to the most recent positive and negative events that had occurred in their relationships, and then to give an explanation for those events. Their explanations (attributions) were coded as to whether they referred to the partner's responsibility, self-responsibility, the relationship, or to an outside influence. These coded attributions were then ranked as to how enhancing they would be to the relationship, according to minding theory. For example, in the case of the negative event, an attribution to the partner would result in a score of only 1 in relationship enhancement, the lowest possible score. An attribution to an outside influence, however, would result in a score of 4, the highest possible enhancement. Self and relationship attributions fell in the middle. For positive events, this scale was reversed: Partner attributions were scored as *most* enhancing and outside influences *least* enhancing.

Using this coding and scoring method, we were able to calculate an overall attributional score for each participant. The higher the attributional score, the more enhancing their attributions. We found no significant relationship between the attributional scores and the relationship satisfaction scores. In spite of this result, there is still some evidence that attributions do contribute to overall satisfaction, as demonstrated by our last set of analyses described below.

We not only wanted to show that each of the four measured

components was individually important to relationship satisfaction; we also needed evidence that the components worked together, building on each other, to create happiness in a relationship. To do this, we first determined what constituted a "high" minding level on each component. For the disclosure component, high minding was demonstrated by a "just right" rating for both self and partner. For reciprocity, it was determined by a median split of the time and effort difference scores. Those below the median reciprocity difference were considered high in minding on this component. For continuity, high minding was shown in an endorsement of the "indefinite" term for the length of the relationship. Finally, for attributions, those participants who had the highest attributional score, enhancing for both negative and positive events, were considered highly minded.

All participants were then given overall "minding" scores, which were calculated by simply counting the components on which they had scored "high" in minding. Thus overall minding scores could range from 0 (high on no minding components) to 4 (high on all minding components). This overall minding score correlated positively with the RAS scores, demonstrating that the higher the minding, the higher the satisfaction ($r = .54$, $p < .01$). Additionally, an analysis of variance showed that, if participants were grouped by their overall minding scores, there was a linear trend to the groups' mean RAS scores. Satisfaction increased with every additional minding component. Thus, we have evidence that all four of our measured components may work together to contribute to overall relationship satisfaction. Having simply one component is associated with lower satisfaction than having two components; two is lower than three; three lower than four.

It is important to note that, in these results, the relationship between the minding components and relationship satisfaction is correlational in nature. It is probable that the lack of minding leads to dissatisfaction with a relationship. It is equally possible, however, that the dissatisfaction may be perceived and experienced first. In other words, those students who are most dissatisfied are also more likely to report unsatisfactory reciprocity, disclosure, and so on. It is pertinent to ask whether or not the reports of low minding and low satisfaction are associated with eventual breakups of relationships.

We were able to contact twenty-two of our participants at the end of the semester, approximately two months after the initial survey. All but three of the couples were still together. This small change in our sample was not enough for us to draw any firm conclusions. However, the three participants who had ended their relationships had previously reported low levels of overall minding (scores of 1, 0, and 0). Two of the three had indicated problems with both partner and self-disclosure. The mean difference between partner and self effort reported for these three was 24 percent (well over the general mean), and only one believed his or her relationship would last more than a year.

FUTURE DIRECTIONS

We continue to work on refining the measurement instruments that we are using to assess the minding components. Currently we are exploring the idea of a minding scale with multiple items designed to assess each component. More long-term research with couples needs to be done, as well as carefully designed experimental studies, when possible. We encourage other researchers to take on this challenge as well.

For now, we can say that our research demonstrates that the minding components are recognized as helpful, perhaps even necessary, to relationships by a sample of the general population. Two samples of couples have reported higher satisfaction with their relationships when they also report higher levels of minding. Finally, it appears that, although one or two minding components are good for a relationship, all of them are better.

This research reinforces our overall ideas about minding. It is a theory that can be simple for real couples to understand and utilize. It has real value in explaining differences between satisfied and distressed couples. It is a synergistic combination of cognitive, emotional, and behavioral components that works best when all the pieces are in place.

CHAPTER 10

An International Perspective on Minding

This chapter presents case study evidence from interviews with couples and single persons conducted by the first author while in Romania working as a Fulbright Research Scholar in the spring of 1998. As is true for the evidence presented in the previous chapter, this research was designed to be illustrative rather than conclusive regarding minding ideas from an international standpoint. Psychologists frequently note the need for more cross-cultural research on psychological phenomena. This work was carried out in part to address that need as it applies to close relationship functioning.

While this evidence is not intended to represent relationship functioning for the whole of such relationships in a country of more than 20 million, it is intended to provide some insights on how social context affects relationships. As Kelley et al. (1983) argued in their theoretical analysis of the dynamics of close relationships, the social environment in which a close relationship occurs may play a vital role in how the relationship functions. That point is certainly true in Romania and some other "transitional" countries in Eastern Europe in the late 1990s. Of all the environmental forces affecting relationships in Romania at this time, the eroding economy is having a major impact on how people function, including their efforts to achieve closeness and have families.

In particular, with inflation higher than 150 percent in 1997 and the average income for most occupations (including many requiring high levels of education) at less than $100 per month, people in Romania often are scrambling so much to make extra income via second and side jobs that they have little time for work on their relationships – if they have them.

Romance flourishes in Romania, as it does around the world. A casual observer of the street scenes in large Romanian cities such as Bucharest will witness scores of young and sometimes older couples revealing the passion of their feelings for one another. But for most Romanians hard practical realities intervene at every point in a typical day to affect plans, energy level, interpersonal relations, and ultimately psychological conditions such as hope and morale. As a sampling of such realities, young couples who are strapped financially sometimes leave newborn children at hospitals for adoption or placement in orphanages because neither they nor their relatives can afford the care of a child.

In present-day Romania, there are thousands of poorly cared-for orphans, with many homeless. Such an external environment greatly influences the planning of families by couples and national pessimism about the possibilities for success in marriage and the family. A great tragedy of Romania is on display at orphanages on a Sunday, or visiting day, when young mothers and grandmothers come to see their children whom they cannot afford to raise at home. As will be seen in this chapter, the external economic difficulties are so great that this reality will probably be a part of the Romanian scene for years to come.

HISTORICAL BACKGROUND

Before presenting case study evidence on minding and relationship functioning in Romania, it may be useful to provide some historical context. Romania has endured for over a millennium waves of armies and migratory peoples representing neighboring and more distant countries and cultures, such as the Ottoman Empire, Czarist Russia, the Hapsburg Empire, and more recently the Nazis and the Communist Soviet Union from 1945 to December 1989. Without question, the most important historical event in Romania in the last century was the toppling of Communist dictator

Nicolae Ceausescu in December 1989. After a week of revolutionary activities in which an estimated 1,000 people were killed, Ceausescu and his wife were captured by the military and executed after a short trial near the end of 1989. Since then, the country has had a parliamentary democracy form of government. From the 1960s to the mid-1980s, Ceausescu wanted the population to increase despite the inadequate resources of most to care for additional children. He made abortion and contraception illegal. This policy led to thousands of illegal, botched abortions. Many deformed children were born. Many thousands were put in orphanages.

Historically, women have held a second-class position in Romanian society. Women married young and their role was seen as that of homemaker and caretaker of children. The man's job and aspirations were viewed as primary in most traditional Romanian families. In the late 1990s these attitudes began to change. There has been an increase in the age at marriage, with the average age for women around twenty-four and for men around twenty-seven in 1998. Many young people simply cannot afford to get married. There are very few large, lavish weddings in contemporary Romania. While women have traditionally been trained to handle a family's domestic chores, increasingly women in their twenties and thirties are requiring that men share in these chores. As in Western cultures, there is a lot of complaining about what men do in private versus what they proclaim in public. For example, in public men may say that they are egalitarian in their attitudes toward women and close relationships, but in private they may demonstrate sexist attitudes and behavior. The changing social mores in Romania are also contributing to a higher divorce rate. The rate jumped to 30 percent of recent marriages immediately after the revolution and now has moved closer to 40 percent.

CASE STUDIES OF MINDING AND RELATIONSHIP FUNCTIONING IN ROMANIA

We interviewed in depth three couples and four single persons. One of the couples was in their early thirties, one was in their mid-twenties to early thirties, and the other was in their late fifties. The single persons were ages twenty-nine, thirty, forty-five, and fifty-five. Three had been married; all were or had been recently involved in close relationships. It should be clear that our sample is biased in many ways. It is small, and all those agreeing to be interviewed were college-educated; some spoke English. This sample very likely does not represent the experiences of thousands of Romanian citizens living in peasant villages.

Nevertheless, in other respects, this small group epitomized the Romanian population fairly well. Many Romanians in larger cities are college graduates. All of the persons interviewed worked or had worked in professional occupations in which they made less than $150 per month in their primary job. Professions represented were journalist, teacher, graduate student, public relations specialist, army officer, dentist, advanced law student, administrator, and (retired) businessman.

The main interview questions in the case studies were: How did (do) you meet people for romantic relationships or to get married, and what factors influenced your romantic choices? When you have been in a relationship, what approaches have you and your partner(s) consciously employed to achieve satisfaction in how you relate to one another? How successful have you been? Given that divorce and breakups are fairly common in Romania, how do you try to make your marriage (or close relationship) work? How has the Romanian culture, including conditions of living such as the economy, affected your close relationships/marriage? How has it affected your plans for having a family?

In asking these questions, we probed specifically regarding the minding criteria of reciprocity, attribution of intent to facilitate the relationship, acceptance, and respect; we inquired as to how often the couples or individuals felt that they consciously adopted approaches involving these or other criteria aimed at enhancing functioning.

Potency of the External Social Environment

Every person we interviewed emphasized the potency of the external social environment to almost entirely control how close relationships progress over time. How was this potency realized? The younger couples indicated that the majority of conflict and quarrels in their families centered around money. One couple, with two young daughters, is trying to pay monthly mortgage installments on an apartment that cost them about $45,000. The monthly installment now takes up about 85 percent of their total pay, approximately $200. The only way they survive is with the help of their parents. The couple pools their money with that of their parents to get by. However, because of inflation, their payments have almost doubled since they bought the flat in 1996. They indicated that if the mortgage goes up another third, they will have to sell the apartment and move in with their parents. They said that there was frequent tension about how to buy what their daughters need for school and how to afford food, much less anything beyond what is needed for simple survival. They said that they had a good approach to their relationship, having become quite knowledgeable about one another well before marriage and having similar attitudes about many life questions and similar backgrounds. Nonetheless, they both spend a lot of time at work and are so fatigued when they get home that they do not spend a lot of time talking or going out alone.

This young couple said that they would not be able to make it without the financial and child care help provided by their parents. Although they do not have children yet, the other young couple interviewed echoed this view. These young couples believed that a majority of young Romanian couples who stay together do so only because this help is provided. They knew of many couples who divorced in part because of the constant financial strain they had encountered and the spin-offs of such strain on their marriages. They suggested that often such couples had only modest, if any, financial and practical support from their families.

One of the most difficult aspects of the economic situation faced by young couples (or singles interested in getting married and having families) is the inability to plan. For both of the young couples interviewed, they felt that they could not make many plans for the future in light of the 150 percent yearly inflation and continued instability in the government and effective economic reform. The one couple without children felt that it was impossible to begin to plan a family under these circumstances. They planned to stay in Romania and hoped to be successful in their careers, hers in law and his in dentistry. However, even with the possible future income from those fields, they could not begin to anticipate whether they would have enough to begin a family within their first three to five years of marriage.

This latter couple spoke of a dilemma that many respondents commented on in our interviews. Romania essentially has no middle class anymore. While a country such as the United States has a substantial middle class, Romania has a small upper class, and perhaps 85 percent of the population in the lower class – those mentioned above who average $100 a month, with expenses twice that in most households. Another fraction of the population is homeless, several thousand of them children. We discuss the issue of whether minding is principally a middle-class concept at the conclusion of this chapter.

The young couple with children indicated that there were other negative influences on their marriage associated with the economy and emergent market-oriented society of Romania. As an illustration, everyone has a television now. On television, they and their children see many new products (e.g., computers and video equipment) being advertised, products bought mostly by foreigners and the wealthy. There is little discretionary money available in the typical Romanian household to buy these products. This young couple and their children experience a degree of frustration in watching television. This couple also is concerned about how the imported violence of U.S. television serials and movies is affecting their children and the children of the country, since these shows did not exist in the Communist-run government prior to 1990. They believe that already the country is starting to experience more violence, including domestic violence in the home, and that such violence has an indirect link to the entertainment media, which is heavily influenced by U.S. imports.

One of the most obvious external environmental factors pertains to divorce. In the Communist era prior to 1990, there were many fewer divorces in Romania than has been the case in the 1990s. The Communist Party frowned on divorce as a decadent Western practice. This view circulated among employers and supervisors who made decisions about people's jobs and whether they were hired. It was not conducive to one's career to have a divorce in his or her personal dossier. But with the end of the Communist era, that sanction ended. Just as the erosion of the influence of the Church and traditional family had primed the culture for the possibility of more frequent divorce, so did the new parliamentary government and social structure.

Traditional Male-Dominated Culture

All of the single persons (including the one male in this group) emphasized the detrimental role of Romania's continuing traditional male-dominated culture in affecting their previous marriages or close relationships. The basic theme was that a substantial double standard continues to exist in the country. According to this double standard, women expect men to "play around" while married. They do not believe (or have little evidence to believe) that faithfulness to one's partner is part of the male repertoire of behavior. In this regard, the report of these respondents is reminiscent of David Buss's (1994) evolutionary psychology thesis discussed in Chapter 3, that it is a biological or an evolutionary condition that causes men to desire multiple sex partners and women to have an inclination to be and stay with one partner.

These educated single people recognized a version of Buss's thesis for Romania, even though such a thesis suggested the continued second-class status of women. They thought that this recognition was common among Romania's younger and middle-aged single population and that it greatly interfered with positive relationship functioning. One interviewee, aged thirty-two, said that she had been engaged to a man who wanted a "traditional" wife, saying that given her background she had all the tools. But she said she broke off the engagement when she decided that "traditional" meant giving up her career to take care of the children and stay in the kitchen.

These respondents believed that men could be faithful in close relationships or marriages for a few years. But, then, the ring would come off, and they would start "playing around." They said that they did not think this belief was self-fulfilling. Rather, it was a "part of the way the country and culture work – as simple as that." This view, too, can be seen as part of the controlling influences of an outside social environment that is very slowly changing toward greater equality between the sexes and greater respect for commitment in close relationships.

The older couple had a somewhat contrary view, suggesting that young people were hurting their prospects for a sound marriage by living together before marriage. This couple felt such behavior was not consistent with the norms of the culture or the Orthodox Church, to which almost 90 percent of Romanians subscribe to some degree. In their home, the male had been the breadwinner, although the female had worked too in order for the couple to survive. The female believed that she had deferred to the male in most important areas of decision making, and they both felt that such deference had been positive in their marriage.

None of the single people interviewed agreed with this older couple's approach or belief system regarding marriage or closeness. However, one older single woman made some perceptive points regarding women's subjugation in the society. She said that traditionally men's domination and women's submissiveness are rooted in a natural and religious order that defies rationality. The functioning of the household and well-being of the home and family generally fall on the wife's shoulders. Such an arrangement frees the husband and father to focus on career and to be the decision maker and interface between the family and community. This respondent suggested that for women, Romanian society poses the stereotype of either beauty without intelligence, or intelligence without beauty, but never beauty with intelligence. Women, therefore, are allowed a mind or a body, but not both (see also Liiceanu, 1998).

USE OF SPECIFIC MINDING CRITERIA

Neither the couples nor the singles articulated the complete set of minding criteria as essential to their relationship. Nonetheless, all were aware that conscious mental and emotional work is necessary to make relationships succeed over time. Each respondent endorsed parts of the minding process. Most indicated that they believed in and used self-disclosure and reciprocity in making their relationships function positively. In terms of self-disclosure, most of the respondents felt that it was important to discuss in general past relationships and to be able to learn from these discussions.

All of the Romanian respondents indicated that it was important to have faith in the nature of your partner (attributions) and to give your partner reason to have faith in you. In addition, all indicated that it was critical to be consistent in one's values and how they were played out in a relationship. They felt that relationships often were failing in part because each partner did not disclose enough critical self-emotional and/or background information. They also felt that relationships were vulnerable when partners held views about one another that were not communicated.

The respondents endorsed the criteria of acceptance and respect. They indicated a belief that a person should be his or her partner's best friend and support the partner in any problematic situation. They saw this friendship as a mark of acceptance and respect. They also felt that in Romania and in light of the influence of the family on whom a person marries, it was possible to feel fairly confident about the character of your partner by knowing well the partner's family.

An interesting feature of all of the young relationships we heard about was the powerful influence of the couples' families in determining the ongoing attributions made about each partner. In the main, these young persons were accepting of their parents' and relatives' attributions. As we note below, this influence probably is greater than what is typically reported in Western countries. Factors involved include the poor economy and continued role of tradition in how relationships start and either flourish or are dampened early in their development.

MAKING CLOSE RELATIONSHIPS WORK IN ROMANIA

Because of custom and the wretched economy, Romania is a country that can best grow healthy relationships when members of one's extended family are instrumentally involved in providing resources and guidance well into early mid-life. For citizens with intact families, the bond among parents, grandparents, and children is stronger than in many Western families of the late 1990s.

Our observations were that young women and to a lesser degree young men were protected for a much longer "developmental" period in Romania than in the United States. Not only is it essential to combine financial resources to cope, but there is less mobility in the country, so relatives stay close by. The Gallup poll in Romania reports that only a small portion of the Romanian population (about 5 percent) has traveled beyond neighboring countries (or at most a couple of thousand miles). Thus, the link across generations is both symbolically and practically quite strong at present in Romania.

The protection afforded those who are fortunate enough to have families who can help is both a blessing and a curse. The blessing part is obvious. The curse part is less obvious, but it comes into play in the development of autonomy in young people. We heard that the young are seldom taught about sexuality or birth control in the home or school; this education occurs in interactions with peers and via television and movies. Young people seem as interested in sexuality in Romania as they are anywhere, and the media are filled with erotic material. The older generations seem to believe that this development will have a harmful effect on Romania's youth in years to come.

We observed an emerging debate in Romania in 1998 about whether the Parliament would create tolerance laws regarding homosexuality. Young people with whom we visited seemed quite at ease with the topic of homosexuality, yet tolerance was not a quality for which opinion polls showed much support. The people "on the street" being interviewed argued that homosexuality was unnatural and that it would destroy the Romanian family. They indicated that they believed that the present heterosexual-dominant culture was vital to Romania's future and that the main or only job of the family was to ensure procreation and care and protection of the young.

Respondents told us that, by and large, families in Romania believe that they have a right to tell young people whom to date and marry and how to live their lives for a long period into the children's young adulthood. This belief emerges in the context of the family's support of the couple, often with the different families living together in the same small apartment.

HAZARDS OF GENERALIZATION AND RECOMMENDATIONS FOR FURTHER WORK

As noted at the outset, there are limitations to any case study, such as a small number of respondents, or the possible nonrepresentativeness of the respondents. Beyond that, to come into a country as foreigners without command of the language and culture and draw conclusions about people's lives and issues confronting the country is quite hazardous. This limitation is offset to some degree by the possible openness and freshness of an outsider's viewpoint.

The major conclusions of our analysis revolve around the potent impact of Romania's economic and social–political difficulties on close relationships and the family. Can Romania's difficulties be extrapolated to those of other countries? The economic, social, and political issues faced by Romania in 1998 are probably comparable to varying degrees to other Eastern European countries that were part of the former Soviet Union, such as Bulgaria, Moldovia, Albania, and Ukraine.

We did check some of our observations with European respondents in further trips to Greece and Poland. In Greece, like Romania, the three women we interviewed indicated that the "macho" male style of relating was one of the central problems in close relationships. It was suggested that males also adopted double-standard rules regarding sexuality, with men preferring wives to be only "slightly experienced" at the time of marriage; whereas they indicated that men "played around" all they wanted before marriage and boasted about their conquests. Interestingly, the Greek women we interviewed believed that American couples were much more advanced in their egalitarian approach than was true in their part of Europe.

On the other hand, the coping issues for relationships described in this chapter can be found to exist to some extent throughout the world. Certainly, there are instances of greater suffering and more daunting circumstances than can be found in contemporary Romania. The current economic situation in Iraq, for example, has led to losses similar to or greater than what is being experienced in Romania.

In the literature of Western psychology, we have little input about countries of Africa that have encountered massive losses due to violence or droughts in recent years. Undoubtedly, close relationships and the family have suffered in such contexts. Large-population countries in Asia such as Indonesia represent powder kegs of potential violence because of a battered economy that has had devastating effects on millions of impoverished citizens.

Thus, with regard to generalizability, it is clear that the ideas and conclusions of the present analysis must be viewed with caution. While daunting, Romania's different dilemmas probably are less imposing in terms of potential solutions vis-à-vis different miseries affecting other groups of people throughout the world. For Western psychology, part of the value of studying Romania now is that there are many knowledgeable, English-speaking psychologists in the country who are amendable to collaboration. The same cannot be said for other parts of the world that are undergoing rapid and large-scale social transition. An exasperating issue for Romanian psychology in the late 1990s is the fact that research is ceasing because of financial deprivations in the universities and the pressure on researchers to work other jobs in order to survive.

As we hope this chapter illustrates, Romania has a richness of psychological phenomena for students of relationships and coping, as well as scholars working in other areas, that should be of great interest to Western psychologists. They and their psychology colleagues in Romania cannot solve Romania's many social problems. But they can study them. There is a wealth of information regarding the orphans' and beggars' obstacles and potential that awaits psychological investigation. Even more potential for discovery is available to interdisciplinary research teams working on these problems.

CONCLUSIONS, QUESTIONS, AND SUMMARY

Based on the evidence from Romanian respondents, a crucial question for minding theory is not, Does it work in different countries? Rather, Is minding relevant to some close relationships given the adversity of the social context surrounding them? How can a couple who has at most a few hours of free time together each week have enough energy for minding activities? Is minding a process that only people who have time, energy, and resources can implement? Is it, in other words, a middle-class idea that has little meaning to those who are struggling for survival?

From our Romanian evidence, there is some truth in the assertion that minding basically is a middle-class idea. At least one of the couples, who had children and two jobs, felt that they had insufficient time to begin to think about "strategies of relating." The other young couple, who do not have children, felt that they indeed have a strategy of staying close and that it was made possible by their somewhat better standard of living than was true for most young couples and by the strong support they received from both sets of parents.

This chapter provided a glimpse of how a country with an eroded economy and flux in the governmental and social institutions may experience influences on close relationships that differ from those found in countries with more stability in these areas. In particular, this chapter revealed the power of the external social environment to affect how people relate and how they plan to develop their family aspirations in the future. These environmental forces include in Romania's case a debilitating economy that makes it necessary for most adults to work two jobs just to get by, and family traditions that likely have both positive and negative impacts on the development of close relationships.

We also discussed the "macho" ethic that seems to continue to have a foothold in Romania, with many men adhering to a double standard in sexual relations. There is widespread belief that after so many years in marriages or close relationships, men begin to "play around" and take mistresses; it is believed that most women do not show this tendency.

Many families tend to protect young women, leading to slower development of the women's own views about relationships and the family. However, women increasingly are becoming vocal about relationship issues and are frequent initiators of dissolution or divorce.

CHAPTER 11

Minding in Couples Therapy and Counseling

When we become wiser, we become sadder.

Anonymous

Faith is the bird that sings when the dawn is still dark.

R. Tagore

God, give us grace to accept with serenity the things that cannot be changed, courage to change the things that should be changed, and the wisdom to distinguish the one from the other.

Reinhold Neibuhr, *The Serenity Prayer*

In this chapter, we discuss how minding might be used in therapy and counseling activities aimed at enhancing close relationships. The quotes that begin this chapter speak to the deep experiential base that we believe is at the heart of minding. We believe that minding can be achieved mainly after people have encountered the pain of serious relationship difficulty, whether or not dissolution occurred. Minding is an adaptive response to the pain that is so frequently found in "closeness."

Minding is like a "bird singing in the dawn light" – the singing being an act of hope and faith that the dawn will come. Such is the synergy of a well-minded close relationship. Minding contributes greatly to the ability to make distinctions between that which can and should be changed and that which cannot and to the courage needed to make such distinctions – Niebuhr's *The Serenity Prayer*. As we argue in this chapter, the couple in a well-minded relationship is engaging, in the final analysis, in a coordinated act of hope and faith.

As should be apparent at this point in the book, our perspective on minding is that its components can be utilized at any point in a relationship, from the first glimmer of people's consideration that they may start a romantic relationship to the bitter end of a drawn-out separation and divorce or dissolution, but it is most fully applied in committed relationships. We also believe that minding is an approach that a therapist can embrace in developing a strategy for a client's relationship problems. That logic unfolds in this chapter. Minding, too, may be followed as a systematic way of thinking and behaving by a couple without therapeutic intervention.

An application of minding that may not be self-evident is that it has implications for how people engage in critical thinking about therapeutic advice regarding close relationships. As we outline in this chapter, some advice is not cogent either on logical or empirical grounds: "Caveat emptor!" (Buyer beware!) Whether the individual is evaluating minding or any other approach to closeness that has applied implications, scrutiny should be given to the coherence of the logic and to whether there is a literature that directly or indirectly offers support for the therapeutic implications.

So often the "therapeutic advice" is hardly compelling even to a novice person who is trying to better understand her or his own relationship or relationships in general. We are complex animals whose relationships usually involve many layers of relevant experience and contemporary issues. Advice that does not recognize such complexity is apt to be incomplete at best, and possibly misleading or harmful. To paraphrase a quote by Oscar Wilde, for every complex problem, there is a simple solution – and it usually is wrong.

In presenting our position on the therapeutic value of minding, we describe some approaches to counseling couples that contrast with or are similar to how minding therapy might work. But first we return to a set of general principles about therapy that may be readily deduced from the minding position.

MINDING PRINCIPLES FOR APPLICATION IN COUPLES THERAPY

The minding approach to therapy with couples involves a set of general principles that follow from the basic argument. They are as follows.

1. The most general principle is that effective therapy (i.e., therapy that strengthens relationships) will enhance minding activities in the relationship. As we describe in this chapter, much that couples therapists suggest to troubled couples boils down to minding-type points. We do not believe that low- or anti-minding approaches are used in any reputable, well-tested therapy currently available in the relationship therapy literature.

2. Therapy with couples will be effective mainly to the degree that both parties accept and follow the prescribed regimen. This principle relates back to the reciprocity criterion, with reciprocity necessary for a well-minded and hence close and satisfying relationship. If only one partner is involved in the therapy and the other partner is uninvolved, it is unlikely the reciprocity criterion can be effectively addressed via what the involved partner does.

3. Therapy with couples will be effective mainly to the degree that each person in the relationship is involved in learning about the partner and being open to the partner's learning about him or her. This principle derives from the knowledge criterion. Couples who mind well will be inquiring about one another's history, state of being, thinking, feeling, and the like; they will want to know. They also will want their partners to want to know and be available for similar scrutiny. This scrutiny is not like what a real scientist might do in studying in minute detail some subject. Rather, it is a human act of natural curiosity and care for a most important other person. As was noted in various chapters, the knowing and being known steps are carried out in different ways by different people. But their goal is knowledge and updating information on a constantly changing landscape, namely, the couple, each partner, and the dynamic unfolding between them.

4. Therapy with couples will be effective mainly to the degree

that the therapeutic activities are practiced regularly by the couple, apart from the therapy setting, and do not end when the therapy ends. This principle follows from the criterion that minding cannot end if a couple is to continue to be close and satisfied. If the therapy approach is to be helpful, it too must be sustained over an extended period.

5. Therapy with couples will be effective to the degree that it makes them sensitive to the vital links among thoughts, feelings, and behavior. This principle relates in part to the attribution criterion. Partners regularly are making attributions about one another and one another's critical relationship-relevant behavior. Couples need to recognize that reality and be open to discussing and challenging one another's causality and responsibility attributions and trait inferences. The same point applies to attributions and feelings of respect and acceptance. There needs to be an openness about these attributions and feelings and willingness to discuss their merit.

Thus, it can be seen that the criteria of the minding conception that were presented in Chapter 1 all lead to certain principles of what needs to happen in therapy. This linkage should not be unexpected. Minding, as has been argued, is quintessentially a pragmatic approach to living. It involves a plan, detail, and execution of the plan. Minding involves regular checking of the plan and the execution of it. These are essential elements of most therapeutic approaches to relationship enhancement.

SPECIFIC COUNSELING APPROACHES AND THEIR RELATIONSHIP TO MINDING

In the following discussion, we will point to a number of approaches to counseling and therapy. These often involve parts of minding, and we can show the threads of minding logic weaving through these techniques. However, we also include approaches found in the vast literature on self-help therapy that do not involve many, if any, of the dynamics posited as important in minding. We view these as "anti-minding" approaches, and do not believe it is feasible to develop "quick and easy" ways to redress relationship problems that involve complex humans, often entangled in complex dilemmas of living. Let's consider some specific therapeutic approaches and how they may be interpreted in minding terms.

Halford and Behrens's Relationship Behaviors

As suggested by Halford and Behrens (1997), there is a set of behaviors that is strongly related to marital satisfaction. Paraphrased from Halford and Behren's analysis, these behaviors include: (1) *Affection*: For example, this may be represented by saying, "I love you," by giving a hug or kiss to the partner, or enjoying a laugh together and saying that you enjoy a partner's company. (2) *Respect*: Listening to a partner's opinion reflects respect, as does introducing a partner to others with pride. (3) *Support and assistance*: This may be represented by doing errands for a partner, or something to save a partner's time and energy. (4) *Shared quality time*: This may be represented by specifically designating a time to do something together and inquiring about one another's well-being. Working together on a project also may reflect this behavior. (5) *Appreciation*: This may be represented simply by saying, "Thank you." Also, in the presence of a partner, telling others how much you appreciate something your partner does may give the partner a greater sense that you are grateful for his or her positive acts.

From a minding standpoint, these are important acts. Minding emphasizes behavior, behavior that is well-conceived in its plan and purpose for the enhancement of the relationship. Each of the foregoing behaviors may reflect minding and consequent behavioral patterns. What is as important as the specific behaviors, however, is each partner's acts of knowing and understanding that go into them. For example, showing affection is essential as long as both partners perceive the act as affectionate. To be felt as affection, the target needs to see the motives of the giver as true to the act and not motivated by some other concern – simply "mindless" behavior with no real meaning. Similarly, the giver needs to perceive the gift as genuinely an act of affection and know the difference between that and an attempt to placate or influence the partner in some way.

The same line of reasoning applies to behavioral classes such as support and assistance, devoting quality time to one another, sharing time with one another, and acts of appreciation. The imputed motives behind the behaviors must support the idea that each partner is acting more in the interest of the relationship than of the self alone. Couples who "know" one another will know whether or not the motives are consistent with this enhancement of the relationship idea. It may take time to have such knowledge, and it should be remembered that time is a criterion of a well-minded relationship. But with knowledge, motivation will not be easily dissembled.

Behavior, therefore, is critical to minding and to relationship growth and closeness when it is contextualized within two people's understandings of their relationship and their sense of what is necessary to make the relationship work. They need to be conscious of plans and subtleties for making their relationship work. The behavior may have potency apart from such understanding, but over time it will not be effective without each partner's interpretation of the behavior as positive for the relationship.

"How to Build Intimacy in an Age of Divorce?"

This heading was found in a May 1989 *Psychology Today* article by Caryl Avery. Avery presented a case that relates partially to the message of minding. One part of the argument is that it is a rather cynical world regarding trust in relationships. Infidelity and deception in close relationships abound and are constantly presented in the media and public messages. Hence, how do we achieve trust in our personal relationship in such a cynical world context? Avery suggests it is important for individuals to take the position that the relationship will last not because of the children or any other factor but because the relationship itself is valued and cherished. To do this, partners need to communicate that the relationship has top priority in their lives.

Our argument about such reasoning is that it makes sense as far as it goes, but it does not go very far. Because of its focus and motivation, minding as such is about as powerful an antidote to cynicism about close relationships as we can imagine. Minding embodies caution because it is based on experience and care in the details of how relationships are carried out. But the caution is toward care in how a new relationship is implemented, not in resistance to consider a new relationship. With minding, a couple does not have to let their prior negative experiences undercut their process of achieving a constructive, satisfying relationship. They will use their positive learning from past relationships and recognize that an enduring, satisfying relationship is within their behavioral repertoire. Like Avery, we believe that the relationship should take a top priority, even compared with other priorities such as work, children, personal growth, and health. But we wish to stress the *acts* necessary to make high priority of the relationship happen. Will to achieve priority is not enough. Will power is realized in behavior. Well-minded relationships require cognitive, emotional, and behavioral planning and execution on a regular, never-ending basis.

Soul Communion

In *Soul Mates*, Thomas Moore (1994) presents the interesting argument that a soul mate is someone to whom we feel profoundly connected and that the communicating and communing that take place between soul mates are tended in as careful a manner as we would tend our most prized plant or artistic creation. This reasoning is congenial to the minding position and is as close to a spiritual aspect to minding as may be found in the literature on relationship enhancement approaches.

Moore quotes the poet John Donne in his emphasis on soul, "Love's mysteries in soules doe grow." Moore said about soulful relating:

> In the final paradox, if we want to light the fires of intimacy we have to honor the soul of the other. A relationship demands not that we surrender to another person, but that we acknowledge a soul in which the parties are mingled and respect its unpredictable demands. All of these paradoxes keep the mind spinning and the heart superficially insecure yet deeply trusting. Our intimacies reach out

and preserve the world around us, so that our movements toward union, grounded as they are in deep threads of soul that reach far beyond human persons, keep the world itself from falling apart. (p. 254)

This discussion of paradox in relationships is reminiscent of the dialectic approaches (e.g., Welwood, 1990; Baxter & Montgomery, 1996) that we earlier endorsed as highly relevant to minding. Another theorist who has emphasized dialectics is Miller (1994). She uses the concept of "resonance" to suggest that couples have to balance the scales of power and responsibility, blend interdependence and intimacy, and enjoy a passionate chemistry that can be renewed over the course of a long-term relationship. She suggests that couples achieve this resonance with focus on their relationship tasks, good intentions in carrying them out, and empathy with their partner in doing the same.

These arguments are compelling because couples frequently show the paradox of uniting with one another, while simultaneously separating from one another. The proverbial yin and yang of lust for freedom and interdependence is found in most couples, even as these qualities are found in most minds. We want and usually are "together" with others in very significant ways from birth to death. Yet at the same time and especially at the very end of our lives, we are all alone. Most of us experientially entertain that recognition that we must die alone and probably fight it from early in life until death. It is the part of death that can be most frightening.

Thus, in the midst of this profound recognition about being alone at the end, Moore's logic of souls having communion is persuasive. While it is compatible with implications of minding, it does not suggest the detailed steps to have closeness. What Moore's logic does do, however, is suggest hope in the context of potential chaos and oblivion. Close relating, fundamentally, is about hope. We said earlier that minding at its core is about the pragmatics of living. We wish to say now that minding also is fundamentally about hope that what we think, feel, and do as humans has meaning and matters. Achieving and preserving closeness with another human, from this perspective, is an ultimate human achievement.

Smart Love? The Sexuality and Closeness Conundrum

Maybe there are some recommendations for relating that are simple and essentially involve "smart love." Consider the following offerings regarding sexuality in relationships posed by Nancy Van Pelt (1997) in a book entitled *Smart Love: A Field Guide for Single Adults*. The author presents a number of benefits to complete sexual abstinence before marriage. Here are some of them:

1. Abstinence before marriage helps prevent divorce. The author cites an article in a well-known journal, but does not provide a direct reference. This article supposedly shows that over a twenty-year period, virgin brides were less likely to end their marriage through divorce than were women who had not been virgins at marriage.

2. Abstinence before marriage helps prevent unnecessary break-ups. Without citation, the author claims that studies show that couples who engage in sex before marriage are more likely to break up than are those who do not. She says that even those formally engaged who have sex before marriage are more likely to break up (no evidence cited). She says that having sex before marriage satisfies the sex drive – hence, why get married?

3. Abstinence before marriage helps both the male and the female in preventing sexual dysfunction. Aside from the general statement, "Some studies indicate half of all American wives have such poor attitudes about sex they cannot achieve orgasm," the author offers only the argument that poor habits, perforce, are established by males and females alike who have sex before marriage. She suggests that this is true even for those who have sexual relations only with their future spouses.

4. Abstinence prior to marriage decreases the likelihood of adultery and helps distinguish "real love" from infatuation. Without referencing research, the author asserts that studies show that those who have had premarital intercourse are twice as likely to engage in adultery as those who have not had premarital intercourse: "People who have had a variety of come-and-go lovers find it difficult to do an about-face at their wedding and commit themselves to a lifetime of fidelity . . ." (p. 204). She argues that sex before marriage

masks areas of concern that should be discussed as the relationship develops.

Smart Love involves some provocative advice. Our argument about the wisdom offered in *Smart Love*, however, is that it may not be so smart at all and that the logic behind minding suggests as much. Although minding says nothing, per se, about sexuality before marriage, satisfying sexuality is a vital part of well-minded relationships.

Further, *Smart Love* does not explicitly discuss the divorced person's situation, but many people who are pursuing new partners have divorced (maybe multiple times). The author probably would assert that it does not matter whether the romantic partners have been divorced before. But realistically it does matter. Some people feel that their other marriage(s) did not work out because of sexual performance reasons. Thus, they want to know about their partner's sexual proclivities before marriage, not after. Only a religious stance on abstinence would suggest that their quest for such prior knowledge is not wise. *Smart Love* mostly hedged its religious, philosophical foundation, although it seems safe to conclude that such a foundation attended the recommendations.

While minding makes no specific predictions about sexuality, it says a lot about how closeness is affected by how people think, feel, and behave toward one another. It is a fact that many people engage in sexual behavior before getting married. Couples who are minding their close relationship development well may decide to have sex before marriage and suffer no negative consequences. Why? Because if they are minding their relationship well, the sexuality will be contextualized within a set of thoughts, feelings, and other behavior that implies to each partner caring and thoughtfulness, as well as self-disclosure. If they are not minding their relationship development well, we believe that such a failure is the major problem – not whether or not they had sex before marriage. For a couple who are considerate and interested in considering long-term bonding, sexuality may help them understand one another.

Sexuality involves acts of self-disclosure or "social penetration," to use Altman and Taylor's (1973) concept. It involves knowledge acquisition and openness to such acquisition. Couples may learn how to care for one another more completely in sexual activities. After all, sex is not simply intercourse. It is an array of acts, as well as thoughts and feelings. Depending on how broad a person's conception of sexuality and relationships, it may even include how sexual fantasies do or do not have relevance for relationship satisfaction. The literature is scant regarding all the questions we could ask about such matters. We probably never will know the sexual nuances of most close relationships. *Smart Love* did not begin to examine even the tip of the sexuality iceberg. In fairness, though, *Smart Love* is like hundreds of other books addressing self-help and relationship issues in its depth of coverage.

Broadly construed, sexuality pervades many types of relationships, and especially close romantic ones. Sex that is done well is a part of minding. It has a broad and deep meaning, but then so do many other important behaviors that people take vis-à-vis one another. Any analysis that does not begin to recognize such depth and breadth of meaning and mores cannot help a lot of people in dealing with their practical questions about sexuality and relating.

Gottman's Approach to Successful Relating

John Gottman's 1995 work on predictors of divorce and recommendations for successful close relationships has been mentioned previously in Chapter 8 comparing minding to contemporary approaches to relationships. In this section, however, we treat his logic in more detail, as that logic is applied to relationship problems. We selected Gottman's approach because it involves probably the most detailed and research-based approach to therapy with couples available in the relationship literature. Gottman is a psychologist and professor at the University of Washington, Seattle.

Gottman's therapeutic techniques are based on his extensive research with couples. In his research procedures, Gottman observes newlywed couples in an apartment-type setting. By videotaping parts of their interaction and obtaining psychophysiological and verbal report information, Gottman claims that he can predict divorce for 90 percent of the couples who participate in this research. In fact, some early participants who indeed did divorce challenged him to develop intervention approaches to complement his success in predicting divorce – a challenge that Gottman and his therapist wife now have tackled with a similarly ambitious program at their Seattle Institute.

To illustrate Gottman's ideas, we abstract points from an article in the magazine *New Woman* (July 1997), in which a wife tells about attending a workshop for couples experiencing problems held by Gottman as part of his Seattle Marital and Family Institute. The woman and her husband are a thirtysomething couple with a young child. Although the couple is quite successful overall, the relationship is showing signs of crumbling in the time devoted to one another and in the degree of distance that is intruding on the couple. The wife notes that her husband is unhappy with their sex life since the birth of their child, while she is unhappy with her husband's lack of recognition of and empathy for her difficult job of caring for a toddler and the household. She says that they have encountered increased episodes of fighting, defensiveness, and each "leaving the field" to get away from the tense times and underlying issues. They recognize their problems, though, and have gone to Gottman's workshop because of his reputation as a scholar and practitioner. She also notes that her husband basically is quite loving and predisposed to Gottman's techniques that do not involve a lot of "talk therapy," in which people discuss childhood wounds and the like.

She goes on to briefly outline what Gottman often asks couples to do in his controlled-intervention setting, including: role-playing and games such as "Love Maps," a board game in which couples are asked questions about their partner's likes, dislikes, fears, and behavioral tendencies; selecting three adjectives from a list of sixty that best describe what a person appreciates most in his or her partner; having psychophysiological recordings of heart rate, for example, taken of each partner; and having each partner observe and listen to the other during the couple tasks.

The wife-narrator notes that the games and other tasks were very helpful. For example, she says that they both learned that they knew a lot about one another's private thoughts and feelings in the Love Maps game; they were reassured in how accurate they could be on matters that require interest in and empathy with a partner in order to learn the content of these thoughts and feelings. They also learned that their heart rate declined significantly from the beginning of the session (with the input from Gottman's research that heart rate usually increases during fights or distancing activities). In general, while the workshop was helpful, the narrator suggests that she and her husband still have many issues to work through on their own in order to reach a point at which they could be satisfied with their attempts at renewal.

In the course of the *New Woman* article, the narrator describes some of the major ideas behind Gottman's approach to relationship therapy. Gottman points to the need for a couple to be alert to what he terms the "Four Horsemen of the Apocalypse" – factors so labeled because of the damage they can do to a close relationship – if they are to develop and sustain long-term closeness and satisfaction. These "Four Horsemen" are criticism, defensiveness (that includes even rehearsing defensive thoughts such as "I'm not going to take this any longer" in one's mind), stonewalling (clamming up about hurt feelings or motivations for acts), and contempt (which can be obvious or subtle, such as a rolling of the eyes that one's partner would not mistake for a more benign sign).

Heart rate considerations (referring more generally to physiological arousal) are important to Gottman. He recommends that during fights and tense moments couples take breaks of at least twenty minutes. Such time-out breaks allow their bodies to calm down physiologically. Gottman emphasizes that time-outs should not be used to rehearse how one will "get back at" a partner or counter a partner's earlier points. Gottman believes that a heart rate of less than ninety-five beats per minute is optimal for these relationship interactions.

Other central ideas in Gottman's approach are the following. (1) Early in their relationships (as newlyweds, for example), couples should "take no guff" from one another: They should, to use minding's term, be respectful. This early interaction pattern is believed to set the tone for the long haul of the relationship. (2) Couples should know how to get out of highly distressful episodes. Couples can exit and maneuver by changing the topic, gossiping about other couples, using humor, stroking the partner with a caring, loving remark, backing down, noting the common ground that underlies their positions, and in general showing by comments and nonverbal signals that one respects and cares for one's partner and his or her viewpoint. (3) Couples should focus on the positive in interactions; Gottman believes that happy couples make five times as many positive statements to and about each other and their relationship than negative statements. (4) Overall, Gottman emphasizes the countless small acts that establish the climate of a relationship that matter most – not necessarily the specific acts taken during times of conflict. These small and sometimes barely discernible acts (e.g., acknowledging what a partner has said or making eye contact that reflects attention and care in conversation) go a long way toward creating a savings account of good will that then will serve the couple well in difficult times.

Gottman's Approach and Acceptance Theory

More recently, Gottman, Coan, Carrere, and Swanson (1998) have compared several models of predicting marital happiness among newlyweds and concluded that most couples who are most satisfied figure out a way to gently raise issues, complain, fight, and deescalate negativity that so often builds up in conflict. Based on their research with 130 newlywed (within the last six months) couples, they also indicate that the relationship interaction is the most satisfying when the husband learns to accept influence from his wife (who in effect has a better sense of relationship balance – an idea that Jesse Bernard, among others, suggested years ago).

In making this proposal, Gottman and colleagues take issue with a well-recognized model for treating conflicted couples proposed by Neil Jacobson and Andrew Christensen (1996) involving acceptance therapy (see discussion below regarding its link to minding). Acceptance therapy emphasizes empathy and active listening. Gottman et al. interpret their own data as not supporting this empathy–active listening approach. They suggest that acceptance therapy involves more potential confrontation than the couple can assimilate. They propose a model of gentleness, soothing, and deescalation of negativity; in their suggested pattern for deescalation, negativity by one spouse is followed by neutral affect by the other. They conclude by suggesting that the therapist concentrate on the husband, mainly in trying to induce him to deescalate his negative affectivity.

Minding and Gottman's Approach

We heartily endorse the bulk of Gottman's recommendations to enhance relationship closeness. Most of these recommendations have been subjected to much more empirical attention than have the minding concept and many other ideas in the close relationship literature. The final idea discussed above about small acts creating large consequences and an overall gestalt-like sense of well-being in the relationship are especially congenial to the minding position.

Along that line of logic, though, we doubt that specific ratios of positive to negative comments are critical to the success of a relationship. Or we would argue that research and theory do not support such specific ideas. Why? Because positive and negative comments are psychologically weighed in people's minds differently across couples and individuals. One person may think that one comment to her husband was very positive, for example 10 on a scale of 1 to 10. However, the husband may give the same comment a rating of 6 on the same scale, and may accord much higher weights to something said that the wife viewed as rather minor. Over time, couples may zero in on one another's differential weighing of comments and meanings attributed to different kinds of acts. But even for golden anniversary couples, we would expect to find much divergence in meaning and perception of statements and acts. That reality is inherent in both the complexity of people and their constantly changing circumstances and natures.

Minding deals with such complexity and fluidity by suggesting that couples must be ever "mindful" of the work necessary in successful communication of meaning, and especially meaning that reflects the respect, acceptance, and affection of one person for another. Minding even amplifies on the complexity–fluidity theme by pointing to the fact that both parties can be sending, receiving, and changing at the same time. Hence, the problem of mindful social interaction is, at this abstract level, rather mind-boggling. Nonetheless, people can mind and do mind their relationships.

Turning to other major ideas in Gottman's approach, we would say that minding is a way to avoid the "Four Horsemen of the Apocalypse." A couple who is minding their relationship well will not have to worry about these specific acts. Minding, for example, suggests that self-disclosure is a responsibility; thus, stonewalling would not be a part of a well-minded relationship. Similarly, there would be no regular stimulus for defensiveness and contempt in a well-minded relationship. When criticism is offered in a well-minded relationship, it is done and received as constructive and not destructive.

Gottman is a bit ambiguous regarding how much people can confront one another regarding perceived mistakes and profit from such confrontation. In Gottman's system, stonewalling is bad, yet a generally positive orientation is good. Minding proposes no difficulty with confrontation, such as raising neglected issues or reporting felt slights; in fact, it probably will occur regularly in a well-minded relationship. But if confrontation occurs, it typically will be accompanied by signs of acceptance and respect for the partner, kindness, and a nonaccusatory tone. Minding emphasizes the great value of this type of regular discussion and not letting delicate psychological matters slide by. An attempt to be positive is not as important in minding as is an attempt to be honest and thoughtful in how such honesty is communicated.

What if conflict ensues in such frank discussion? What does minding say? Conflict is inevitable in human relationships, including the best ones. Couples who are minding well will learn how to address the conflict, which may include "cease and desist" and time-out type strategies, as suggested by Gottman. There is lot of individuality in heart rate response to different situations, and even greater idiosyncrasy in people's conscious or unconscious connections among heart rate and other physiological responses and their understandings and perceptions. Thus heart rate alone cannot tell in a definitive way how people will perceive and send meanings in relationship interactions. However, it will help to know when one is "very upset" and to not act in a precipitous way when one is.

Important questions may be raised about the theoretical process posed by and therapeutic suggestions deriving from Gottman et al. First, it is not clear that the gender differences (for example, the emphasis on the need for the husband to deescalate negative affect) would hold for couples who are more advanced in their relationships; well-minded relationships should involve this principle of attempted deescalation by both partners, and older, more experienced couples may more readily exhibit this collaborative activity. Even if deescalation of negative affect is central to cooling down and smoothing out a relationship at any stage, Gottman and colleagues' work implies a "minding-type" activity that underlies the deescalation attempts (and the decision to permit the wife or partner to lead regarding the issues under discussion). At a deeper psychological level, activities such as listening to one's partner, being thoughtful in considering behavioral impacts on one's partner, and making attributions that are fair and positive about one's partner are implied by the pattern of recognition and deescalation suggested by Gottman and his co-workers. Similarly, carrying out such activities connotes active empathy with a partner, and empathy very definitely goes into making the types of thoughtful attributions suggested by minding. Thus, we do not see how Gottman and colleagues are providing a statement of process that necessarily involves elements different from those involved in acceptance therapy or minding.

All of our qualms notwithstanding, a great value of Gottman's ideas is the high degree of specificity of the ideas. People often desire specifics when trying to fix the problems with their relationships. Our overriding caveat, though, is to suggest care in evaluating how well specifics apply across couples and situations. Although Gottman and colleagues are leaders in doing the research to support their ideas, they have not sampled couples across the lifespan and across the myriad types of situations that couples encounter. We also could be concerned about the possibly different responses that couples, who are being paid to participate in research, will show in artificial settings as opposed to their private dwellings. At the same time, these mostly young twenty- and thirty-year-old couples are providing invaluable evidence when they serve as research respondents in these involved studies. We as investigators cannot ethically go into people's homes, bedrooms, and other private settings and collect comprehensive evidence of the quality collected by Gottman and colleagues.

We have argued that minding is valuable as a package of specifics. There are many ways to achieve the criteria of minding – not unlike what Gottman at some points seems to argue regarding "creating positive atmospheres." Compared with a very specific approach, such as what is found in much of Gottman's writing, minding is more abstract and geared toward advocating that people emphasize the general principles in their own individual ways.

A final point about Gottman's approach is that it rises to the challenge of combining research with intervention. Such a direction is needed for minding, or any conception that purports to help people better their relationships. Relative to what one so often sees in the self-help literature regarding relationship enhancement, Gottman's ideas – based often on sound empirical foundations and careful, clinically relevant experience and logic – represent rare beacons of light for a public that is starved for persuasive arguments about how to find and maintain closeness.

SUMMARY AND CONCLUSIONS

In this chapter, we have discussed minding and related ideas for helping couples deal with close relationship problems. We initially outlined a set of principles for applying minding in therapy with couples. These principles flow from the criteria of minding described in the first two chapters.

The chapter next addressed a set of therapeutic approaches, some of which involved ideas similar to those of the minding conception, and some of which involved ideas that seem closer to nonminding behavior in close relationships. We noted our strong concern about simple theories to explain complex phenomena, such as those involved in maintaining a close, satisfying relationship.

We gave considerable attention to Gottman's (1995) approach to successful relating. We noted the several points of similarity between Gottman's ideas and the minding approach, as well as a few points of divergence. We were, for example, concerned about offering couples exact guidelines for what to do or not do. We noted the differences in how people interpret the same act and that minding was a way to address these natural differenes. But minding is more an emphasis on general principles than a highly specific set of recommendations. Minding does recommend specific acts, but it recognizes the diversity of how these acts may be carried out, received, and interpreted.

In visual, oral, and tactile interactions, both members of a couple are almost always simultaneously interacting, even if one person is only "passively" communicating nonverbally. Hence, there is ample opportunity for miscommunication and resultant conflict. Minding is a package approach to how to deal with miscommunication and conflict. Different couples will do minding in different ways. But do it they will if they are to achieve and continue to preserve long-term closeness and satisfaction.

Paul Newman on the secret to his long, lasting marriage to Joanne Woodward: "Lust, respect, and determination" (on *The Larry King Show*, CNN, February 28, 1998).

CHAPTER 12

Limitations and Future Directions

The brain is wider than the sky – put side by side,
you decide.

Emily Dickinson

In this chapter we discuss questions regarding minding and its limitations, alternative types of processes that may be instrumental in the creation of intimacy and satisfaction in close relationships, and finally, some of the intriguing directions for future work on minding, especially as it links both cognitive and social approaches to understanding close relationships.

QUESTIONS AND SOME ANSWERS

Is minding more idealistic than anything else? This concern may be broached because of the demands on time, thought, attention, and behavior required to "mind" a relationship. While there may be lesser or greater examples of minding revealed in different relationships and at different points in time in the same relationship, we believe that its existence and durability in a relationship represent a powerful vehicle for continued satisfaction and bonding. A well-minded relationship involves a mixture of equity, equality, empathy, negotiation, friendship, and deep commitment. It is not a mythical possibility. Many couples achieve it. Many also do not.

Does this conception give adequate attention to the impact of emotion on close relationships? We believe that behavior reflecting sentiments of caring and empathy for a partner reflects emotional behavior. To wonder about, care for, or inquire about someone's thoughts and feelings are acts often based on strong positive emotion. Further, affect has been found to be a part of the connective tissue of mutual storytelling in close relationships (Veroff, Sutherland, Chadiha, & Ortega, 1993).

Can one talk or think a relationship "to death"? If so, is that the same as saying one can mind a relationship "to death"? Labored discussion, whining, and verbally obsessing about issues are examples of behavior that can be irritating, if not divisive. A person may think about a relationship for hours on end without reaching any new insights or understanding. However, there likely can never be too much quality talk, problem-solving, negotiation, and thought about a relationship. The minding process keeps as its focus the goal of learning about one's partner and expressing respect for and commitment to the relationship, as opposed to the goal of expressing one's own feelings and complaints. It is the reciprocation of this process that leads to the feelings of understanding and acceptance that in turn make unproductive discussion less likely to occur. Periods of "over-thinking" or labored discussion that lead to no new understanding would thus serve as symptoms that minding is *not* being well done.

Can one learn "too much" about someone while engaging in this process? Well-minded relationships involve agreement on what is a useful amount or type of talk to address issues. Well-minded relationships are disciplined regarding the rules of engagement. Quality talk and thought evolve in the process of caring for and learning about one another that a couple will have implemented if they are minding their relationship. It is likely that in any relationship, some negative events will occur, some negative information will be revealed, or some hurtful words will be said. This happens regardless of whether or not minding is occurring. The advantage of minding as a process is that it gives couples a tool to deal with unpleasant discoveries, and a background of stability and intimacy to support them during times of conflict or insecurity.

It might be suggested that our conception of minding implies that each partner engages in the same kinds of acts that epitomize this

202

process. We do not suggest that partners must adopt similar styles. One partner may emphasize direct verbal expression, while the other may display nonverbal acts of kindness that reveal understanding of the other. As we have implied, the couple in such instances will acknowledge what has been shared and the value of sharing. Both partners may show little verbal expression regarding their thoughts and feelings. If they are minding the relationship, however, they somehow communicate knowledge of and caring about one another.

Nor are couples "stuck" with some structured, prescribed method of minding. Since minding is an activity that requires effort, couples can be flexible in how they implement it. It can take many forms over time, depending on the changing needs of the people involved in the relationship. For example, at one point in a relationship, a couple may decide that regular family discussion of issues needs to occur; at other points, the same couple may use more informal or spontaneous exchanges. This process will be most effective when dealing with content reflecting issues of moment to both partners, including relationship or family concerns (Larson & Richards, 1994).

It might be suggested that one partner's minding may be enough for a relationship that is satisfactory to both. While that is conceivable, our position is that the partner who does not feel that her or his partner likewise is minding the relationship will become dissatisfied over the long run. To not mind essentially may come to mean "to not care" that much about one's partner and the health and welfare of the relationship. Once an attribution with such meaning (e.g., "He thinks only about himself and seldom cares to find out about me") comes to fruition in the thinking of the minding partner, the relationship surely will be less satisfying to him or her.

Does everyone who finds satisfaction in a close relationship have to engage in minding? To the best of our knowledge, there are no good examples in the extensive literature that show that processes quite different from or opposite to minding are positively related to relationship satisfaction. Knapp and Vangelisti (1991) allow for a type of relationship that stabilizes at a low level of involvement, with no further coming together nor apparent coming apart. It is a sort of "empty-shell" marriage, after the term used to define couples staying together without much intimacy and out of convenience, or because of their concerns about the impact of separation on children or their reputation. Our own view is that such relationships are not "close," in that there is no emotional significance to the relationship beyond that of material need or convenience. There is no sense of emotional synergy.

It has been found that some couples spend a relatively great amount of time with one another alone, not talking (Larson & Richards, 1994). Is it not possible that time spent together alone without a process such as minding occurring may lead to satisfaction and closeness? Possibly, but more likely these couples do not suspend their thinking about and feeling toward one another even in such quiet moments of togetherness. The smallest acts of perception are imbued with learning and contribute to knowing.

It also is conceivable that independent of what people do in their minds, they may be biologically and temperamentally well matched such that their behaviors will lead to satisfying long-term relationships (a possibility perhaps implied in some work having a psychological evolutionary foundation; see Simpson & Harris, 1994). To the extent that this possibility might be theorized to exist independent of a couple's interactions, it is highly speculative and will require considerable further theoretical and empirical scrutiny.

A critic might readily point to cultures in which many couples indicate that they are satisfied with their close relationships, and yet there is little apparent indication that couples in those cultures self-disclose or communicate their feelings. However, self-disclosure and other aspects of the minding process may be implemented in more subtle ways in different cultures. Without more evidence of process in these relationships across different cultures, minding cannot be ruled out.

A culture's history of mores regarding close relationships also may affect the nature of what is viewed as satisfying in close relationships. Cultural norms and social structures of a particular time may have placed less emphasis on emotional closeness within a romantic dyad, with more intimacy needs being met through friendship or extended family networks. Later generations of couples may now look back and wonder how these earlier couples could possibly have been satisfied without more dialogue and manifestations of what they conceive of as intimacy. The embrace of principles obtaining in peer marriages and companionate or friendship-oriented relationships by contemporary generations of couples has set the table for our creation of the term minding and analysis of its current cherished stature in close relationships.

WHY ISN'T MINDING LEARNED AND THEN IMPLEMENTED AUTOMATICALLY?

If minding is an ability that we learn, as has been proposed in this book, then why do we not learn this ability and then perform it in an almost automatic way as we conduct our close relationships? We do believe that minding is an ability that is learned. Like other abilities, however, it must be practiced regularly in order to be effective. A basketball player who is an accomplished outside shooter may take hundreds of shots in practice every day during the basketball season and during a good portion of the off-season as well. As important, it is critical that the practice shots be taken in the manner that is correct for accurate shooting. The shooter should consider how the practice conditions differ from or simulate real game situations. In all of this, the shooter will be focused.

Relating closely to another human being over time requires abilities that must be practiced with no less intensity, care, and focus than that displayed by the successful basketball player. Each performance may involve a degree of scripted behavior that involves little thought. But much thought went into the practice, and in general much thought goes into achieving the desired long-term goals. The close relationship literature too long has been silent about the nuances of learning required in the skills to achieve and maintain closeness.

FUTURE DIRECTIONS: CONNECTIONS TO THEORIES OF BASIC HUMAN PROCESSES

There are several important directions for future work on minding theory and research. In other chapters we have pointed toward some of those directions, such as necessary empirical tests. One interesting direction is to develop further theoretical directions as minding interfaces with basic theories and ideas in the social and behavioral sciences, not unlike the linkage suggested for plans and the structure of behavior (Miller et al., 1960). An overarching view about the value of minding guides this discussion: We believe that as formulated, minding has the capacity to be a bridging concept that brings basic cognitive psychology concepts closer to social psychology, and vice versa.

Metacognition

Metacognition generally refers to people's thinking about thinking. Specifically, it may refer to people's thoughts, feelings, and perceptions about how they are performing, will perform, or did perform (Metcalfe & Shinamura, 1994). It encompasses, also, attributional logic: how people use their own immediate experiences to generate more complex judgments, not unlike the self-perception process posited by Bem (1972) and discussed in Chapter 4. Metacognition relates closely to minding in that minding presupposes that people do think about their thoughts and that such self-reflection is critical to how they mind and implement their close relationships. Further, minding suggests that people think a lot about their partner's thought processes (often in distorted ways), and that these thoughts also are instrumental in interaction patterns.

Speaking of distortions, basic metacognition work makes important contributions to our formulation of minding. As articulated by Metcalfe (1998), people are often unduly optimistic about how much they know. She reviews work showing the following: (1) We sometimes think that we will be able to solve problems when we will not. (2) We sometimes think we know the answers to questions when we do not. (3) We sometimes think that the correct answer is on the tip of our tongue when in fact there is no right answer, or the answer we know is wrong. (4) We sometimes believe that we have mastered learning when we have not, or that we have understood when we have not.

The reader familiar with cognitive social psychology will recognize the "cognitive heuristic ring" in these conclusions (Tversky & Kahneman, 1974). Such heuristics are shortcuts to decisions, and they are sometimes based on inadequate and/or nonrepresentative information. Heuristics are commonplace in our thinking about our close relationships and our partners. They make us overconfident, and as such they run counter to the minding process, which depends so much on careful checking and rechecking of information and comparison of information with one's partner.

Research has pointed to the value of well-conceived optimism in dealing with severe stressors in our lives (Taylor & Brown, 1994). But "well conceived" is the key descriptor here, and it may hurt less to be overly confident about recovery in some life-threatening situations (e.g., battling cancer) than it is in a normal relationship process situation. In the life-threatening situation, the over-optimism may be motivating, which is even more important than having accurate information about the disease. In minding a close relationship, we need both the information on how to make the relationship work and the motivation to make it work.

Another aspect of metacogniton theory and research focuses on automaticity processes in how people perform and interact (Bargh, 1997), processes that were discussed in Chapter 7. There is impressive evidence that people do a lot of what they do everyday in relatively automatic ways, without much thinking or planning. Such a conclusion probably holds for what people do in close relationships much as it does for driving, walking, and countless other behaviors. Nonetheless, as we have argued previously, it is hardly the case that automaticity in close relationship habits works in the interests of the relationships. It may, if the automated patterns are subjected to checks and revised as needed. But in general, automated patterns probably get us in more trouble than they spare us in efficiency.

Folk Psychology

Folk psychology may be viewed as a type of metacognition (Jost, Kruglanski, & Nelson, 1998). This work reflects a field of cognitive and cognitive social psychology to which minding may be profitably related. Folk psychology refers to our everyday understanding of mind and behavior (Lillard, 1997). As such, it bears a striking parallel to Heider's (1958) naive psychology, which formed the foundation for attribution theory in social psychology. Folk psychology relates to minding most closely as it pertains to people's theories of mind. Folk psychology, like attribution theory, suggests that people spend a great deal of time and energy considering others' mental states and their reasons for acting as they do. As argued for metacognition, minding emphasizes the importance of care in this process of developing a theory about others' mental states – and especially our close others' mental states. Not unlike a careful scientist, we need to test and evaluate our theories and be open to revising them and admitting that there are lots of areas of others' mental states that we probably will never understand very well. But theorize we will!

Folk psychology has another interesting application to minding. In the developmental psychology literature, some theorists such as Fodor (1992) have taken the position that much of what a child knows is inherited, or inborn knowledge. This argument seems to have its greatest merit regarding knowledge of language and related symbolic processes (including quantitative skills). With close relationships, it is unlikely that many geniuses in effective relating are born that way. If they were, there would be much less turbulence in interpersonal relationships than we observe. On the other hand, acquisition of knowledge that often takes many years and much trial and error seems to be the norm in learning how to have successful relationships. Such reasoning does not rule out the possibility that temperaments conducive to facilely learning closeness do not exist at birth. They probably do. We all know people who from early on were quick to show anger – a style that must be moderated if these people are to relate well to others.

What would be fascinating for future work on minding and folk psychology would be to investigate more thoroughly young children's theories of their own and others' mental states as such states pertain to close relationships. It is likely that such theories begin to develop early, and perhaps are inborn (Wellman, 1990). Work is needed to explore these theories empirically and determine when and how children begin to understand how to relate well, and in particular when and how they learn to love others.

A general criticism of both metacognition and folk psychology conceptions is that they give too little credit to people's ability to evolve adaptively in their understandings and theories of the way events unfold in life. As has been argued by Dennett (1996), there is strong evidence about the evolving nature of the human nervous system that is closely related to adaptation. We have suggested in this book that reading a book about minding should help people better structure their minds and behavior so as to have stronger close relationships. Dennett makes a similar argument in suggesting that it would help airline pilots to read a book about all the flying contingencies they may encounter. This act would not guarantee success (or adaptation) to a crisis situation in flying. But it likely would not hurt, either, and may provide clues to solving difficult problems encountered in the act of flying. Dennett goes on to say that through inheritance or acquisition, humans must obtain information in dealing with their environments. We have contended that learning minding skills is one method of information acquisition that is essential to adaptation in close relationships, which in turn means greater adaptation in other areas given the association between successful relationships and well-being (Argyle, 1987).

Chaos Theory

A linkage exists between minding and "chaos theory," which has been posited in physics and in behavioral sciences such as psychology. Chaos theory has been used to study complex phenomena, and a close relationship could be one example. The use of chaos theory for modeling complex social and psychological phenomena avoids the unduly restrictive nature of traditional linear models.

According to West (1997), chaos theory involves factors that are nonlinear or mutually interdependent (versus independent for linear factors). Chaos theory also pertains to emergent processes. Chaos theory follows the Gestalt logic involved in minding that indicates that "the whole is greater than the sum of its parts." West points out that chaos theory posits that a minor change in the input to a system can have a catastrophic change in the output. West also notes that for chaos modeling, qualitative models are as important, and sometimes more important, than quantitative models.

This link between chaos theory and the minding conception may seem farfetched. But the reader will note the similarity of terms, such as interdependence, emergent processes, nonlinearity, and the phrase "the whole is greater than the sum of its parts." As we conceptualize minding, it usually embodies all of these elements. It emerges synergistically through the interdependent behavior, thoughts, and feelings of two individuals. What they create together is different from and greater than what each can create alone. Further, we also have embraced the idea that qualitative knowledge may be just as important, or sometimes more important, than quantitative knowledge in understanding minding processes.

How Can Minding Theory Help Cognitive Social Psychology Be More Social?

Minding by definition refers to our thoughts and feelings about others, as well as to behavior directed toward them and in reference to them. In effect, minding is inherently a social psychological process. It specifies a package of thoughts that relates to the self and to the other, as well as patterns of interaction with the other and self–other interfaces. Minding suggests that such a necessary bond is part and parcel of closeness and that cognition and social interaction cannot be analyzed separately when the question is how to enhance closeness.

The reciprocity component of minding also makes it equally a cognitive and social process. The reciprocity idea is that each person in a close relationship often is thinking, feeling, and acting relative to the partner. Minding theory does not posit that people can learn this skill and how to do it well, or without making a lot of mistakes. But it does argue that they will learn it if they are to succeed over an extended period of relating closely to others. In this learning, we have implied in our conception that the work of the mind *must simultaneously be focused* both on itself – its contents and processes – and outside events, including the minds of and interaction with close others. That is both a scary proposition and an eminently feasible proposition. Just think about all the activities we sometimes catch ourselves doing at the same time. For example, consider the proverbial driver who is listening to the radio and talking on the phone, all the while driving 70 mph down the freeway! We invite the reader to use that analogy to consider how in close relationship interactions (sometimes not even involving face-to-face interaction), both partners are also thinking, feeling, and behaving all at the same time. Like the driver who is busy with a variety of tasks, lovers must learn how to juggle and balance and not crash on the "matrimonial freeway."

CONCLUSIONS

This book presented an analysis of what we define and describe as minding activity in the development of satisfying and potentially long-term close relationships. We defined minding as a process involving attribution, thought, feeling, and behavior designed to know the partner, actions based on that knowledge that have the goal of facilitating the relationship, and acceptance of and respect for what is learned in the process. It is essential that both parties be involved in minding activities and believe that each is involved and sincere in their efforts. We have suggested that this process model is similar to models of reciprocal self-disclosure and intimacy, but that the minding model involves important differences as well. Those differences include: the continuous quest for knowledge about the other and the relationship, the role of attribution in a person's designation of causality and responsibility for the other's and his or her own behavior, and perceptions about one another's effort and sincerity in engaging in the knowing process. Overall, we believe that the minding analysis provides a further integrative link between attribution theory and close relationships.

The late short story writer Laurie Colwin (1981) said about the transformative power of love, "Love transforms a difficult person into a charming eccentric; points of contention into charming divergences." We would suggest that it is the process of minding that leads to transformations in meaning such as these

It is also our contention that minding can create more than just increased feelings of closeness. Couples who "mind" the relationship well may often perceive themselves as stronger together than apart. More romantically inclined partners may describe themselves as "soulmates" or as "meant" to be together. For these couples, this belief or feeling is a serious and fairly consistent one over time, not simply inspired by the first passion of courtship. While not losing their individuality as people with separate minds and identities, individuals in well-minded relationships may develop the Gestalt-like sense that their relationship has an importance and meaning beyond that of their two separate lives.

Harold Kelley (1979) concluded his analysis of the structures and processes of personal relationships with the following eloquent observation about the difficult quest each human faces in trying to connect intimately with another mind:

> The unavoidable consequence of human social life is a realization of the essentially private and subjective nature of our experience of the world, coupled with a strong wish to break out of that privacy and establish contact with another mind. Personal relationships hold out to their members the possibility, though perhaps rarely realized in full, of establishing such contact. (p. 169)

We believe that the process we have called minding offers us the best means by which we can attempt to break out of our private, subjective experience and connect intimately with another human mind and life. Minding makes people feel special, and it makes our relationships meaningful. Minding helps us solve relationship problems and plan how to make relationships work better. Minding over time creates and sustains a sense of connection between two minds and lives.

References

Abelson, R.P., Aronson, E., McGuire, W.J., Newcomb, T.M., Rosenberg, M.J., & Tannenbaum, P.H. (1968). *Theories of cognitive consistency: A sourcebook*. Chicago: Rand McNally.

Acitelli, L.K., & Holmberg, D. (1993). Reflecting on relationships. The role of thoughts and memories. In D. Perlman & W.H. Jones (Eds.), *Personal relationships* (Vol. 4, pp. 71-100). London: Kingsley.

Ahrons, C. (1994). *The good divorce*. New York: HarperCollins.

Akeret, R.U. (1992). Every picture tells a story. *New Woman*, October, 78-82.

Alberoni, F. (1983). *Falling in love*. New York: Random House.

Altman, I., & Taylor, D. (1973). *Social penetration: The development of interpersonal relationships*. New York: Holt, Rinehart & Winston.

Anderson, S.M., & Bem, S.L. (1981). Sex typing and androgyny in dyadic interaction: Individual differences in responsiveness to physical attractiveness. *Journal of Personality and Social Psychology*, 41: 74-86.

Argyle, M. (1987). *The psychology of happiness*. Oxford: Oxford University Press.

Aron, A., & Aron, E.N. (1986). *Love as the expansion of self: Understanding attraction and satisfaction*. New York: Hemisphere.

Aron, A., & Aron, E.N. (1996). Self and self-expansion in relationships. In G.J.O. Fletcher & J. Fitness (Eds.), *Knowledge structures in close relationships: A social psychological approach* (pp. 325-344). Mahwah, NJ: Erlbaum.

Aron, A., & Westbay, L. (1996). Dimensions of the prototype of love. *Journal of Personality and Social Psychology*, 70: 535-551.

Bargh, J.A. (1997). The automaticity of everyday life. In R.S. Wyer (Ed.), *Advances in Social Cognition* (Vol. 10, pp. 1-48). Mahwah, NJ: Erlbaum.

Baxter, L.A., & Montgomery, B.M. (1996). *Relating: Dialogues and dialectics*. New York: Guilford.

Baxter, L.A., & Wilmot, W.W. (1985). Taboo topics in close relationships. *Journal of Social and Personal Relationships*, 2: 253-269.

Beck, A. (1988). *Love is never enough*. New York: Harper & Row.

Bem, D.J. (1965). An experimental analysis of self-persuasion. *Journal of Experimental Social Psychology*, 1: 199-218.

Bem, D.J. (1972). Self-perception theory. In L. Berkowitz (Ed.), *Advances in experimental social psychology* (Vol. 6, pp. 1-62). New York: Academic Press.

Berley, R.A., & Jacobson, N.S. (1984). Causal attributions in intimate relationships: Toward a model of cognitive-behavioral marital therapy. *Advances in Cognitive-Behavioral Research and Therapy*, 3: 1-35.

Bernard, J. (1982). *The future of marriage*. New Haven: Yale University Press.

Berscheid, E. (1994). Interpersonal relationships. *Annual Review of Psychology*, 45: 79-129.

Blumstein, P., & Schwartz, P. (1983). *American Couples*. New York: Simon & Schuster.

Bochner, A.P., Ellis, C., & Tillman, L.M. (1997). Relationships as stories. In S. Duck (Ed.), *Handbook of personal relationships* (2nd ed., pp. 307-324). Sussex, England: Wiley.

Bowlby, J. (1969). *Loss: Sadness and depression*. New York: Basic Books.

Bradbury, T.N., & Fincham, F.D. (1990). Attributions and behavior in marital interaction. *Journal of Personality and Social Psychology*, 107: 3-33.

Brehm, S.S. (1992). *Intimate relationships*. New York: McGraw-Hill.

Burleson, B.R. (1995). Personal relationships as a skilled accomplishment. *Journal of Social and Personal Relationships*, 12: 575-581.

Buss, D.M. (1994). *The evolution of desire*. New York: Basic Books.

Carver, R. (1986). *Where I'm calling from: New and selected stories*. New York: Atlantic Monthly Press.

Chelune, G.J., Robinson, J.T., & Kommor, J.J. (1984). A cognitive interactional model of intimate relationships. In V.J. Derlega (Ed.), *Communication, intimacy, and close relationships* (pp. 11-40). Orlando, FL: Academic Press.

Clark, M.S., & Mills, J. (1979). Interpersonal attraction in exchange and communal relationships. *Journal of Personality and Social Psychology*, 37: 12-24.

Cohn, N.B., & Strassberg, D.S. (1983). Self-disclosure reciprocity in preadolescents. *Personality and Social Psychology Bulletin*, 9: 97-102.

Coles, R. (1989). *The call of stories*. Boston: Houghton Mifflin.

Collins, N.L., & Miller L.C. (1994). The disclosure-liking link: From meta-analysis toward a dynamic reconceptualization. *Psychological Bulletin*, 116: 457-475.

Colwin, L. (1981). *The lone pilgrim*. New York: Harper & Row.

Conway, M. (1995). *Flashbulb memories*. Hillsdale, NJ: Erlbaum.

Csikszentmihalyi, M. (1982). Toward a psychology of optimal experience. *Review of Personality and Social Psychology*, 3: 13-26.

DePaulo, B.M. (1992). Nonverbal behavior and self-presentation. *Psychological Bulletin*, 111: 23-243.

Darley, J.M., & Fazio, R.H. (1980). Expectancy confirmation process arising in the social interaction sequence. *American Psychologist*, 35: 867-881.

Davis, M.H. (1993). *Empathy*. Dubuque, IA: Brown & Benchmark.

Dennett, D.C. (1996). *Kinds of minds*. New York: Basic Books.

Derlega, V.J., & Chaikin, A.L. (1976). Norms affecting self-disclosure in men and women. *Journal of Consulting and Clinical Psychology*, 3: 376-380.

Derlega, V.J., Metts, S., Petronio, S., & Margulis, S.T. (1993). *Self-disclosure*. Newbury Park, CA: Sage.

Deutsch, M. (1973). *The resolution of conflict: Constructive and destructive processes*. New Haven: Yale University Press.

De Villers, L. (1997). *Love skills*. San Luis Obispo, CA: Impact Publishers.

Downey, G. & Feldman, S.I. (1996). Implications of rejection sensitivity for intimate relationships. *Journal of Personality and Social Psychology*, 70: 1327-1343.

Dunn, J. (1988). *The beginnings of social understanding*. Oxford: Basil Blackwell.

Ellis, C. (1996). On the demands of truthfulness in writing personal loss narratives. *Journal of Personal & Interpersonal Loss*, 1: 151-178.

Fabry, J., Bulka, R.P., & Sahakian, W.S. (1979). *Finding meaning in life: Logotherapy*. Northvale, NJ: Jason Aronson.

Fehr, R. (1988). Prototype analysis of the concepts of love and commitment. *Journal of Personality and Social Psychology*, 55: 557-579.

Felmlee, D. (1995). Fatal attractions: Affection and disaffection in intimate relationships. *Journal of Social and Personal Relationships*, 12: 395-411.

Fincham, F.D. (1985). Attributions in close relationships. In J.H. Harvey & G. Weary (Eds.), *Attribution: Basic issues and Applications* (pp. 203-234). New York: Academic Press.

Fincham, F.D., & Bradbury, T.N. (1992). Attributions and behavior in marital interaction. *Journal of Personality and Social Psychology*, 63: 613-628.

Fiske, S.T., & Taylor, S.E. (1991). *Social cognition* (2nd ed.). New York: McGraw-Hill.

Foa, U.G., & Foa, E.B. (1974). *Social structures of the mind*. Springfield, IL: Charles C. Thomas.

Fodor, J.A. (1992). A theory of the child's theory of mind. *Cognition*, 44: 283-296.

Frankl, V.E. (1959). *Man's search for meaning*. Boston: Beacon Press.

Franzoi, S.L. (1996). *Social psychology*. Madison, WI.: Brown & Benchmark.

Gergen, K.J. & Gergen, M.M. (1987). Narratives of relationships. In R. Burnett, P. McGhee, & D.C. Clarke (Eds.), *Accounting for relationships* (pp. 269-315). London: Methuen.

Glasser, W. (1995). *Staying together*. New York: HarperCollins.

Goffman, I. (1959). *The presentation of self in everyday life*. Garden City, NY: Doubleday.

Gottman, J. (1994). *What predicts divorce? The relationship between marital processes and marital outcomes*. Hillsdale, NJ: Erlbaum.

Gottman, J. (1995). *Why marriages succeed or fail*. New York: Fireside Books.

Gottman, J.M. & Krokoff, L.J. (1989). Marital interaction and satisfaction: A longitudinal view. *Journal of Consulting and Clinical Psychology*, 57: 47-52 .

Gottman, J.M., Coan, J., Carrere, S., & Swanson, C. (1998). Predicting marital happiness and stability from newlywed interactions. *Journal of Marriage and the Family*, 60: 5-22.

Halford, W.K., & Behrens, B.C. (1997). Prevention of marital difficulties. In P. Cotton and H. Jackson (Eds.), *Early intervention & prevention in mental health* (pp. 21-58). Sydney: Australian Psychological Association.

217

Harvey, J.H. (1987). Attributions in close relationships: Research and theoretical developments. *Journal of Social and Clinical Psychology*, 5: 8-20.

Harvey, J.H. (1995). *Odyssey of the heart: The search for closeness, intimacy, and love*. New York: Freeman.

Harvey, J.H., & Omarzu, J. (1997). Minding the close relationship. *Personality and Social Psychology Review*, 1: 223-239.

Harvey, J.H., & Weary, G. (1984). Current issues in attribution theory and research. *Annual Review of Psychology*, 35: 427-459.

Harvey, J.H., Hendrick, S.S., & Tucker, K. (1988). Self-report methods in the study of personal relationships. In S. Duck & W. Ickes (Eds.), *Handbook of research on personal relationships* (pp. 99-113). New York: Wiley.

Harvey, J.H., Orbuch, T.L., Chwalisz, K., & Garwood, G. (1991). Coping with sexual assault: The roles of account-making and confiding. *Journal of Traumatic Stress*, 4: 515-531.

Harvey, J.H., Trevino, E.A., Omarzu, J., Clutts, J., & Busch, C. (1997). *Minding and close relationship satisfaction. Paper presented at the conference of the International Network for Personal Relationships*, June 1997, Miami University, Ohio.

Harvey, J.H., Weber, A.L., & Orbuch, T.L. (1990). *Interpersonal accounts: A social psychological perspective*. Oxford: Basil Blackwell.

Hatfield, E., & Rapson, R. (1993). *Love, sex, and intimacy*. New York: HarperCollins.

Hazan, C., & Shaver, P. (1987). Romantic love conceptualized as an attachment process. *Journal of Personality and Social Psychology*, 52: 511-524.

Heider, F. (1944). Social perception and phenomenal causality. *Psychological Review*, 51: 358-374.

Heider, F. (1958). *The psychology of interpersonal relationships*. New York: Wiley (reprinted by Erlbaum).

Heider, F. (1976). A conversation with Fritz Heider. In J.H. Harvey, W.J. Ickes, & R.F. Kidd (Eds.), *New directions in attribution research* (Vol. 1, pp. 1-10). Hillsdale, NJ: Erlbaum.

Hendrick, S.S. (1988). A generic measure of relationship satisfaction. *Journal of Marriage and the Family*, 50: 93-98.

Hendrick, C., & Hendrick, S.S. (1986). A theory and method of love. *Journal of Personality and Social Psychology*, 50: 392-402.

Hendrick, C. & Hendrick, S.S. (1989). Research on love: Does it measure up? *Journal of Personality and Social Psychology*, 56: 784-94.

Hochschild, A. (1989). *The second shift*. New York: Viking.

Holmberg, D., & Veroff, J. (1996). Rewriting relationship memories: The effects of courtship and wedding scripts. In G.J.O Fletcher & J. Fitness (Eds.), *Knowledge structures in close relationships: A social psychological approach* (pp. 345-368). Mahwah, NJ: Erlbaum.

Holmes, J.G., & Rempel, J.K. (1989). Trust in close relationships. In C. Hendrick (Ed.), *Close relationships: Review of personality and social psychology* (Vol. 10, pp. 315-359). Newbury Park, CA: Sage.

Ickes, W. (Ed.) (1996). *Empathic accuracy*. New York: Guilford Press.

Ickes, W., Stinson, L., Bissonnette, V., & Garcia, S. (1990). Naturalistic social cognition: Empathic accuracy in mixed-sex dyads. *Journal of Personality and Social Psychology*, 59: 730-742.

Jacobson, N.S., & Christensen, A. (1996). *Integrative couple therapy: Promoting acceptance and change*. New York: Norton.

Jones, E.E., & Davis, K.E. (1965). From acts to dispositions: The attribution process in person perception. In L. Berkowitz (Ed.), *Advances in experimental social psychology* (Vol. 2, pp. 219-266). New York: Academic Press.

Jones, E.E., & McGillis, D. (1976). Correspondent inferences and the attribution cube: A comparative reappraisal. In J.H. Harvey, W.J. Ickes, & R.F. Kidd (Eds.), *New directions in attribution research* (Vol. 1, pp. 389-420). Hillsdale, NJ: Erlbaum.

Jost, J.T., Kruglanski, A.W., & Nelson, T.O. (1998). Social metacognition: An expansionist review. *Personality and Social Psychology Review*, 2: 137-154.

Jourard, S.M. (1971). *The transparent self*. New York: Van Nostrand Reinhold.

Kayser, K. (1994). *When love dies*. New York: Guilford Press.

Kelley, H.H. (1967). Attribution theory in social psychology. In D. Levine (Ed.), *Nebraska Symposium on Motivation* (Vol. 15, pp. 192-240). Lincoln: University of Nebraska Press.

Kelley, H.H. (1979). *Personal relationships: Their structures and processes*. Hillsdale, NJ: Erlbaum.

Kelley, H.H., Berscheid, E., Christensen, A., Harvey, J.H., Huston, T., Levinger, G., McClintock, E., Peplau, A., & Peterson, D. (1983). *Close relationships*. San Francisco: Freeman.

Kelly, A.E., & McKillop, K.J. (1996). Consequences of revealing personal secrets. *Psychological Bulletin*, 120: 450-465.

Kleinke, C. (1978). *Self-perception: The psychology of personal awareness*. San Francisco: Freeman.

Knapp, M.L. (1978). *Nonverbal communication in human interaction* (2nd ed.). New York: Holt, Rinehart and Winston.

Knapp, M.L. (1984). *Interpersonal comunication and human relationships*. Boston: Allyn & Bacon.

Knapp, M.L., & Vangelisti, A.L. (1991). *Interpersonal communication and human relationships* (2nd ed.). Boston: Allyn & Bacon.

Langer, E.J. (1989). *Mindfulness*. Reading, MA: Addison-Wesley.

Langer, E.J., & Rodin, J. (1976). The effects of choice and enhanced personal responsibility for the aged: A field experiment in an institutional setting. *Journal of Personality and Social Psychology*, 34: 191-198.

Larson, R., & Richards, M.H. (1994). *Divergent realities: The emotional lives of mothers, fathers, and adolescents*. New York: Basic Books.

Levinger, G. (1980). Toward the analysis of close relationships. *Journal of Experimental Social Psychology*, 16: 510-544.

Liiceanu, A. (1998). Loss of collective identity: Self-sacrifice, beauty contests, and magical practices. In J.H. Harvey (Ed.), *Perspectives on loss: A sourcebook* (pp. 293-302). Philadelphia: Taylor & Francis.

Lillard, A.S. (1997). Other folks' theories of mind and behavior. *Psychological Science*, 8: 268-274.

Loftus, E.F. (1993). The reality of repressed memories. *American Psychologist*, 48: 518-537.

Manusov, V., Floyd, K., & Kerssen-Griep, J. (1997). Yours, mine, and ours: Mutual attributions for nonverbal behaviors in couples' interactions. *Communication Research*, 24: 234-260.

Mauriac, F. (1947). *The desert of love*. New York: Farrar, Strauss, and Giroux.

May, R. (1969). *Love and will*. New York: Norton.

McAdams, D.P. (1988). *Power, intimacy, and the life story*. New York: Guilford Press.

McAdams, D.P. (1989). *Intimacy: The need to be close*. New York: Doubleday.

Metcalfe, J. (1998). Cognitive optimism: Self-deception or memory-based processing heuristics. *Personality and Social Psychology Review*, 2: 100-110.

Metcalfe J., & Shinamura, A. (1994). *Metacognition: Knowing about knowing*. Cambridge, MA: MIT Press.

Miller, G.A., Galanter, E., & Pribram, K.H. (1960). *Plans and the structure of behavior*. New York: Holt, Rinehart and Winston.

Miller, L.C., Berg, J.H., & Archer, K.L. (1983). Openers: Individuals who elicit intimate self-disclosure. *Journal of Personality and Social Psychology*, 44: 1234-1244.

Mills, J., & Clark, M.S. (1982). Exchange and communal relationships. *Review of Personality and Social Psychology*, 3: 121-144.

Murray, S., & Holmes, J.G. (1993). Seeing virtues in faults: Negativity and the transformation of interpersonal narratives in close relationships. *Journal of Personality and Social Psychology*, 65: 707-722.

Murray, S.L., Holmes, J.G., & Griffin, D.W. (1996). The benefits of positive illusions: Idealization and the construction of satisfaction in close relationships. *Journal of Personality and Social Psychology*, 1: 79-98.

Omarzu, J., Harvey, J.H., & Chavis, A. (1997). To tell or not to tell. Paper presented at Midwestern Psychological Association, Chicago, IL, May 1997.

Orvis, B.R., Kelley, H.H., & Butler, D. (1976). Attributional conflict in young couples. In J.H. Harvey, W. Ickes, & R.F. Kidd (Eds.), *New directions in attribution research* (Vol. 1, pp. 353-386). Hillsdale, NJ: Erlbaum.

Parks, M.R. (1997) Communications networks and relationship life cycles. In S. Duck (Ed.) *Handbook of Personal Relationships*, pp. 351-372. New York: John Wiley & Sons.

Pennebaker, J.W. (1990). *Opening up: The healing power of confiding in others*. New York: Marrow.

Pennebaker, J.W., & Beall, S.K. (1986). Confronting a traumatic event: Toward an understanding of inhibition and disease. *Journal of Abnormal Psychology*, 95: 274-281.

Pennebaker, J.W., Kiecolt-Glaser, J.K., & Glaser, R. (1988). Disclosure of traumas and immune function: Health implications for psychotherapy. *Journal of Consulting and Clinical Psychology*, 56: 239-245.

Pennington, N., & Hastie, R. (1991). A theory of explanation-based decision making. In G. Klein, J. Orasanu, & R. Calderwood (Eds.), *Decision making in action: Models and methods* (pp. 115-142). Norwood, NJ: Ablex.

Petronio, S., & Martin, J.N. (1986). Ramifications of revealing private information: A gender gap. *Journal of Clinical Psychology*, 42: 499-506.

Phillips, A. (1997). *Monogamy*. New York: Pantheon.

Planalp, S. (1987). Interplay between relational knowledge and events. In R. Burnett, P. McGhee, & D.D. Clarke (Eds.), *Accounting for relationships: Explanation, representation and knowledge* (pp. 175-191). New York: Methuen.

Prager, K.J. (1995). *The psychology of intimacy*. New York: Guilford.

Rabin, C. (1996). *Equal partners, good friends: Empowering couples through therapy*. London: Routledge.

Reis, H.T., & Patrick, B.C. (1996). Attachment and intimacy: Component processes. In E.T. Higgins & A. Kruglanski (Eds.), *Social psychology: Handbook of basic principles* (pp. 523-563). New York: Guilford.

Reis, H.T., & Shaver, P. (1988). Intimacy as an interpersonal process. In S.W. Duck (Ed.), *Handbook of personal relationships* (pp. 367-389). Chichester: Wiley.

Riley, G. (1991). *Divorce: An American tradition*. New York: Oxford University Press.

Rogers, C.R. (1975). Empathic: An unappreciated way of being. *The Counseling Psychologist*, 5: 2-10.

Ross, M. (1989). Relation of implicit theories to the construction of personal histories. *Psychological Review*, 96: 341-357.

Rubin, L.B. (1985). *Just friends*. New York: Harper & Row.

Rusbult, C.E. (1980). Commitment and satisfaction in romantic associations: A test of the investment model. *Journal of Experimental Social Psychology*, 16, 172-186.

Rusbult, C.E., Zembrodt, I.M., & Gunn, L.K. (1982). Exit, voice, loyalty, and neglect: Responses to dissatisfaction in romantic involvements. *Journal of Personality and Social Psychology*, 43: 1230-1242.

Rutter, M., & Rutter, M.E. (1993). *Developing minds and continuity across the lifespan*. New York: Basic Books.

Schank, R.C., & Abelson, R.P. (1977). *Scripts, plans, goals, and understanding*. Hillsdale, NJ: Erlbaum.

Schank, R.C., & Abelson, R.P. (1995). Knowledge and memory: The real story. In R.S. Wyer (Ed.), *Advances in social cognition* (Vol. 8, pp. 1-86). Hillsdale, NJ: Erlbaum.

Schonbach, P. (1992). Interactions of process and moderator variables in account episodes. In J.H. Harvey, T.L. Orbuch, & A.L. Weber (Eds.), *Attributions, accounts, and close relationships* (pp. 40-51). New York: Springer-Verlag.

Schrof, J.M. (1998, January 19). Married . . . with problems. *U.S. News and World Report*, 56-57.

Schwartz, P. (1994). *Peer marriage*. New York: Free Press.

Shaver, K.G. (1985). *The attribution of blame: Causality, responsibility, and blameworthiness*. New York: Springer-Verlag.

Simpson, J.A., & Harris, B.A. (1994). Interpersonal attraction. In A.L. Weber &

J.H. Harvey (Eds.), *Perspectives on close relationships* (pp. 45-66). Needham Heights, MA: Allyn & Bacon.

Snyder, M., Tanke, E.D., & Berscheid, E. (1977). Social perception and interpersonal behavior: On the self-fulfilling nature of social stereotypes. *Journal of Personality and Social Psychology*, 35: 656-666.

Spence, D. (1982). *Narrative truth and historical truth: Meaning and interpretation.* New York: Norton.

Surra, C.A., & Bohman, T. (1991). The development of close relationships: A cognitive perspective. In G.J.O. Fletcher & F.D. Fincham (Eds.), *Cognition in close relationships* (pp. 283-304). Hillsdale, NJ: Erlbaum.

Swann, W.B., Jr. (1996). *Self-traps: The elusive quest for higher self-esteem.* New York: Freeman.

Swann, W.B., Jr., De La Ronde, C., & Hixon, J.G. (1994). Authenticity and positive strivings in marriage and courtship. *Journal of Personality and Social Psychology*, 66: 857-869.

Tannen, D. (1990). *You just don't understand: Women and men in conversation.* New York: Morrow.

Taylor, S.E. (1981). The interface of cognitive and social psychology. In J.H. Harvey (Ed.), *Cognition, social behavior, and the environment* (pp. 189-212). Hillsdale, NJ: Erlbaum.

Taylor, S.E., & Brown, J.D. (1994). Illusion and well-being: A social psychological perspective on mental health. *Psychological Bulletin*, 103: 193-210.

Tversky, A., & Kahneman, D. (1974). Judgment under uncertainty: Heuristics and biases. *Science*, 185: 1124-1131.

Van Pelt, N.L. (1997). *Smart love.* Grand Rapids, MI: Feming H. Revell.

VanYperen, N.W., & Buunk, B.P. (1991). Equity theory and exchange and communal orientation from a cross-national perspective. *Journal of Social Psychology*, 131: 5-20.

Veroff, J., Sutherland, L., Chadiha, L., & Ortega, R.M. (1993). Newlyweds tell their stories: A narrative method for assessing marital experiences. *Journal of Social and Personal Relationships*, 10: 437-457.

Wallerstein, J., & Blakeslee, S. (1995). *The good marriage.* New York: Warner.

Wegner, D.M. (1986). Transactive memory: A content analysis of the group mind. In B. Mullen & G.R. Goethals (Eds.), *Theories of group behavior* (pp. 185-202). New York: Springer-Verlag.

Wellman, H.M. (1990). *The child's theory of mind.* Cambridge, MA: Bradford.

West, B.J. (1997). Chaos and related things: A tutorial. The *Journal of Mind and Behavior*, 18: 103-126.

Wicklund, R.A., & Gollwitzer, P.M. (1982). *Symbolic self-completion.* Hillsdale, NJ: Erlbaum.

Index

Acceptance and respect, 15–16, 39, 85–91

Acceptance therapy, 87–88, 195–196

Accounts, 15, 35–37

Ahrons, Constance, 110

Altman, Irwin, 40–42, 104–105

Aron, Arthur and Elaine, 34, 100, 125–126

Attachment styles, 50–51

Attention, 132

Attraction, 101

Attributions: relationship-enhancing, 13–15, 75–77, 161–162, 165, 185; dispositional/situational, 13, 66; finding meaning, 27; simple vs. complex, 62–63; motivation, 63–64; covariation principles, 65–67; correspondent inference, 69–71, 131; self-perception, 71–72; distortions, combating, 77–81

Automatic behavior or thoughts, 23–24, 139–141, 207

Baxter, Leslie, 43–44, 88

Beck, Aaron, 8, 23, 97, 127, 138–141

Bem, Daryl, 71–72

Berscheid, Ellen, 41, 93

Bradbury, Thomas, 75–77

Burleson, Brent, 55–56

Buss, David 45–46

Careers and relationships, 146

Carver, Raymond, 39

Chaos theory, 209–210

Children, 54–55, 209

Christensen, Andrew, 88

Closeness, measuring, 19–20

Cognitive sets, 34, 79, 126

Cognitive shortcuts, 63, 79, 207

Commitment, 8, 31, 53, 107; and investment, resource exchange, and trust, 131

Common sense psychology, 65–67

Communication, 12, 39, 49

Companionate relationships, 149

Competition, 27

Communal relationships, 92–93, 124–125

Confiding in close other, 35

Continuity over time, 17–18, 94–95, 165

Control, 22, 26, 69, 152–154

Cultural differences, 29, 174–176, 204

Dating couples, 31, 129

Davis, Keith, 13, 65–71

Decisions, 26

Derlega, Valerian, 32, 42

Dialectics, 189

Divorce, 57, 110, 192–195

Education, 25, 146; in Romania, 177

Elliot, T.S., 52

Ellis, Carolyn, 37–38

Empathic accuracy, 57–58

Empathy, 36, 57–58

Equality, 92, 142–148
Evolutionary psychology, 45–46, 174

Facial expressions, 47–48
Fincham, Frank, 75–77
Flow, 17
Folk psychology, 208–209
Frankl, Viktor, 133–135

Gender differences, 45–46, 93, 154,
    159–160, 198
Gergen, Kenneth and Mary, 128–129
Goffman, Irving, 38
"Good marriage," 113, 148–150
Gottman, John, 19, 85–87, 192–195
Greek couples, 178–179

Harvey, John H., 15, 22, 25, 35–37,
    43, 63
Hazan, Cynthia, 50
Health, 22, 33, 35–36, 52
Heider, Fritz, 7, 13–14, 27, 65–67, 78
Hendrick, Clyde and Susan, 22, 99–
    100, 124–125, 161
Holmes, John, 80–81

Ickes, William 57–58
Interdependence, 16, 68, 78–79, 210
Intimacy, 34, 40, 51–52, 121–124

Jacobson, Neil, 88
Jones, Edward, 13, 69–71
Jourard, Sidney, 32–33, 105

Kelley, Harold, 16, 67–69, 77, 94
Kerr, Norbert, 3
Knapp, Mark, 42
Knowing one's partner, 11–12
Knowledge, 11–12, 31–60, 63, 90,
    184

Langer, Ellen 22–26
Loftus, Elizabeth, 38
Loss, 36
Love: enough for maintenance, 97–
    98, 138–141; falling in love, 98–101;
    styles, 100, 124–125; prototype,
    100; as self-expansion, 34, 125–126;
    and meaning, 132–135

Marriage: "starter," 57; the "good,"
    113, 148–150; peer, 142–148
May, Rollo, 52
McAdams, Daniel, 51–52
Measurement issues, 19–22
Memory, 81–82
Metacognition, 206–207
Metts, Sandra, 32
Minding: definition, 11; meaning (re-
    lation to minding), 27, 135–136;
    variables reflecting, 18–21; devel-
    opmental considerations, 54–57;
    beginnings, 101–103; fundamental
    questions, 106–108; predictions of
    permanence, 109–110; endings,
    110–117; never-minded relation-
    ship, 111–113; crisis-driven break-
    ups, 113–114; winding down, 115;
    salvaging a dissolving relation-
    ship, 116–117; comparison of inti-
    macy and minding, 122–123; and
    the "good marriage," 150–151;
    and staying together, 151–154; and
    couples therapy, 184–199; and
    Gottman's approach, 196–199;
    learning automatically, 205; and
    metacognition, 205–207; and folk
    psychology, 208–209; and chaos
    theory, 209–210; and cognitive so-
    cial psychology, 210–211
Mindless vs. mindful, 22–25
Montgomery, Barbara, 88
Murray, Sandra, 80–81

Nonverbal behavior, 47–49, 76

Omarzu, Julia, 43, 105, 157–167

Peer marriage, 142–148
Pennebaker, James, 35
Petronio, Sandra, 32, 41
Plans and planning, 94–95

Planalp, Sally, 126
Power, 152–153
Prager, Karen, 121–124
Priorities, 26–27
Proximity, 48

Reciprocity, 16–17, 91–94, 161, 164, 184
Reconstructing relationship memory, 81–82
Reis, Harry, 34, 121–123
Relationship skills, 54–56
Resbult, Caryl, 131
Rogers, Carl, 58
Romania, evidence about minding, 10, 168–181
Romantic relationships, 149
Rubin, Z., 53–54

Schemas and scripts, 23, 62–63, 92–93, 126–128, 143, 205
Schwartz, Pepper, 8, 142–148
Seinfeld, 16
Self-disclosure, 32–35, 164; and personality, 50–52; and sexuality, 52–54; at beginning of relationships, 104–105
Self-fulfilling interaction, 23, 73–75
Self-verification, 129–130
Sexuality, 29, 52–54; in social pene-

tration theory, 42; in evolutionary psychology, 45-46; and love, 100; and meaning, 135–136; and equality, 146; and the *Good Marriage,* 149–150; in Romania, 177; and *Smart Love,* 191
Shaver, Philip, 34, 50–51, 121–122
Social construction, 128–129
Social context, 25–26, 46, 78–79
Social environment, 172–174
Social penetration, 40–43, 104–105
"Starter marriage," 57
Stereotyping, 23–24, 26
Story-telling and self-disclosure, 36–40
Students, 2, 4, 15, 148
Surra, Catherine, 126
Swann, William, 129–130
Synergy, 5–6, 16

Taylor, Dalmus, 40–42, 104–105
Taylor, Shelly, 79
Taboo topics, 43–44
Traditional relationships, 142–143, 174–175

Values, 23
Vangelisti, Anita, 42–43

Wallerstein, Judith, 8, 148–150

ance should all be continuous processes that create the synergy of a lasting, close relationship.

ACCEPTANCE AND RESPECT

Acceptance and respect are two concepts that are high on the list of the prototypical features of love (Fehr, 1988). Minding emphasizes finding out a great deal of information about a partner, sharing innermost thoughts and feelings, and revealing the past. We need to accept what we come to know about our close other through this process, and to respect the other based on this knowledge. If we have doubts or cannot accept major parts of who our partners are, then minding is much more difficult to implement.

Researchers who follow couples over time and study their interactions have found that those who display positive types of social behavior together are more satisfied with their relationships. These positive behaviors include listening respectfully to another's opinions, working out compromises that accept another's needs, paying attention to the other during conflicts, and accepting the other's responses. All of these kinds of behaviors are illustrative of respect for the other and acceptance of the other's feelings and thoughts. Less happy couples, on the other hand, tend to display less respectful behavior toward each other, such as verbal attacks, withdrawal, or criticism of the other's ideas (Levinger, 1980; Gottman & Krokoff, 1989).

Gottman (1994, 1995) has done extensive work with couples, observing their interactions and conflicts in a controlled experimental setting. He has followed many couples over time, some for several years. Based on his observations, he has argued that couples who stay happily married for long periods of time are good at repairing conversations when they become corrosive and negative. They do not let negativity become habitual or a common reaction to stress. They are good at soothing and neutralizing tensions and anger. At the core of this behavior is respectful negotiation. They are, essentially, rewarding one another much more often than they are punishing one another.

As will be evaluated in Chapter 11, Gottman has described the factors he perceives to be the signs of a relationship headed for failure. One of the primary factors is pervasive criticism; a second is contempt; and a third is stonewalling, or avoidance. All of these types of interaction (or lack of interaction) can destroy a relationship, and all reflect a lack of respect and acceptance for the other.

Gottman avers that discussion of complaints and disagreements in a relationship can be a healthy, good thing. Criticism, on the other hand, is not. He distinguishes between criticism and complaint by identifying criticism as an attack on the other's personality or character. While a legitimate complaint involves a description of behavior, "doing" something negative, destructive criticism blames a partner for "being" a certain way. He also maintains that while healthy complaints focus on a specific instance of behavior, criticism is more global and therefore more difficult for the criticized partner to handle. For instance, if one member of a couple neglects the other by working nights and weekends, the abandoned partner may *complain* to the other, "You've been working so much recently. I didn't see you at all this weekend. " *Criticism*, on the other hand, might sound more like, "You are so selfish. All you care about is money and your job. You never think about me at all."

When contempt (read lack of respect) creeps into a relationship, it signals a level of unhappiness and dissatisfaction that, Gottman's research indicates, often results in the dissolution of the relationship. In Gottman's hierarchy of relationship problems, contempt is stronger than criticism because it involves the intent to "insult [or] psychologically abuse your partner" (p. 79). He lists four common methods of expressing contempt: insults and name-calling, hostile humor directed at each other, mockery of the other, and disrespectful/disgusted body language. Contempt boils down to a lack of respect or admiration for the partner and can lead to a third destructive factor: avoidance.

Gottman pinpoints avoidance or defensive behavior as contributing to relationship breakdown in what he terms "stonewalling." Stonewalling is virtually avoiding communication with a partner, either by physically distancing oneself so that communication is impossible or by emotionally withdrawing until it seems futile for the other partner to try. To withdraw or avoid contact with a partner in this way also signals a lack of respect for the partner's desire to engage in discussion or social interaction. It is tantamount to ignoring one's partner, which is an effective silent way of conveying disapproval or lack of acceptance.

Gottman's program of research into close relationships makes clear that almost all couples display negative patterns of interaction at one time or another. One way of avoiding destructive effects is to concentrate on keeping negative interactions specific and "complaint"-oriented (focused on behaviors). In other words, it can be healthy for couples to argue or to disagree. It is not healthy to let arguments degenerate into the lack of respect typified by criticism, contempt, and avoidance.

The second key to handling negative interactions, Gottman says, is to consistently express more positive than negative communications toward each other. Some couples who appear to argue a great deal of the time may thus remain stable and satisfied together if they are simply a highly emotional pair whose positive interactions *still* outnumber their negative ones (Gottman, 1994, 1995).

Minding emphasizes the positive forms of interaction by specifically incorporating respect and acceptance into its principles. Couples who are minding their relationship well will be alert to the potential corrosion of a continued period of negativity in communication, feelings, and family atmosphere. They will be aware of the destructive power of criticism, contempt, and avoidance. They will recognize that each partner needs to have a voice and feel affirmed in the behavior and decisions that characterize the relationship (Rusbult, Zembrodt, & Gunn, 1982).

Recently, attention has been focused on a new type of marital therapy that also emphasizes acceptance and respect (Schrof, 1998). Termed "acceptance therapy," this technique helps couples learn to change their ways of thinking about partners. Rather than setting up a program of behavioral changes, something that has been traditional in marital therapy, acceptance therapy highlights tolerance of previously annoying behaviors and personality characteristics. Ultimately, the goal is to learn to not only tolerate but to appreciate a partner's differences, even to develop affection for them. Neil Jacobson and Andrew Christensen (1996) are currently exploring the effectiveness of this type of therapy and have reported that it seems to be especially successful with couples who have not been helped by other kinds of traditional marriage counseling. Acceptance therapy's successes make sense from the perspective of minding theory. It is not change in outward behavior that produces satisfaction in marriages, but change in thinking. Specifically, it is an increased ability to accept and respect another's unique past and personality.

The search for knowledge about a potential partner begins quickly and problems may be uncovered before serious commitments are made. This allows partners time to reflect on whether they are capable of accepting the implications of such negative information. It allows them to search for enhancing attributions and to build those attributions into their overall cognitive schemas about the partner and the relationship. It also allows partners to disengage from a relationship early on, before too much time and emotion have been invested. This knowledge search requires that partners open up to each other, disclose personal backgrounds, and share experiences.

Acceptance is important, even early in a relationship, to ensure this type of adequate disclosure occurs at all. There are inherent risks involved in revealing information about oneself to another that may prevent individuals from disclosing important information about themselves to others. Communication scholars Baxter and Montgomery (1996) have identified four possible risks of disclosing: rejection by the listener, reduction of one's autonomy and personal integrity, loss of control or self-efficacy, and the possibility of hurting or embarrassing the listener. All of these risks affect willingness to open up to a new partner; an atmosphere of respect and acceptance reduces these risks.

Kelly and McKillop (1996) discuss how individuals often "test" potential confidants by observing their reactions to others' disclosures or by sending up "trial balloons": introducing delicate topics at a general level while gauging the listener's response (i.e., "I have